TEACHERS' STORIES

TEACHERS' STORIES: FROM PERSONAL NARRATIVE TO PROFESSIONAL INSIGHT

MARY RENCK JALONGO
JOAN P. ISENBERG
WITH
GLORIA GERBRACHT

Jossey-Bass Publishers • San Francisco

Substantial discounts on bulk quantities of Jossey-Bass books are available to corporations, professional associations, and other organizations. For details and discount information, contact the special sales department at Jossey-Bass Inc., Publishers. (415) 433-1740; Fax (415) 433-0499.

For international orders, please contact your local Paramount Publishing International office.

TCF Manufactured in the United States of America on Lyons Falls Pathfinder Tradebook. This paper is acid-free and 100 percent totally chlorine-free.

Library of Congress Cataloging-in-Publication Data

Jalongo, Mary Renck.
    Teachers' stories : from personal narrative to professional
insight / Mary Renck Jalongo, Joan P. Isenberg. — 1st ed.
        p. cm. — (The Jossey-Bass education series)
    Includes bibliographical references (p.   ) and index.
    ISBN 0-7879-0048-6
    1. Education—Biographical methods. 2. Teaching—Case studies.
I. Isenberg, Joan P., date. II. Title. III. Series.
LB1029.B55J35 1995
920'.0071—dc20   94-24227
                                                              CIP

FIRST EDITION
HB Printing   10 9 8 7 6 5 4 3 2 1   *Code 9505*

CONTENTS

FOREWORD

by F. Michael Connelly

I like this book because it is a storytelling book. Every chapter is filled with cases, anecdotes, and short stories, written warmly, sympathetically, and invitingly. I like the authors, although I have never met them, and the teachers, although I probably will never meet them either. The book conveys a sense of humanity, a personalizing of our educational literature. I believe that you too will like the authors and the teachers.

Teachers' Stories: From Personal Narrative to Professional Insight teaches us about teaching. The lessons to be learned are partially found in Mary Renck Jalongo's and Joan Isenberg's own words, as they use the stories to illustrate their ideas about teachers and teaching. The lessons are also in the way we readers view the stories.

Students of literature know that stories can have surprising multiple interpretations by literary theorists and literary critics as well as by lay readers. The pages of critique often outnumber the pages of original text. The stories in this book are no exception. The authors reveal wonderful and important things about teachers, teaching, and the uses of story; the stories themselves reveal many more wonderful things. A book such as this inevitably goes beyond the limits of the imagination of its authors, because stories interact with listeners, readers, and other storytellers. Vicariously, you may see yourself and your teaching colleagues in this book, or you may imagine new possibilities for your own teaching.

Not only have there been recent shifts in the frames of reference for inquiry, there have been shifts from the *researchers'* experience to the voice of those *in* the experience. These shifts in focus in the social sciences are reflected in educational studies. Curiously, perhaps, the study of teaching rather than the study of learning has been in the forefront of these new educational modes of inquiry.

This book takes its rightful place within a ferment of ideas on inquiry in the social sciences, adding phenomenological, interpretive, and humanistic methods to the "look and record" descriptive research traditions. Not many years ago, it might have been seen as teacher gossip, stories better left for the staffroom. But narrative is now quite widely accepted as a legitimate research approach, and teacher storytelling is accepted as a legitimate mode of professional development. It is within this new mix of research and professional development that this book takes its place.

I find this book especially interesting because of the way it raises the matters of voice and authorship. Is this a book of teachers' stories or is it a book of stories about teachers? Is it a collection of teachers' inquiries or is it an inquiry into teachers? All are true. This is a book of teachers' stories, as the title suggests, but it is also Mary Renck Jalongo's and Joan Isenberg's book about teachers. It is a collection of teachers' inquiries in the form of reflective stories, but it is also the authors' inquiry into teachers. I like this ambiguity — it elegantly marks the crumbling boundary lines between researcher and researched. This book challenges sacred notions of the preeminence of theory over practice. As such, it is a harbinger.

But of what? Therein lies part of the excitement for researcher teachers and teacher researchers alike, who know that a new landscape of teaching and thinking about teaching is on the horizon and will emerge from such works as *Teachers' Stories*. It will be, as my colleague Jean Clandinin and I hope and believe, a landscape where the boundary lines between theory and practice are blurred and faded—just as they are in this book. Mutual respect will replace hierarchical relations. And this, say the authors, is one of their fondest hopes for the book. They wish to validate and put teachers' knowledge on par with their own. They have done so.

November 1994   F. Michael Connelly
                                                                  Toronto, Ontario

To Felicia Gemmellaro Renck, who knew these stories, who thoroughly approved of this book, and who, in the fall of 1993, confronted her story's end. During the twelve days between her diagnosis and her death, she gave me the privilege of showing what I had learned about love and care from her lifelong example.

Dedicated with love and written during loss, this book is for my mother.

M.R.J.

To my prospective and practicing teachers, whose passion for learning and willingness to share their stories have enriched my world beyond words and made this book a reality.

And to Shayna, Joanna, Ari, Oriana, Ramey, and David—whose stories of childhood have enriched the lives of many teachers.

J.P.I.

PREFACE

Becoming a teacher is a complex process characterized by conflicts and challenges, uncertainty and contradiction. A teacher certification program is barely a starting point for the journey to competent teaching, much less professional excellence. Over the years, many proposals for furthering teachers' professional development have been offered. Do teachers need more status, as proponents of career ladders suggested? Do they want a voice in administrative functions, as those supporting the shared decision-making trend concluded? Or do they simply need to improve their technique, as critics on so many bygone bandwagons have asserted? The premise of this book is that the needs of teachers run much deeper than any of these superficial tinkerings with systems and methods would address. Both in professional literature and in our personal experience, one message is clear: the focus of good teachers is to foster student learning despite distractions, obstacles, and disappointments. How do teachers achieve this? It is the thesis of this book that they approach it one student at a time; that expert teachers, by their very nature, reason and reflect on a case-by-case basis. In this book, when we refer to "teachers' stories," we mean classroom incidents and situations that are completely honest, deeply personal, carefully considered, and conscientiously evaluated.

As teacher educators for the past eighteen years, we have regularly witnessed the use of story. To illustrate how teachers think narratively, consider the example of a teacher and graduate student who tells a small group of her classmates that she will be working with a Down's Syndrome child for the first time. Her peers give advice and reassurance in story form, using narratives that begin with statements like, "I had a Down's Syndrome child in fourth grade last year. At first, I was really concerned about whether I had the proper training, but then . . . " Another colleague offers, "I have taught children with Down's Syndrome, but my best experience was with my own child who is now seven years old. Let me tell you about the experience of Jason, my son, from a parent's perspective. I think that might help . . . " Still another teacher begins, "I have been in special education for five years and my classes over the years included three children with this syndrome. I've found that . . . " Another adds, "There was a wonderful article I read that was written by a teacher. She told the story of a child in her class who was afflicted with Down's Syndrome. You should read it. I'll get a copy for you . . . " Talks like these with teachers underscore our assertion that teachers use true stories from the field — those personal narratives of teachers interacting with learners — to learn, to respond, to reflect, and to evaluate.

Purpose of This Book

Throughout this book, we argue that teachers' stories, these positive and negative personal accounts of our lives in classrooms, are central to the type of inquiry and reflection that lead to professional development and personal insight. Educators must delve beneath the routine, the surface, the business-as-usual if they are ever to unearth the heart of teaching and, in the process, nurture their souls as teachers. The word *soul* is used deliberately here, not to raise religious eyebrows but to refer to our inner being rather than our professional facades. Our focus on teachers themselves will not, we hope, be interpreted as thinly disguised narcissism. On the contrary, we contend that it is through careful examination of real-life classroom experiences—both lived one's self and borrowed from other teachers—that teachers explore the complexities of what it means to teach. It is in the narrative mode that teachers consider daily dilemmas, examine their motives and misgivings, savor their successes, and anguish over their failures.

Put simply, playing a role in students' growth and development is what nurtures teachers' own growth and development. What, then, of the students who falter or fail? For the worst in our profession, those students become the enemy, a constant reminder of their own inadequacies. The best in our profession do the best they can, realizing that it is sometimes not good enough. When they encounter a student who can be helped very little, good teachers forgive themselves for being less than perfect, allow themselves to take a lesson from that student, and go on without resentment, only with regret. That student's story becomes like a case file a teacher will return to often as a tool for closely examining what he or she did and thinking about what might be done differently next time. In moments of discouragement, teachers will also draw upon their reservoirs of success stories as a source of strength and support.

The good teacher's life is not an orderly professional pathway; rather, it is a personal journey shaped by context and choice, perspective and values. Narrative is uniquely well suited to that personal/professional odyssey. It is primarily through story, one student at a time, that teachers organize their thinking and tap into the collective, accumulated wisdom of their profession.

Uniqueness of This Book

This book is different from most other books you will encounter on the topic of teachers' stories. To date, much of the writing about teachers has been either narrative research or unexamined anecdote. Narrative research undertakes the careful, in-depth examination of a teacher's or teachers' lives. We value this research and acknowledge that our efforts are grounded in it, yet we do not claim that *Teachers' Stories* is a research book. A primary purpose for this project was to make narrative theory and research more accessible to the classroom teacher, to help him or her see that, unlike some of the studies that seem divorced from classroom lives, narrative itself speaks to practitioners. As readers become more familiar with narrative theory and research, we hope these things will, as F. Michael Connelly suggested in an earlier review of this manuscript, "help them to enter into a tradition of respect for teacher experience and the telling and retelling of lives in education."

The opposite of narrative research is the overly simplistic and superficial reporting of classroom events. There is no teacher voice in such anecdotes, no examination of how, why, or why not things happened. Some of these accounts are highly romanticized versions of teaching events and portray teaching as one fun-filled day after another; others are the notoriously negative teachers' lounge conversations that can deteriorate into chronic complaint.

Our goal is to abandon rather than contribute to superficial accounts that undermine or trivialize teaching. We seek to encourage more reflective practice and to show rather than tell teachers just how this can be achieved. In support of this goal, we have tried to write a book that is equally at home on a desk or bedside table, one that offers food for thought and study, yet could also qualify as pleasurable reading for teachers. The best way of achieving this, we concluded, was to talk with novice and expert teachers across grade levels and urge them to write the stories of their lives, to deliberately mix styles and voices, all the while weaving together story with theory and research.

The teacher narratives contained in our book were gathered in a variety of ways. Some of them were entries in student teaching journals written by new teachers. Some were written as part of a professional development course or in a graduate class. A few were written in response to conference sessions on teacher narratives. Several stories were simply solicited—we asked the most admirable teachers we know to recall stories they had told and commit them to paper. Still other stories were provided by the Southcentral Pennsylvania Writers' Workshop fellows, experienced teachers who enrolled in a summer program led by Lynne Alvine and Carole Bencich, two English professors at Indiana University of Pennsylvania. The stories that were written in case study format were composed by a team of teachers led by Joan Isenberg and Shirley Raines at George Mason University. These case studies were based on the real-life experiences of the team members. Many stories were ones that we had experienced ourselves and had been wanting to share. As we worked on the project, stories continued to surface and resurface, even after the book went into production.

We realize that in creating a hybrid of this sort, a book that is neither research nor light reading, there is always the danger that it will be judged successful at neither rather than at both. Yet we hope the book's strength is in the fact that it makes research on teachers' lives more accessible and encourages teachers to look to themselves for answers about what it means to teach and learn. We also want teachers to realize that the roles they advocate for children apply equally to themselves. It is common today to hear teachers and teacher educators describe a different perspective on the learner. Learners are no longer the blank slate upon which others imprint their mark but active, imaginative problem solvers; individuals who exercise choice, grow in self-evaluation, learn by doing, and work collaboratively. If we demand this for students, can we expect anything less for teachers? For too long, teachers have been urged to accept others' ready-made answers and search for panaceas. Isn't it time for teachers to assert the authority that derives from extensive classroom experiences and the unique perspective they bring to education?

Clearly, for those who stand to benefit from teachers' silence and complacency, the answer is "No." To us, it seems beyond ironic that teachers are called upon to articulate their philosophy of teaching when it is barely formulated—upon completing student teaching. From that day forward, nobody asks. Yet when beliefs, values and attitudes that undergird teaching are neglected, deliberately or otherwise, teaching becomes an assignment, a routine, a drudgery. We propose that teacher narrative is an important way to counteract the temptation to succumb to the mundane, to embrace apathy, to follow the book and teach to the test. Skeptics will no doubt argue that teachers' stories are too humble a tool to exert a positive influence. Those unaccustomed to the practice of reflection find it difficult to conceive of teacher dialogue that is more than complaint or gossip. But when we refer to teachers' stories, we are not talking about any of these things. Rather, we are talking about the essence of teaching, raised by questions like, "What led you to teaching in the first place? How do you conceive of your role in students' lives? How have you matured as a teacher? Where do you hope your career will lead? What enables you to teach well? What obstacles get in your way? Of what are you most proud professionally? Most ashamed? How do you deal with disappointment and despair? What success stories can you share? What are your aspirations for the future? What does it mean to teach and learn?"

Audience for This Book

Our primary audience is practicing teachers, administrators, and teacher educators. *Teachers' Stories* was not conceived of as a textbook, yet it would be ideal for a student teaching seminar, graduate class, or inservice education program designed to foster more reflective practice. Although the book is undeniably written for educators, we found that when our prepublication copies were being reviewed by family, friends, colleagues, and graduate students, the stories had a way of being shared, even with those outside the field of education. This led to both questions about why each teacher selected his or her own particular story to share and a dialogue about the meaning of teaching: "Did something like that ever happen to you?" "You mean teachers really have to do this sort of thing?" we were asked. Connections were sometimes forged with the noneducator listener's background: "Somebody should put together a book like this in library science," "We use cases in business, too, but these are more personal," we heard. Human beings learn from the stories of others to the extent that a particular story causes them to rethink and reexamine their own experience. Our real audience, then, is anyone for whom these stories can become a tool for reflection and a stimulus to tell or write factual accounts of their own personal or professional lives that lead to deeper insights.

Both of us are deeply committed to elevating the status of the teaching profession. We suggest that helping teachers to find their voice, to tell their stories, to be heard—not only by one another but also by noneducators—is a key element in attaining that objective.

Overview of the Contents

In writing this book, we encountered themes in stories that were consistent with narrative theory and research as well as with the recurring issues uncovered during our daily interactions with teachers. The first chapter sets the stage by asserting the authority of teachers' knowledge, their particular ways of knowing what they know. Chapter Two examines the ways in which narrative connects practitioners. In it, we argue that each well-wrought teacher story has the power to connect teachers with one another and link educators with other audiences as well. The stories of an individual teacher are also linked, because story connects past experience with present concerns and future goals as a teacher tells and retells, interprets and reinterprets. In Chapter Three, we examine the reciprocal natures of teaching and learning. By this, we mean that children do not simply learn from teachers, as is commonly assumed, but that the best teachers know how to learn from students.

Much has been written lately about the importance of reflection in the journey from novice to expert teacher, so Chapter Four shows readers how narrative works as a tool for looking beneath the surface of teaching. And because teachers find conflict with peers, parents, and administrators to be especially troublesome, we selected story as a problem-solving tool for Chapter Five's focus. Chapter Six is devoted to helping teachers develop as professionals via story. The seventh and final theme we discuss is "entering the dialogue." It is linked to the feminist literature about voice and dialogue and the notion that when social groups are silenced, they are disregarded or ignored. Throughout

Chapter Seven, we build the case that story is a fundamental way for teachers to be heard and to participate more fully in educational dialogue, which is an ongoing conversation now dominated by politicians and administrators in higher education. Chapter Eight, the final chapter, takes our recommendation one step further by suggesting practical strategies for readers to tell, write, use, and publish their own stories.

Our toughest critics will no doubt be those with a technological mentality about teaching, readers who aspire to break teaching down into its component parts and reduce it to a set of methods and procedures. They may be inclined to disparage the narrative mode as soft and subjective. Yet before they abandon teachers' stories in favor of hard-headed objectivity and facts, we remind them that while numbers provide a useful way to summarize, they are also a way of depersonalizing our decisions. Educators gird themselves with statistics as warriors do with armor; statistics are frequently used by educators to protect themselves from the slings and arrows of the public. Then they are off the hook: it wasn't their considered professional opinion that a child needed remediation in reading, it was the test score that decided.

Numbers can also be used to distance ourselves. It is easy to love all children in theory, yet despise one, some, or most students in practice. Then children can be dismissed completely, not merely at the end of the school day. From this "professional" distance, experts can look at statistics about drug-exposed children, project those figures onto a screen, and debate the issues involved. But the reality of the numbers pales in comparison with the story a teacher can share about the living, breathing body of a drug-exposed child, now assigned to his or her classroom, a child who demands attention, requires care, and needs to learn. A teacher narrative puts a face back on the statistic. Just as real reading ceases when comprehension is lost, we submit that real teaching is sacrificed when we become disinterested in or incapable of understanding individual cases, thinking only in collective terms. We ask that the harshest critics among our readers only consider how narrative can be a constructive force in teachers' lives.

As critical readers look through the themes that we discovered, they may discover themes of their own that seem even more powerful. To them, we say, "Explore that theme and share it with others." *Teachers' Stories* should serve as a beginning, not an end. Teaching is a personal experience as much as a professional one. The book can be read in our sequence or out of it. Its effect will depend on what the reader brings to it. We hope that readers will want to return to the book, bringing new levels of meaning and different experiences with them on each occasion.

To further encourage our readers in telling, writing, sharing, and discussing teachers' stories, we provide additional support in the appendixes. Appendix A includes published teachers' stories for reading and savoring. Appendix B gives resources for authors, examples of published stories by teachers, and suggests publication outlets for teacher narratives.

Acknowledgments

We know that our book owes much of its power to the authentic voices of both prospective and practicing classroom teachers. In fact, the most delightful part of this entire project was working with the teachers we know to help them revise and reflect on their work until their stories communicated as clearly and powerfully as possible. For most of our contributors, this book represents the first experience with writing for publication. They have enriched our lives as teachers by allowing us to function as facilitators in that process. One particular person, Gloria Gerbracht, contributed her thoughts and responses in the form of a chapter. As the book was reshaped and revised, the chapter she originally submitted was incorporated into several other chapters and strengthened each one. Gloria also contacted several of her former students and obtained permission to use excerpts from their journal entries. It is worth noting that Gloria began this project while engaged in doctoral study, read and commented thoughtfully on the manuscript while in the throes of dissertation, and will see the publication of *Teachers' Stories* shortly after she receives her degree. Two other doctoral students who read the entire manuscript, contributed stories to it, and offered support and encouragement also merit special recognition, Jyotsna Pattnaik and Laurie Nicholson Stamp. We also acknowledge the contributions of Nancy Maldonado and Mariann Winick at Lehman College who graciously shared their ongoing research on teachers' personal written accounts of their work. A composite of their research appears as Appendix A.

We are deeply obligated to Lesley Iura, our editor at Jossey-Bass. She instantly recognized the value of sharing teachers' professional lives through story and offered enthusiastic support throughout the project. When the book was at various stages ranging from a difficult infancy to an awkward adolescence, her gentle guidance and keen insight proved invaluable. We would also like to recognize the anonymous reviewers who read an earlier draft of the book and provided extensive feedback that improved the quality of the finished product. We are appreciative also of the work done by Pamela Berkman, our production editor, and Jean Schiffman, our copyeditor, who applied their skills to polish the manuscript. Each of these relationships with our editors, reviewers, and contributors enhanced our learning, something that we value beyond measure.

Writing a book places demands on those who struggle to live peaceably with us. Things like home upkeep and social occasions are routinely sacrificed. For their forbearance, we thank our families and friends. Several of them read the book in part or whole, some listened as we read passages aloud, and some lent unwavering support to this project. Mary Renck Jalongo especially thanks her husband, Frank, whose patient listening and editorial commentary is reliably helpful and enlightening. Joan Isenberg once again thanks her children, Jennifer and Michelle, and her loyal friends, Marsha and Don, who patiently endured her distractedness and unavailability during critical periods in this book's development. To them, she expresses her heartfelt love and appreciation.

From our multiple perspectives as teacher educators, authors in the field of education, and former classroom teachers, we elaborate on the general thesis that human beings perceive the world narratively. It is natural for people to reason, remember, and reflect in story form and we apply that premise specifically to the field of education. Because teaching is, above all, a human enterprise, story is central to our profession. As collaborators on this project, it is our fervent hope that this book will help in some small way to promote teacher narratives. We are convinced that story can and should be used to improve teaching. For teachers' lives, bereft of narrative and reflection, are, as has been said of the unexamined life, hardly worth living.

November 1994   Mary Renck Jalongo
                                                  Indiana, Penn.

                                                  Joan P. Isenberg
                                                  Fairfax, Va.

THE AUTHORS

After graduating from the University of Detroit — Mercy, MARY RENCK JALONGO joined the Teacher Corps in order to work with migrant children. She earned a master's degree in teaching from Oakland University — against the advice of nearly every adult in her life, who pushed her toward more scholarly endeavors. After teaching first grade, second grade, and preschool, she went to the University of Toledo, where she joined the doctoral program, worked in the laboratory school and gained additional experience with two- to five-year-olds.

Jalongo has been a mentor and teacher in the Indiana University of Pennsylvania's Professional Studies in Education Department for the past sixteen years. She has written four other books (*Young Children and Picture Books, Early Childhood Language Arts, Creating Communities: The Role of the Teacher in the 21st Century,* and *Creative Expression and Play in Early Childhood Education* with Joan Isenberg) and published a wide variety of articles in professional journals such as *Educational Leadership, Childhood Education, The Reading Teacher,* and *Young Children.* Three of her manuscripts have received national awards for excellence in writing. In 1991, she was named Indiana University of Pennsylvania's

Distinguished Professor. She is a consultant for Phi Delta Kappa and is involved in the international lecture circuit.

She says, "As I reread this book in its entirety, the word that comes to mind is *keepsake* because this book is a documentation and validation of stories from my students, my colleagues, my own experiences in classrooms. These educators' lives, these autobiographical and biographical accounts, serve to illuminate our way as we pursue the path of becoming better teachers."

JOAN P. ISENBERG is a professor of education at George Mason University in Fairfax, Virginia, where she received a distinguished faculty award for teaching excellence. She teaches graduate courses in teacher development and early childhood education in the Graduate School of Education, where she also coordinates three teacher education programs for both prospective and practicing teachers. Integral to her teaching is the use of personal narrative to enable teachers to make meaning of their teaching and of the teaching profession through the stories they share and analyze with colleagues.

Isenberg has published books, journal articles, and review articles on childhood education and childhood teacher education, particularly in the areas of teachers' professional development, school change, and children's creative behavior. Her major publication is *Creative Expression and Play in the Early Childhood Curriculum,* coauthored with Mary Jalongo.

She currently serves on the governing board for the National Association of Early Childhood Teacher Educators and is past president of the Washington Metro branch of the Association for Childhood Education International. Isenberg earned her Ed.D. degree in elementary education from Rutgers University. Her personal interests include her family, bridge, reading, the arts, and the ocean.

THE CONTRIBUTORS

At the heart of this book are the stories written by teachers and students about their lives in classrooms. We would like to thank all of those who so generously shared their stories and, in so doing, made a substantial contribution to this book.

Hollace Abrams
Sonya Marie Barclay
Jamie Barron
Hope Brady
Joy Brewer
Rosemary Burton
Anna Chacko
Kathryn Chaumont
Mark Connelly
Dina DeEulio
Lori Deluca
Eileen Foulger
Isabelle Hoag
Harriet Houghland
Joan Isenberg
Charlotte Jaeger

Lijun Jin
Gail Keller
Elizabeth Klein
Aneta Large
Karen Liard
Nancy Lusk
Harlan Mathers
Loraine Miller
Jane Mize
Pamela Nelson
Jyotsna Pattnaik
Shannon Patton
Shawneen Peterson
Shirley Raines
Gail V. Ritchie
Loletta Rupe

Stacey Sanders   Paula Treiber
Marshann Snyder   Pam Von Bredow
Lucille Sorenson   Rose Mary Weber
Kenena Spalding   Leanne Weigel
Laurie Nicholson Stamp   Donna Witherspoon
Patricia Tarwater

INTRODUCTION

When the words "teachers' stories" are used, they elicit a wide range of responses from educators. While one educator will offer a brief, amusing anecdote as an example of a teacher story, another might equate teachers' stories with research; whereas one educator will cite a published teacher autobiography as an example of a teacher story, another will associate stories with casual faculty lounge conversation.

This book operates on a different set of assumptions about teacher narratives. Our aim is not to compile unexamined shop talk, nor to attempt ethnographic research, nor to publish an in-depth autobiography. Rather, we want to address educators directly and validate their practical knowledge. We want our readers to use these teacher narratives as tools for more reflective practice, and we want our readers to tell and write teaching stories of their own.

With these purposes in mind, we approach the teaching/learning process in an admittedly and unabashedly subjective way—through teachers' own descriptions of memorable experiences, first lived out within classrooms, then interpreted and reinterpreted through various perceptual lenses.

Throughout this book, we also include the comments of scholars who study narratives as they apply to the lives of teachers we respect and children we have known personally or through story.

To demonstrate what we mean by a teacher narrative, we begin with one teacher's story. Jamie Barron (1993) wrote this success story, which she first shared in a graduate class meeting and then published at our invitation, not only because it captures the essential satisfactions of her work but also because it is an efficient way of communicating her passion for teaching and her compassion for the functionally illiterate.

DON
Jamie Barron

While watching television one evening, Don and his wife saw a public service announcement about a local literacy program for adults. The next day, Don's wife called the number that she had seen and was referred to me, the teacher of the class. She reported that her husband, Don, needed assistance with reading and math. When asked why he did not place the call himself, Don's wife explained that he worked full time during the day, which made it difficult for him to make any personal calls. She also indicated that Don was very sensitive regarding his academic problems and that he was somewhat reluctant to begin classes. Arrangements were made for Don to meet with me, an adult basic education instructor, and attend an evening class.

Being aware that Don was apprehensive about beginning classes, I decided to wait outside the building where we were to meet, instead of in the classroom. About ten minutes before the appointed time, I saw a man who appeared to be in his early thirties drive past slowly. Soon the car made a U-turn and circled the building. Then the driver parked near the curb, shut off the engine, and sat staring at the entrance of the school. The car door opened and then closed.

As the driver restarted the engine, I approached the car and knocked on the window. I asked if the driver's name was Don, and he nodded. I introduced myself and expressed my interest in meeting with him. I reassured him that no other students were expected for an hour and that we could take that time to get acquainted and discuss his goals. With that, Don took a significant step in his literacy growth by crossing the threshold of that imposing building and entering my classroom.

Don and I sat at a conference table and began talking. Don reported that he had had to drop out of high school in the ninth grade. He stated emphatically that he had been mislabeled and placed in special education classes in the third grade. He had been ridiculed by his peers as being "slow and stupid" and eventually stopped trying to learn. Then Don dropped out of high school at age seventeen and began working full time at a construction job. Within two years, Don changed jobs, began working in a local coal mine, and was married. He preferred working underground because "people don't usually expect you to do much reading in the dark." Whenever he was asked to read something, Don would avoid the situation by saying that he had "forgotten his reading glasses" (which he did not need or own).

Unlike many adult literacy learners, Don was realistic. He knew that it would take a long time to learn everything he wanted to know about reading and math. In fact, he expressed concern that his children, now in elementary school, would be in college by the time he mastered the "art of literacy." He quickly added that his wife was "pretty smart" and that she always assisted the children with their homework. Don was grateful for this because it kept his children from being limited by his own low-level reading and math skills.

When asked about his motivation to enroll in the classes at this time, Don was a bit evasive. Finally, he revealed that the primary reason for attending classes was because he wanted to take his family on a vacation to the beach. Don was fearful that he would not be able to read the signs in a new place and become hopelessly lost. As a result, he had never driven beyond two counties in any direction from his home. Because Don's wife had never learned to drive, he could not rely on her for help. "One of the worst things" about being a low-level reader, from Don's perspective, was the feeling of being trapped in the area where you live. Don despised the fact that he had to rely on friends and relatives for transportation outside of the area with which he was familiar.

As if to underscore these feelings, there was a critical incident that occurred while Don and his family were camping on the weekend at a local state park. Don overheard one of his children talking with a friend who had been on vacation at the New Jersey shore. Don's daughter stated that she would love to see the ocean but that she didn't think her father would ever take her there. Don was devastated by her words. For the first time in his life, Don felt that his low-level reading skills were having a negative effect on his family. He went on to say that he too had always dreamed of seeing the ocean and he didn't want his children to grow up deprived of this experience and wondering what it would be like to take a beach vacation.

Don purchased an atlas and several maps but was unable to decipher them. He knew that he needed assistance, but he was too embarrassed to ask a friend for help. Don could ask a friend to travel with him and his family, but he wanted to do this himself for his own family. I explained to Don that even the most proficient readers are often reluctant to drive in new areas, particularly cities. I also assured him that I believed his goal would be attainable in the months ahead before summer and that many of the adult basic education students did travel considerable distances without incident. Then I had a brainstorm. There was another student, a professional truck driver, who was attending a math class later that evening. It seemed that they might be able to work together. Don agreed to the pairing and arrangements were made to begin classes.

Don was persuaded to take the test of Adult Basic Education after I explained that I was required to test him in reading and math and that I would use the results to select appropriate learning materials. Don scored in the primary range in both areas. He was visibly upset by the low scores but appeared determined to begin classes.

In addition to the basic materials, I added materials on Don's level regarding the ocean, sea life, traveling, and map reading acquired from the Adult Education division of the State Department of Education. Colorful, descriptive materials about the New Jersey shore area were obtained from the local AAA.

Don attended classes faithfully six hours per week. He soon came to enjoy language and creative writing and wrote very moving stories about his family, his work in the mine, and his hobbies. Learning more about the ocean became a family project as Don read various books about the ocean, and his children checked out additional books on the topic, then read them aloud to their father.

Don also worked with his partner, Bill, the professional truck driver. Bill was a wealth of information and an unwavering source of moral support. He gave Don a copy of his truck driver atlas and they spent many hours together decoding the symbols and outlining Bill's delivery routes. Bill explained how route numbers related to directions, told him the meanings of certain signs, and gave him various driving tips. Don was entranced by Bill's knowledge of the road. To practice his new skills, Don accompanied Bill on a few short runs and, just before summer began, Don rode with Bill on the very route that Don would be using on his family vacation to the New Jersey shore.

After seven months, the literacy program was drawing to a close for the academic year. Don was retested. His reading and math scores had increased by an average of four levels. He was now reading the newspaper and subscribed to several magazines. He felt more comfortable in forced reading situations although he still attempted to avoid them. Even more important to Don, he felt prepared to take his family on their vacation to the ocean.

Three weeks after the academic year ended, I received a postcard that pictured a family with two children walking joyfully along

the ocean shore. The postcard read, "I did it!!!!
We made it without getting lost. We never had
so much fun. The kids are having a great time.
I brought my books. I read them every day at
the beach. This is the life. See you in the fall.
THANKS! THANKS! THANKS! Don."

It is interesting to note how sharing this incident altered
other teachers' perceptions of Jamie Barron. Because she tends
to be rather quiet in a group setting, her classmates in graduate school did not know her well. Yet after sharing her experience, other teachers came to know and respect her more. Several
of her classmates were moved to tears by Don's triumph over
illiteracy. One teacher said, "You should publish this." Another
teacher spontaneously wrote a success story that she had been
wanting to tell for years. Yet another teacher remarked afterwards, "I loved the ending, but I didn't want the story to end.
I guess it doesn't have to because she must have so many good
stories to tell. I hope she tells them." Barron's account of her
teaching experience—and the teachers' responses—illustrates
several things: how appealing and evocative teachers' stories can
be; how a teacher's personal and professional lives are inextrica-
bly interwoven; and how stories help members of a class to develop a sense of community, and, similarly, bind us together
as individuals and as educators.

But the impact of story continues beyond its entertain-
ment value and the immediate response—it leads to reflection.
Reading about Don's success, for example, raises many significant questions about teaching: what does Barron's story reveal about her as a person and as a professional? About Don
as a person and as a learner? About the plight of other illiter-
ates? How does Barron seem to define her role as teacher? In
what ways has her work influenced her? What role does her practical knowledge apparently play in her decision making? How
does she conceptualize the curriculum? In terms of relationships,
what does this story tell us about Don's family? About interactions between teachers and students? About colearners like Don
and Bill, the truckdriver? With respect to contexts, what does

this story imply about Barron's teaching/learning situation? How might it shed light on other teachers facing similar challenges in different contexts? What glimpses do we have about the conflicts she faces? What questions do we still have for her and about her, what do we yearn to know? And finally, which stories of our own are sparked into consciousness by Don's and his teacher's?

We use this example of a teacher narrative and some reflections upon it both as a point of departure and as a way of setting your expectations for what is to come in the pages that follow. We begin by building a case for the authority of teachers' knowledge: the wisdom derived from daily classroom experience and reflections upon that experience. We believe that teachers' stories and stories of teachers hold great promise for improving the images of teachers and schools and thus improving the lives of teachers, children, and families.

TEACHERS' STORIES

ONE

TEACHERS' STORIES, TEACHERS' KNOWLEDGE

Throughout this book, we argue that teachers' stories are simultaneously an expression of care for our students and care for ourselves. To help justify that position, we begin with a true story about real teachers, a story that resurfaced after many years while we were in the process of writing this book.

MARLA
Mary Renck Jalongo

When I stopped by the school office at noon, I noticed a fifth-grade girl sitting in one of the three chairs usually reserved for children who had misbehaved or who were ill and waiting to be picked up by a parent or neighbor. I didn't see any professional staff members around, so I greeted the girl and asked, "Do you need to call someone? Are you sick?" "No," the girl said sullenly, "my teacher sent me down here because she says I stink." This was one of the few times in my life that I was left speechless. I was stunned by the child's candor

1

and outraged that a colleague could treat a student so insensitively. My first impulse was to
protest that there must have been some misun-
derstanding or to say that Ms. S. had no right
to do that, but clearly, she already had. I also
knew that Ms. S. was an attractive, young
southerner who had thoroughly charmed our
old, northern principal, so I doubted that he
would act impartially on behalf of the student,
whose name, I later learned, was Marla. What
I did instead was talk to Ms. G., the other
fifth-grade teacher, a kind soul and assertive
advocate for children. Her political acumen led
Ms. G. to approach the issue in a surprising
but effective way. She made an appointment
with the principal and told him that the class
sizes in fifth grade were rather imbalanced because two of her students had moved away after a new student was placed in Ms. S.'s class.
She hinted vaguely that there were some problems that might be resolved. The principal had
already exceeded my expectations by telling
Ms. S. that she could not continue to leave
Marla sitting around the main office day after
day. It also became clear that he had lowered
his opinion of Ms. S. considerably as a result
of this situation, but that did nothing to allevi-
ate the child's suffering. Although children were
virtually never moved to another class in
midyear, the principal not only removed Marla
from Ms. S.'s classroom, he also thought it was
his idea.

The child who had been previously
degraded by her teacher and peers because of
her body odor was assigned to Ms. G.'s class
and given a fresh start, both figuratively and
literally. There had been no question that
Marla carried a repugnant body odor, but

investigating her living conditions helped to explain why. She resided with her large family in a wooden shack that had no indoor plumbing. The mother had abandoned the children years ago and the father was attempting to raise them. Marla slept with a younger sister who wet the bed every night. Ms. G. was a pragmatist. She knew it would be difficult to change Marla's living conditions so she arranged for Marla to shower during opening exercises and provided her with clean secondhand clothes outgrown by her own daughter. She also provided basic toiletries and complimented Marla on her progress. Eventually, Ms. G. persuaded Marla's father to accept a sofabed donated by another teacher so that the fifth grader would have her own bed. Four weeks after the transfer, Ms. S. was standing around drinking coffee when an attractive, lively fifth grader delivered a message. The secretary told us that after the child left, Ms. S. asked, "Who was that? She looks familiar," to which the secretary replied, "Why, that was Marla, your former student."

This teacher's narrative has the traditional story elements — setting, characters, theme, plot, style — but it also moves beyond basic elements and into the realm of reflections on teaching. Throughout this book, we describe how teachers seek and share stories about life in classrooms because these narratives offer reassurance and renewal, show teachers at their best and worst, and afford us the luxury of examining closely and thinking deeply about education. To us, Marla's story is a triumph of the teacher's self-sacrifice and resourcefulness over the self-centeredness of Ms. S. The story inspires us in the original sense of that word. We "breathe in" its message, and it reminds us of our ideals, prompts us to become better child advocates. Now that we have recorded the story, we can all bring personal experiences and perspectives to bear upon it. Some teachers might begin with criticism, worrying about all the things that might have gone wrong and generating a list of reasons for deciding not to intervene. The father could have become angry and suspicious. Ms. S. might have resented the transfer. The school is not in the business of providing showers and clothes; there could be legal ramifications. Perhaps even more basic is the ethical dilemma: just how far are teachers really expected to go in helping children? Surely Ms. G. went beyond her job description. The litany of reasons to do nothing could go on and on, and yet the teacher accepted the personal and professional risks and responded humanely to a neglected, hurting child. Just as we can identify the dangers, we can also marvel at Ms. G.'s perceptiveness about people and skill in working the system to the child's advantage. We take heart from the story because it shows how one teacher's inner strength has the power to affect children's lives profoundly. Even though the story speaks for itself, there is so much to be said about it.

Ways of Defining Narrative

We have presented "Marla" as an example of a narrative. But will we define *narrative* or *story*? Specifically, in this book, we focus on a subset of narrative that has particular relevance for educators at all levels, the teacher personal narrative, so we define the term by referring to each word in the label: *teacher*, written by (autobiographical) or about (biographical) classroom teachers; *personal*, educational incidents that were personally experienced and are used as tools for reflection; *narrative or story*, event-structured material, told or written, that documents lived classroom experience.

Psychologist Donald Polkinghorne (1988) highlights three key features of the narrative:

1. Ascribing meaning to temporal experience and personal actions
2. Synthesizing everyday actions and events into episodic units
3. Structuring past events and planning future events

We are using the terms *teacher narrative* and *teacher's story* interchangeably to refer to actual accounts of classroom experience, shared via written or oral language, and used to help teachers think more deeply about the meaning of teaching and learning and to grow and change, both personally and professionally.

A Rationale for Narrative

It is understood that narrative is a basic way of responding to the avalanche of information that we encounter daily. Perhaps the single most important attribute of the human brain is its ability to perceive patterns and organize otherwise fleeting images and perplexing experiences, usually in the form of a narrative. In fact, Bruer (1993) contends that the human brain actually "runs" on stories, and many of the greatest contemporary thinkers argue that the narrative mode is a supreme means of rendering otherwise chaotic, shapeless events into a coherent whole, saturated with meaning (Bruner, 1986; Coles, 1989; Rosen, 1988).

Nor is the recognition of the importance of story a new concept. Traditionally speaking, story has been credited with wielding sufficient power to preserve and transmit culture (Silko, 1977). Barbara Hardy (1977, p. 12) attests to the value of narrative when she writes, "We dream in narrative, daydream in narrative, remember, anticipate, hope, despair, believe, doubt, plan, revise, criticize, construct, gossip, learn, hate, and love by narrative. In order to really live, we make up stories about ourselves and others, about the personal as well as the social past and future."

Part of the power of narrative is its ability to present many interesting paradoxes. To illustrate, here is a short, simple story about a colleague.

GREAT SAVE
Mary Renck Jalongo

The building where I taught elementary school was the oldest structure in the school district. This particular elementary school had been an exclusive boys' academy at one time, so even though the building was originally constructed of durable materials, the effect of years of wear was evident. The centers of the granite steps leading into the school, for example, were deeply cupped from nearly a century's worth of students' shoes scuffing the stony surface. One day after recess, a column of children clambered back into the building. Carla, my fellow first-grade teacher, was at the top of the stairs leading her class while I was at the bottom, following with mine. I looked up to see a child out of line, teetering on the second step and beginning to fall backwards. I shouted to Carla, who turned and in a single, deft motion grasped the boy's parka hood while lifting him safely to the landing. "Great save!" I called out from the bottom stair as we both laughed with relief. Throughout the day, I eagerly shared the story and our colleagues congratulated Carla for her pivotal role in averting a dangerous fall and possible injury to a child in our care. It was a relatively minor incident, yet I find myself thinking about it often and sharing it occasionally with preservice and in-service teachers. There are several reasons for this, I think. One is that it celebrates an admirable quality in teachers that isn't, as far as I know, an objective in any teacher preparation program or the focus of educational research. Whether we call it aplomb, poise, unflappability, calm in a crisis, or grace under pressure, great teachers cultivate it and use it in the service of children.

This story illustrates several of the interesting features of narrative:

- Historical/contemporary. Although it has a "here and now" quality, it also captures and preserves the past. The "great save" occurred twenty years ago, but the message of the story remains current, and it continues to elicit contemporary stories with a similar theme. Narrative preserves traditions, yet leads to the creation of new stories. After reading "Great Save," for example, one first-year teacher told the story of intercepting crack cocaine from a second grader who thought it was candy, and one retired teacher described how she intercepted a shattered thermos filled with shards of glass just as a child was about to drink from it. As educators, we are autobiographers — originators, creators, and constructors of our life stories and of the thoughts, feelings, and actions therein (Tappan and Packer, 1991). We can use narrative as both a mirror — when we learn something about ourselves by transforming daily experience into something profound (Livo and Rietz, 1986) — and as a window — when we use it to examine the beliefs, behaviors, and insights of fellow teachers, past, present, and future.

• *Individual/group.* Stories illuminate one person's life experience, yet in doing so, evoke stories from others and remind us of our interconnectedness. After reading "Great Save," one class of teachers began talking about why it seems that most districts use their oldest buildings for their youngest students. They composed the following paragraph for group discussion: "Think of preschool through high school in a school district as a giant ice cream cone. The good stuff — the two scoops at the top — represents high school and junior high school, presumably because they are the pinnacle of a long climb through the school system. The middle school is the widest part of the cone and the elementary school, the narrowest. Our elementary buildings are like the very bottom of the cone, dripping, broken, and not worth the time or trouble it would take to repair them. That is because in American public education, they always defer to those students who are closest to exiting the system. We think it should be just the opposite." As their group response indicates, a teacher's story may be individual, yet other members of the profession can respond to it in surprising ways, both as individuals or in groups.

• *Thinking/feeling.* Narrative contradicts deeply rooted dichotomies in Western thought by connecting knowing with feeling and by linking thought with action. For decades, the paradigm of behaviorism has been allowed to dominate our thinking. Human activity was reduced to stimulus-response and learning, to a system of reward and punishment, observable and measurable. But we are undergoing a major change in the prevailing world view, a paradigm shift. Gradually, educators are reacting "against an antiseptic, value-free, purely rational view of teaching and learning" (Sparks-Langer and Colton, 1991, p. 40). "Great Save" is a good example of how narrative seamlessly connects thinking with feeling (and action), how story combines our personal and professional selves.

• *Simplicity/complexity.* Although stories appear simple and are often taken for granted, narrative is well suited to capturing the complexities of what it means to teach. Much has been written lately about caring as our first responsibility, our ethical obligation as teachers (Noddings, 1984). By using a simple story like "Great Save," this guiding principle is made more concrete, showing a teacher who is expressing care and concern by rescuing a child from a hazardous situation. Narrative can break down the theory/practice dichotomy by being simultaneously abstract and concrete (Clandinin, 1993).

Teachers' professional growth and children's authentic learning do not follow an orderly, hierarchical progression. Rather, they are embedded in contexts—the particular people, places, artifacts, and cultures of school. As we have seen, story is a useful way of portraying life in schools because it is equal to the task, providing a sufficiently flexible, complex, and individualized format to accurately document authentic experience.

The experiences, concepts, and themes of teaching are the way we educators fulfill what should always be the irrefutable, overriding purpose of teaching, which is to help every student to learn. Personal narratives—our own stories—are ideally suited to the essential task of educators everywhere who want to understand not only the whats (subject matter) and hows (methodology) but also the whys and whens of teaching.

Features of a Teacher's Story

What are the distinguishing features of teachers' stories, those attributes that make a story more than just entertaining, but a *bon penser,* a good thing to think with? Because teachers' personal narratives center on teaching and learning, they might actually be better termed *professional stories,* or *stories of practice.* Take, for example, a story that we have used many times, the "Angel Brown Story." Angel Brown was a first grader who was instructed by the teacher to write her name on her paper. Angel came up to the teacher and said, "But teacher, I don't know how to write my name yet." The teacher thought for a moment, then suggested cheerfully, "Angel, I printed your name for you on your crayon box. Just take it out of your desk and copy your name." Angel seemed satisfied with this solution to her problem and returned to her desk. She laboriously printed the letters on her paper with an oversized pencil, her tongue turned up at the corner of her mouth as a visible sign of the effort. She continued to write. Then she wrote some more. The teacher was mystified by what could possibly be taking that long. Then she walked over and looked at her paper. It read, "Angel Crayola Brown the Great American Crayon."

When teachers hear this story, they laugh, partly, we think, at the suspense and surprise elements of the story and partly at the charm and innocence of childhood. At first, we thought this story was just a humorous anecdote and shared it often. But it is a story that can be interpreted and reinterpreted — as an example of the need for more developmentally appropriate language tasks, as an example of the role of teacher expectation, as an illustration of a child's drive to communicate, or as a metaphor for risk taking in the learning process. The "Angel Brown Story" did not realize its potential as a teacher narrative until it became a tool for reflection, until the teller and listener, writer and reader, delved beneath the surface of anecdote to examine motives, implications, and connections.

As this story illustrates, personal narrative is taken from a direct experience, explained in some detail, structured by events or episodes, told or written in story form. Narratives are often used to communicate meaning and explore underlying values and, as such, these personal narratives are frequently the basis for reflection, discussion, and debate. Personal stories have three components: experiences, concepts, and themes. According to Smith (1989), "Experiences are the 'facts' that happen to us.

They are the people, places, and events that become part of our history. . . . Concepts are beliefs or ideas we have about ourselves and others that we use to screen and interpret experiences and to guide our behavior . . . . Themes are general, abstract principles that summarize and consolidate experiences and concepts. Themes give unity to personal stories. They are like templates that organize the concepts of a personal story into a coherent, meaningful whole" (pp. 8–9).

Like the "Angel Brown Story," teachers' stories are much more than charming anecdotes. Rather, they are experiences that evoke stories from others, encapsulate professional perspectives, and lead to professional insights about the meaning of teaching. A good and useful story of practice has at least four key characteristics (Jalongo and Isenberg, 1993):

1. *It is genuine and rings true.* "A good story and a well-formed argument are different natural kinds. Arguments convince one of their truth, stories of their lifelikeness" (Bruner, 1986, p. 574). A real teacher story resonates within each of us, is not contrived to be cute, not edited to show the teacher in the best possible light, not sensationalized to evoke public reaction. Elizabeth Vance's (1990) diary of a child with AIDS is a fine example. At one point in the story, she acknowledges that although the situation is tragic, the crisis that binds her staff together and gives them a shared sense of higher purpose can be exhilarating at times. She admits that a part of her was enjoying the challenge even though the emotional strain was difficult to bear and the family's distress was horrible to witness.

2. *It invites reflection and discourse, which are fundamental to reflective practice.* A good teacher story leaves us fairly bursting to respond, sometimes with comments about the story told, sometimes with questions or insights about the underlying issues, sometimes with a story of our own, or sometimes with strenuous opposition. Sue's story is a good illustration. She is a fifth-grade teacher in what might appear to the casual observer as an easy assignment, twenty-seven students from a small town in a spacious, modern building. Yet because she cares, one particular academic year was stressful for Sue in unprecedented ways. Between September and June, one child's father died,

another went home to find that the family trailer had been repossessed, and a third lost everything in a fire. In addition, the mother of a new girl called the school and left the message that she would be checking into a psychiatric hospital. Because the girl had no other family or friends who would or could care for her, Sue took her home to live with her own family for three weeks. Sue's story invites discussion of critical issues, such as how far teachers can be expected to go in supporting the children in their classes and the legal ramifications of the decision that she made. Because the story is powerful, it stimulates dialogue.

3. *It is interpreted and reinterpreted.* Authentic teacher narratives go beyond "kids say the darndest things" and look beneath the surface again and again to discover underlying meanings. The experience does not change, but the concepts and themes used to interpret it change as we amass other experiences and become more reflective practitioners. The same story can be viewed from different vantage points. In Greg's elementary school, for example, all of the children had been involved in a child sexual abuse prevention program that emphasized resisting uncomfortable touch. After three fourth-grade girls were in physical education class with Greg, they went to the principal and said that he had been "touching them." Greg asked to see the girls with the principal present and began by asking, "What did we do in class today?" The girls said that they were working on the balance beam. "Did we ever use the balance beam in class before?" Greg asked. "No," the girls agreed. "And what do I do whenever we are trying something new in gymnastics?" "Spot us," one of the girls answered. "Yes, I spot you so that you won't fall and get injured. That's what I was doing today." With that discussion, the girls felt satisfied that their concerns had been addressed and the complaint went no further. This particular story began as an unjust accusation story. But as time passed, Greg interpreted it in other ways; he later cited it as an example of the importance of questioning strategies and later still, viewed it as an instance where staying calm in a crisis averted a career-ruining incident.

4. *It is powerful and evocative.* Teachers' stories can elicit strong emotions. Consider the story of Glenna, who was asked

by the parents of students in her fifth-grade class to meet with the children following the tragic death of a classmate in an auto accident. She was in a summer session graduate class at the time, and agonized over what she would say, how she would say it, and what she could do to help. The instructor empathized with her apprehensions but reminded her that it was because she was a sensitive, caring person with the right instincts that the parents had made this request in the first place. Glenna decided to change the topic of her paper for her child development class to helping children cope with death. To her disappointment, no book or person could give her specific directions on what to say or do when she met with the children except to be honest about her own feelings and to respond directly to the children's concerns rather than follow some prepared agenda. When Glenna returned to the university, she told her colleagues, "I decided to follow the children's lead and it was amazing. They wanted to remember Tyler—to look through samples of his work, to relive his funny stories, to admire his drawings. It was a way of coping with their grief that any therapist would endorse. We recalled many of our happy times together. Finally, I asked if there were any questions or comments, and Cheryl said softly, 'It makes you afraid because *anybody* could die any time, like your parents or your brothers and sisters.' That quiet comment just hit me and I started to cry. Many of the children cried too, and we were all trying to comfort one another. I reassured them by saying that it *was* unusual for children or young adults to die, that it usually happened to older people. Then someone had the idea of packaging up all of Tyler's work and sending it to his parents, along with a letter from all of us. Afterwards, I thought about the intensity of my emotional reaction. It's strange because my father died when I was eleven and I have really had a problem handling death. But I learned so much from my students on that day, and I think they felt relieved that I grieved *with* them."

Authenticity, reflection, reinterpretation, and response—we believe that these are the features that elevate a teacher's story from the realm of idle talk.

Respecting Teachers' Knowledge

Yet no matter how powerful the story, in order for teachers' stories to realize their full potential, we must validate the types and uses of educational knowledge. Unfortunately, in the world of education, personal perspectives on what it means to teach and to learn often take second place to hard data, facts, and figures. Stories are soft, subjective, and value-laden — or so the argument goes. This controversy between soft data and hard data is much more than a minor disagreement; it is a philosophical and pedagogical conflict of enormous proportions (Bogdan, 1980; Greene, 1992). Darling-Hammond (1993) says that conflict in education is largely based upon "issues concerning the types of knowledge sought and the uses to which knowledge should be put. Is the goal to discover the 'one best system' of educational practice and thus control curriculum and teaching? Or is knowledge to be used for illuminating the complexities of human learning for the purpose of enriching teachers' own thinking about their practice and empowering them to see teaching and learning through many lenses?" (p. 768).

In many ways, the controversy is an aesthetic truth versus objective truth debate (McLaren, 1988). Aesthetic truth involves a holistic evaluation of what "works" based on an admittedly intuitive appraisal of the total performance. A good example is the orchestra conductor who knows, based on years of experience and professional insight, when the performance is superlative. Why do we trust the intuition of artists and question the intuition of educators? Most of us would think it ludicrous for a choreographer to use a rating scale to assess each member of a dance troupe's performance, yet in attempting to assess student learning or teaching effectiveness, superficial measures of quality are the norm. We must realize that in education, as in the arts, the questions with easy-to-measure answers are seldom the most important ones.

As a group, outstanding teachers tend to favor aesthetic truth and mistrust objective truth when it resorts to measuring and fragmenting information (Jackson, 1992; Glasser, 1990).

Why? Because far too often in education, we make mistakes when we attempt to answer questions of quality through quantity. How many volumes in the library? How much homework is assigned? How does this child's performance on this test compare with that of peers? Although this information is of interest, it falls short of addressing important questions, much less arriving at answers. More often, it is the aesthetic truth question that tells the tale. How do children respond to literature? How can we reconceptualize home/school communication? How can we optimize every child's learning?

The actual stories of practicing teachers address these issues and get to the heart of the matter; that is one reason why we educators find accounts by teachers about teaching so appealing. In addition, it is through work with story that educators can achieve a multiplicity of perspectives. Therefore stories should not be held in low regard, like an unsubstantiated opinion in comparison with a research report. Rather, they are part of an emerging case study literature that experts from all fields use to organize their thinking, develop professional repertoires, reinvent curriculum, and contribute to their growth as professionals (Ambrose, 1993; Jalongo, 1992; Shulman, 1992).

Moreover, the issues of what qualifies as knowledge in teaching—as well as whose knowledge matters—affect teachers' lives and constitute many of the most pervasive, frustrating philosophy/reality conflicts. Suppose that a kindergarten teacher's practical knowledge of child development leads her to endorse a more child-centered, informal style of teaching while her curriculum supervisor insists upon a rigid schedule, direct instruction, workbooks, and tests. Their conflict has to do with power and authority, with whose knowledge "counts," the teacher's personal, practical, and professional knowledge or the supervisor's brand of knowledge, borrowed from other sources, primarily the textbook and test publishers. Now imagine a group of high school teachers who seek to make changes in their program. About half of them want to "detrack" the students into heterogeneous groups while the other half want to keep the students sorted by ability. The principal and superintendent listen, but they are uncertain how to proceed. What evidence is there to support the point of view that secondary students are best taught in homogeneous groups, as some of the teachers contend? What evidence is there to suggest that detracking would be worth all the effort? As these commonplace incidents suggest, what we know, how we come to know it, and the sources that we use to construct educational knowledge are important. This is not to say of course that a teacher's knowledge is infallible, only that it is no less perfect than other highly touted sources: the teacher's manual, the end-of-unit test, the visiting consultant. As Clandinin (1986) points out, "Teachers are commonly acknowledged as having had experience but they are credited with little knowledge gained from that experience. The omission is due in part to the fact that we have not had ways of thinking about this practical knowledge and in part because we fail to recognize more practically oriented knowledge" (p. 177).

Teachers' Ways of Knowing

Teachers can "know" something in a variety of ways: directly through lived classroom experience, vicariously through the observed or described experiences of other teachers, formally through professional reading and study, or intuitively through their value systems. Belenky and her coauthors (1986) have argued that there are different "ways of knowing." One research team that studied women extensively suggests that there are some fairly predictable milestones in the growth of knowledge (Belenky, Clinchy, Goldberger, and Tarule, 1986). The sequence of these common themes is dependent upon teachers' views of knowledge and their ability to articulate their ideas. Belenky and her colleagues describe the progression as follows:

> *Silence* is experiencing the self as voiceless, without the capacity to receive or generate knowledge.
> *Received knowing* is seeing knowledge as absolute and always in the possession of "authorities."
> *Subjective knowing* is distrusting authority and understanding knowledge as personal and originating within oneself.

Procedural knowing is perceiving knowledge as objective
and rationally derived, though subject to multiple perspectives.

Constructed knowing is understanding knowledge as "constructed," the knower acknowledging and taking responsibility for shaping knowledge (Ashton-Jones and
Thomas, 1990).

It has been posited that, taken as a group, women tend
to favor more subjective, narrative-based approaches. But it
would be wrong to conclude that to choose teacher narratives
is a gender issue or a mere preference. Rather, narratives are
key components in the authentic study of teaching, for until we
understand the context and appreciate the perspectives of those
involved, any understanding of what it means to teach and learn
will remain fragmented and disconnected from the real world
of teaching. Each day, in myriad ways, teachers get the message that their knowledge is inferior. Someone else, usually someone far removed from the daily realities of the classroom, always knows better. William Ayers (1992) asserts,

Who understands the peculiar demands of teaching, the mind-wrecking and back-breaking moments of it, the forests of paperwork that surround
it, the endless preparation for it, the invasiveness
of it into every corner of a life? Who knows the ec-
stasies of it, its specific satisfactions, its dazzling
transformative possibilities—and these are not
merely for the learners, but, in an elusive and won-
derfully interactive way, at least as powerfully for
the teachers themselves? Who can say what teachers
are up to, what they take to be the point of what
they are doing, what it means for teachers to teach?
Who, indeed. To say that teachers are the ones who
understand, who know, and can say seems so obvious that it is beneath reporting. But in the often
odd, sometimes upside-down world of social research, the obvious news must be reported and

repeated: teachers can be the richest and most useful source of knowledge about teaching; those who hope to understand teaching must turn at some point to teachers themselves [p. v].

Moreover, if we regard ourselves constructors of knowledge rather than purveyors of someone else's ready-made answers, teachers' knowledge assumes even greater importance: "What is missing from the knowledge base of teaching, therefore, are the voices of the teachers themselves, the particular contexts in which teachers work, the questions teachers ask of themselves and others, the ways teachers use writing and intentional talk in their work lives, and the ways that teachers interpret experience as they strive to improve their own practice" (Cochran-Smith and Lytle, 1990, p. 2).

A Teacher's Story, A Student's Story

The following stories within a story help to illustrate the ideas presented throughout this chapter. During the summer of 1993, one of the authors of this book—Mary Renck Jalongo—met with the Southcentral Pennsylvania Writing Workshop teachers about writing for publication and invited them to contribute to this book. In the weeks that followed, Loletta Rupe, one of the workshop participants, wrote a story she had been wanting to tell for a long time. The student she describes preferred to remain anonymous, so we named her "Kate" to conceal her identity.

EVERYBODY MAKES MISTAKES
Loletta Rupe

She sat alone behind the old upright piano in the first-grade classroom. Her straight, dark hair framed her thin face. A secondhand plaid dress hung loosely from her shoulders. She didn't talk to the other children. She didn't want to play with them. She just wanted to play with the cards, the little ones with the

writing on them. At six, the child formed sentences from the dozens of tiny word cards.
Looking back on it now, I understand the at-
traction of those cards. They were pieces of her
world that she could control and fit together.

She sat alone in my fourth-grade classroom too. Her grey-green eyes peered out from
under shaggy bangs. She tugged uncomfortably
at the hemline of a too-short blue plaid skirt.
She wanted to stay inside during recess and
finish her math homework, using a pen if I
would permit it. Now I see how putting ink on
the page must have appealed to her. There was
a permanence about it.

In later years, she sat alone at the
smooth, round table in the library. Her long,
brown hair was pulled back severely from her
face. The style of the gaudy-print dress fit
Kate's growing body, but not her years. She
didn't want to join her sixth-grade class in the
cafeteria for lunch, to be expected to laugh at
their jokes, to pretend to enjoy them. She
wanted to select the books she would read that
weekend: stories of other people's lives, other
people's pleasant realities.

Many years later, she stood alone in the
open doorway of my classroom. "Hello," she
said quietly. "Do you know who I am?"

"Yes," I nodded. "Come in. Sit down. It's
so nice to see you again after all these years.
How long has it been?"

"I was in your fourth-grade class fourteen
years ago. You wouldn't let me do my math
with a pen." She smiled wistfully. "I didn't
make mistakes, you know. Really I didn't."

"Everybody makes mistakes," I countered.
"Nobody's perfect."

"You're right," she agreed. "I — I'm here because a mutual friend said I could talk to you. She said I could trust you with anything." Her eyes met mine for an instant, then fixed their gaze on the sunlit carpeting.

"I'll do anything I can for you. How can I help?"

The story came in bits and pieces over the next few months. Sometimes Kate screamed it; more often she whispered it. Kate said she was tired of trying to find safety in the realities of other people's lives when there was none in hers, tired of trying to create permanence and stability in a world where she couldn't depend on anything, weary of the search for sense in what had happened to her.

"I'm sorry," I sobbed. "I'm so sorry. I didn't know! I just didn't know."

"Everybody makes mistakes," Kate said. "Nobody's perfect."

For nearly ten years before her parents' divorce, Kate had been violently and repeatedly violated by her alcoholic father. The sexual abuse began when she was four years old and remained unnoticed by every teacher in elementary school, junior high, and high school — including me.

When Kate left home and went to college, she was no longer able to silence the wounded child inside. Her world came apart. Self-abuse took many forms. At the insistence of college counselors, Kate went into therapy. The few months of treatment did little more than stir up the pieces of her broken life. In time, she sought out her elementary school librarian and one of her fourth-grade teachers to help her put her world back together again.

It has been ten years since she came to me for help. During those years, Kate has courageously shared with me the terror-filled details of her ordeal. In an attempt to prepare myself to support her, I read book after book about sexual abuse—professional writings, self-help guides, personal narratives. At first I read for her, to help her. Later, I read for me. Being a listening partner for a survivor of childhood sexual abuse is a difficult, draining experience. Yet having become a trusted confidante for Kate, I couldn't abandon my role to spare myself discomfort.

That decade has brought about many positive changes for Kate. Those years have changed me, too. They've changed how I look at the children in my classroom. I know that statistically speaking, I could have at least one sexually abused child in my class every year. I now recognize the effects of abuse. I'm aware of behaviors that sexually abused children may exhibit. I know that what they won't say, what they can't say with words, may be expressed in other ways. I look for clues now, clues that may help save a child.

I hope that my heightened awareness will help me see and aid more quickly the next "Kate" who comes to my classroom. I realize that nobody's perfect, but my students, these children in my care, cannot afford for me to make the same mistake again.

After Loletta shared her story with other teachers, they asked if "Kate," her former student and adult friend, might write a companion piece from the child's perspective. During the time that this book was being revised, Kate grew stronger and ultimately decided to write the story she had endured as a child. Here is the story she shared within that community of writers.

INVISIBLE
"Kate"

Getting ready for the first day of school would be no problem. Everything I had to wear was new — the plaid dress was still starchy, the shoes were shiny, the underwear was still in the package. Everything was laid out on the dresser, totally in order.

Morning came bright and warm into the room. I thought if I dressed before venturing downstairs, I would be safe. On went new underwear, new socks, new shoes. I was removing the dress from the hanger when the doorknob began to turn. He came in, locking the door behind him. Silence and the smell of whiskey and sweat from his too-close body. No struggle. I had long since learned to yield — he was so much bigger and stronger than I was. The bright clarity of the morning began to cloud in a foggy haze. Afterwards, I moved automatically, eating soggy corn flakes that seemed to collect halfway down my throat, grabbing the new pencil and notebook, opening the front door. I didn't need anyone to walk me to school. I knew all eight blocks and the places where I was allowed to cross the street.

Slowly I made my way to the building, which was already crowded by dozens of other children, squeaky-clean in their first-day clothes. Shamefully, I stumbled up the stairs believing that my first day of first grade would be marred when the teacher found out. I couldn't smell the soap from the night before. All I could smell was man sweat, whiskey, and that other smell. The teacher would surely discern that my underwear was not new and clean like everyone else's and I would be sent home in disgrace.

I took a seat toward the back of the room and was horrified when I realized my name was on one of the desks in the middle. A kindly, middle-aged teacher came and put her arm around me to lead me to my desk. She pinned on my name tag and never said a word about the sullied underwear. How could she not notice? But day after day she let me stay.

Whenever I could get away from the other children, I would. Behind the big piano in the corner, I sat with word cards and made sentence after sentence, never forgetting the period at the end. The teacher was always surprised that I could read so well. She didn't know I was reading long before I came to her room. No one noticed anything different about me, good or bad. I was well on my way to becoming invisible.

Another year, another teacher. I always chose the chair in the back corner by the door. By fourth grade, we were allowed to choose our own seats after the first few weeks. School had become a haven. There was enough going on there to block out the sights and smells of home. At school, I absorbed everything and made no mistakes. That way I could not be distracted and the teacher would never single me out.

By sixth grade, I stopped playing altogether. I went to the library at recess. Books were calming. I couldn't bear to be around the other kids with their constant laughter and jokes. I just wanted it quiet. Besides, I was not like them.

The librarian was one of the best people I knew. She didn't care if I was different. On Fridays, I would check out more books than I could carry, so she would drive me home with

my weekend "sedatives." On Monday, she
would quiz me about each book. My librarian
didn't think it was possible I'd read them all,
but I answered every question correctly.

After I learned how to be relatively invisible, my classes were never a problem. School
and the rest of my life were in no way related.
Friends were very few. Most of my classmates
seemed petty or dull, and since I had lived in
the world of books and ideas at school instead of
learning to socialize as they did, I was far removed from them intellectually.

I graduated very near the top of my class
and was admitted to the university of my
choice. When I finally went to college, the life I
had so ardently tried to hold together began to
crumble. Unsocialized and unable to relate to
anyone, I fell into a tailspin of destructive behavior. I tried to destroy anything that was left
of self after years of being abused sexually,
emotionally, and psychologically. Eventually,
even my intellectual stronghold failed, and I
was recommended for counseling by school
officials. Cat and mouse games were all that
came of the first counselors, people I saw as in-
competents. Finally, they scheduled me with
the head of the department. He was smart and
at least had some grasp of the problem. He was
careful to leave the door open and allow me access to an escape route. We intellectualized the
whole story so it could be discussed, but the
pain was never mine, nor the guilt, nor the
shame.

A few years later, I struck another low in
my life when the pain caught up with me. A
call went out to the librarian, that friend of my
childhood who had kept up at least an intermit-
tent relationship ever since fourth grade. There

were visits to her house before and after her
divorce, long discussions about the wisdom of
remarriage, an announcement when her son
was born, letters back and forth. I related
quickly, sketchily what had happened to me.
She invited me to her home—we'd work it out.
I spent a couple of months at her house, talking. No one else on earth knew where I was.
Finally, we decided I would return home.
Mother had long since divorced her hus-
band/my father and married a good and decent
man. He loved her children as much as if they
had been his own, with none of the extra atten-
tions I dreaded from fathers.

My librarian friend told me that my
fourth-grade math teacher (who didn't let us
use pens lest we make mistakes) was still at the
school and was someone I could trust.

That was ten years ago. I am dealing
much better with the past now. Although I can
see how it clouds my vision of the present, I
am not totally limited by it. We talk a lot, my
teacher friend and I, about the abuse and how
it happened that I passed through the entire
system without anyone ever guessing that there
was a problem. Sometimes she cries because
she didn't realize it and because she realizes
there must be others she never knew about. We
excuse it because when she taught me, she was
young and inexperienced and in those days one
didn't look for those things. Now she is very
careful about leaving doors open for children.
The system still doesn't encourage her to look
for things that are wrong, but she's smart
enough to know the possibility exists.

Some children act out their pain. They
are the lucky ones. More often, they hide behind the facades they build to protect themselves. Then they become invisible.

Shortly after I (Mary Renck Jalongo) read these stories, a mature woman stood in the doorway of my office at the university with an envelope in her hand. "What's this?" I joked, "a special delivery?" Her face looked familiar to me, but I knew she was not a college student. She smiled. "Loletta Rupe asked me to bring another story to you. She said you liked our other stories, the one she wrote and the one I wrote." Now I was confused. Was she saying that she was "Kate," the author of "Invisible"? At first, I was surprised that she would reveal her identity. Then I wondered what sort of breakthrough the writing might represent for her. She said that it didn't take her long to write the story, that she wanted to share her experience with as wide an audience as possible. Her goal was to have the story read by teachers so that other children could be protected from the nightmare she lived. When she reminded me that I had probably seen her from time to time at her workplace and told me her real name, I felt entrusted with an important confidence.

That night, I said to my husband, "I had the most unusual experience today. I'll explain more after you read these two stories."

He read them and agreed, saying, "You have an ethical obligation to keep this confidence. Don't tell anyone, not even me." Then he said, "I thought the part about how she thought all the adults knew was so—"

"Poignant," I offered. "Yes, and the rituals that she invented to try and protect herself, the new clothes, getting fully dressed, they so accurately portray a young child's perspective. Also, it was amazing to me how she sought out the librarian and the teacher so many years later."

"I would do that, I think, if they lived nearby," he said. "In fact, I used to go and see my old teachers when we still lived in Detroit. There are some teachers who I really miss and I keep thinking that I didn't fully appreciate them at the time."

This summer afternoon, I will share Loletta Rupe's story and the story of "Kate" with my doctoral seminar class, "The Acquisition of Literacy," a group of twelve fine educators who will surely have much to say. But now, the story will change because of the context. Because we have been focusing on reading in this graduate course, we have been talking about literacy all semester as though it were the be-all and end-all of existence. I think these two stories, one written from the teacher's heart, one written from the child's, will help to put reading ability back in perspective.

In the fall, Loletta Rupe decided to sit in on a writing for publication course that I taught. She also brought along "Kate." As Loletta shared her story about Kate with yet another group of teachers, they began to talk about children whose suffering they might have misinterpreted or even overlooked. By the final class meeting in December, Kate was part of a community of writers and felt sufficiently comfortable with her classmates to confide that she was a victim of sexual abuse. I urged her to continue writing, to come back to school, that haven. Rupe's and Kate's stories are tools for exploring the nature of the teaching commitment, the connection between our personal and professional lives, the despairs and satisfactions of teaching, and our continuing obligation to care. We might wonder why Loletta went to such lengths to help a former student and why "Kate" did not persist in seeking expert psychiatric help even after her bad experiences with counselors. Yet both women made choices that seemed right to them and both place great value on the friendship that resulted.

Conclusion

As we have seen, authentic teachers' stories serve a variety of important purposes:

- They give us a professional voice and material to stimulate professional dialogue.
- They enable us to explore principles underlying practices (Atwell, 1987).
- They help us to communicate beliefs to a wider audience, particularly parents.
- They build our self-confidence as we confront professional dilemmas.
- They describe and document our professional experiences.
- They provide us with insight into teacher-student relationships.

- They contribute to our overall "wisdom of practice" (Shulman, 1992).

Philip Jackson (1992) speaks to the intangible rewards of using our stories, our experiences to become better teachers: "In the process of teaching subjects . . . teachers at all levels also teach, through example and through shared forms of social exchange, the virtues of diligence and persistence, of commitment to truth, of listening to and caring for the contributions of others . . . we put our best foot forward in the classroom. We project to our students not who we are but the kind of person we would like to be or what we would like others to think of us as being. . . . After years of such trying, we often wind up better than we were at the start, which is surely one of the great rewards of teaching" (pp. 242–243).

TWO

HOW NARRATIVE
CONNECTS

We speak so often of context when speaking of story — and with good reason. The word *context* originates from a Latin verb meaning "to weave together," and that is exactly what compelling stories do — they weave together the themes throughout one teacher's lifetime, connecting them to the lives of many different teachers. The best teachers have learned to transcend the boundaries of time, place, and distance by looking to the past, the present, and the future (Jonquiere, 1990), and narrative is a useful tool for achieving and balancing these perspectives. Story has an immediacy about it; every good story, whatever its era, seems to be happening right now. Yet, story also enables us to preserve events, to hold them constant and study them. Through story, teachers can examine past events and impressions as if they were current, reflect on different teaching contexts, or even anticipate future courses of action as if they had already occurred. Freema Elbaz (1991) speaks to this unifying feature of story when she observes, "Unity is something we seek to accomplish in our lives, and if the teacher achieves this in her working life, it is because she has been able to arrange matters in a consistent story line. The accomplishment of story thus always involves both the creation of a coherent meaning and the successful resolution of whatever conflict threatens meaning" (p. 95). To illustrate the interconnectedness of narrative and its contributions to meaning, consider how Laurie Stamp (1993) weaves together her contemporary circumstances with past experiences and uses a particular story to examine values. As she participated in a doctoral seminar on multicultural education, she began to ask the questions we all ask as our sensibilities change: what was I like *before* I knew this? Did I, in the past, behave in ways I would now criticize? To answer these questions, she turned to story and reflected on her years as a teacher in a cooperative nursery school long before awareness or acceptance of cultural diversity was a distinct component of teacher preparation.

BODY LANGUAGE
Laurie Nicholson Stamp

Because of its proximity to a major university campus, our little nursery school enrolled many children of international graduate students. It was my first experience with children who were not native speakers of English. I was scared out of my wits! There were two little Chinese fellows in my three-year-olds' class who were evidently even more frightened than their teacher. Day after day, I watched Nam Sun and Hale Cho arrive with their mothers and cling to them. Both mothers were very patient and understanding, but they also expressed to me their fervent desire for their children to "fit in." Within a couple of weeks, the boys were working and playing well with the other children and growing in self-confidence. I noticed though that at departure time, they still seemed a bit uncomfortable. Many of the American children would run over to me for a hug before leaving with their parents, but Hale Cho and Nam Sun always shied away, choosing instead to bow to me from a distance before

departing. One day, Nam Sun bowed to me in
preparation for going home and I bowed back.
He looked astonished, then dashed to his
mother's side, smiling and speaking in a very
animated way. Nam Sun took his mother's
hand and headed for the door while looking
back over his shoulder. Then he paused, turned
around, and walked slowly back. I watched him
approach, and when he came close, he raised
his open arms and looked at me. Then I bent
down, hugged him tightly, and he responded
with obvious delight. That fond memory of the
day we learned to say goodbye in two languages will stay with me always.

As Laurie's story illustrates, experiences from a distant
time and place can become tools for reflection here and now
as situations jar them into consciousness.

However, stories are so pervasive in our lives that it is
easy for us to overlook them just as a bird disregards the air
or a fish ignores the water. For example, when we asked an
elementary school teacher to share some stories from her fifteen
years of experience, she instead named some popular children's
stories and books. She did not understand that we were asking
for her own stories about her life in classrooms and was surprised to learn that her stories were of interest to anyone else.
After further discussion and clarification, she agreed that her
teaching behaviors were firmly embedded in stories. She also
realized that not only her current realities but also her experiences as a child and her future actions were woven together by
narrative. Until the moment that she was asked to share and
reflect upon her personal narrative, this veteran teacher failed
to realize the real function and role of story in the continuum
of her personal/professional development. Gradually, she began to recognize that connections existed among her stories, the
stories of other teachers, her students, and learning contexts in
general. As a result, she began to make her tacit knowledge more
explicit and speak in her own "unadulterated teacher's voice"

(Butt and Yamagishi, 1988). As Elbaz (1991) points out, story is particularly useful in making the teacher's voice public because there are distinct similarities between storytelling and teachers' ways of relating experiences; both, for example, do the following:

- Link thought and action and make them public
- Connect the teller with an audience, sometimes creating a dialogue that changes the story
- Take place in a context that affects meaning
- Call upon tradition, yet create new forms
- Allow the teller to express harsh criticism in socially acceptable ways
- Involve a lesson or a moral

Personal narratives are an effective way for educators to arrange, understand, and organize their experiences, giving them a shape, a theme, a frame. After such structuring, stories can be "saved" as teachers preserve the events of their lives in story form (Livo and Rietz, 1986). Regardless of when they occur, stories can serve as guideposts in the course of a teacher's life. When viewed individually, they may seem little more than markers, but when taken together, those narratives indicate both existing and possible courses of action as well as pathways to self-discovery.

To further illustrate the theme of forging connections via story, we present a narrative that illustrates connectedness at three levels: first, at the literal level (incidents in two physical education classes), second, at the abstract level (taking something positive from negative experiences), and third, along a time continuum (connecting past with present).

PHYSICAL EDUCATION
Mary Renck Jalongo

Whenever I visit another university, I
usually find myself looking through the campus
bookstore at the required and recommended

textbooks for various courses. This might seem
like strange behavior, but for a teacher educator and textbook author, it is a quick way to
identify which books are in use and the text
features that are shared or unique. On this particular day, I happened to pick up a book that
I would normally overlook because it is outside
my range of interest — a textbook for a methods
course in physical education. I noted that the
fundamental goals of physical education, as explained in the book, were to develop children's
physical abilities, to introduce them to a variety
of physical pursuits, to help them appreciate the
benefits of exercise, and to encourage students
to make a lifelong commitment to some form of
regular physical activity. My experiences, both
in junior high school and in high school many
years ago, had just the opposite effect, for they
not only convinced me that my body was inferior, they also resulted in an enduring aversion to sports and exercise.

    In seventh grade, I had a gym teacher
who was a former military officer. Every week,
she would line us up in squads, and the squad
leaders — the most athletic girls in the class —
would inspect us, then report back to the
teacher. We were obligated to have clean socks,
pressed gym suits, and freshly polished white
gym shoes every day of class. The week before
Easter vacation, I accidentally left my gym
clothes in my locker. Since the building was
locked until the first day back, I had no alternative but to appear in my rumpled gym suit
and await the squad leader's official report of
my transgressions to the teacher. One other
student and I had been singled out when the
teacher flew into a rage. She ordered both of us
to get dressed, to draw a bucket of water, to

get a bar of soap, and then return to the gym. We washed our gym suits while the rest of the class watched in silence born of fear and embarrassment, then spent the remainder of the class in the bleachers, holding our dripping wet suits. For the first time in my life, I felt cold-blooded hatred. I also understood the meaning of not wanting to give someone the satisfaction of seeing you upset. Ironically, the other girl who sat with me that day became my best friend, for in the midst of our public humiliation, she managed to whisper comments that were both defiant and funny.

Three years later, when I was a sophomore in high school and my sister was a senior, our family was transferred, and we moved from a high school of three hundred to a high school of three thousand. Neither of us was particularly well coordinated. In the middle of the year, we got a new physical education teacher who had a passion for gymnastics. Instead of following the usual curriculum of exposing us to a smattering of various individual and team sports, she devoted the remainder of the year entirely to gymnastics. A student who was on the gymnastics team, headed for the state competition, was brought in to demonstrate. She flipped over the horse, stood on her hands, swung around on the uneven parallel bars, and generally cavorted about like an Olympic hopeful. No member of the class was ever successful in imitating what she saw that day, but my sister and I were the least successful in our respective classes. The teacher informed us that there were certain tasks we had to perform in order to get a passing grade. Failing at any one of them would have jeopardized our plans to attend college. Although my sister and I really

tried, we had little to show for it, other than
huge eggplant-purple bruises all over our legs
and arms. Our mother was so incensed by
these weekly batterings in the name of gymnastics that she wanted to go to school and complain, but we talked her out of it, fearing that
the teacher's obvious disgust for our physical in-
eptitude would only escalate as a result.

In the interest of moral support, my sister and I arranged to meet and commiserate
during the fifteen minutes that sophomores' and
seniors' lunchtimes overlapped. At home in the
evenings, we would sit on our beds in the
bedroom we shared and speculate on all the
evil things we would visit upon that teacher if
we only had the power, then laugh as our im-
aginations grew wilder.

One of the accomplishments that had to
be demonstrated in order to pass was a flip
over the top uneven parallel bar. This was not
exactly something you could practice at home,
as I had done with volleyball and softball.
When the testing date arrived, I stalled a bit
and reviewed the standards before I attempted
the flip: "I pass if I do a flip off the bar, right?
It has to be the top bar, correct? Are you sure
the bottom bar isn't good enough? And even if
I break both arms and legs, you won't take off
points or make me do it over?" The teacher
confirmed all of this and then shaking with
fear, I managed to get to the halfway point,
twisted around, but not on the ground. The
teacher put down her clipboard and pushed my
rump. I landed on the mat, and I passed the
course. My sister had managed to pass too.

The only positive thing that came from
this class was, as with my seventh-grade experience, interpersonal. Up until that point, my sister and I had always had a hierarchical big

sister/little sister relationship. After that year, we became best friends and still are to this day.

It seems ironic that while none of the basic physical education goals were met by junior and senior high school experiences, both of them led to the unintended outcome of enduring and satisfying human relationships. There is yet another positive that emerged from these experiences: I find that in my role as a teacher, they have served me well. Every time that I encounter a student who is struggling mightily with the subjects that I find most interesting and tasks that I consider to be easy, there is this message posted in my brain that reads, "Don't forget gym class." It is a constant reminder that I need to give support and encouragement, that I have to treat students fairly and with respect. In recent years, I have begun teaching a summer reading and study skills course for incoming freshmen, and my reminder is particularly useful with those students who are convinced that reading is their nemesis.

An adult literacy teacher and graduate student I know, Jamie Barron, told me that she begins her classes by asking her students to teach something that they feel very confident in doing. Over the years, she has been the rather inept student in a lesson on elaborate cake decorating, basic auto maintenance, and wood carving, just to name a few. She has taken what for me is a reminder, made it concrete, put it into action, and allowed students to really see it.

So now, my story of positive and negatives in gym class comes full circle. It starts with my life as a student and comes around to my life as a teacher educator who is learning from her students.

This story illustrates several points about connections via story. First, it shows how teachers integrate their reminiscences of childhood and their present and future actions. Secondly, it reveals links among story, personal and career-oriented reading, thought, and dialogue. Finally, the incidents are connected in the teller's mind to the issue of caring/failing to care for and about students. The sections that follow address each of these topics in greater depth.

Stories and Our Childhood Pasts

Stories from the classroom involve the lives of teachers and children, values and beliefs, teaching and practice. This is particularly evident when we turn to the stories of our lives as children. Educators frequently overlook the significance of their own childhood experiences in shaping their attitudes about teaching and learning. Those early experiences often become "hidden curriculum" lessons that we remember far better than any of the thousands of content coverage lessons directly taught.

Some of these lessons show how easily children's feelings and aspirations are crushed. We have a friend who speaks with great emotion about being forbidden to sing by an elementary school teacher, another who remembers a kindergarten teacher's note on a report card, "Cries easily," a third who recalls being severely punished in a parochial school for saying, "Hey! Dog is God spelled backwards!" All of these educators have transformed those negative messages into positive action. The first has taken music and voice lessons throughout her life, sings in the church choir, and is an advocate for the arts in the curriculum. The second is a nurturing teacher who was voted by her students as the best at the university. And the third, as a continuing act of defiance, is witty and articulate. For all three, childhood experience has made them the teachers they are today.

Of course, there are also many positive experiences and messages that are translated into action in teachers' lives, the stories of playing school as children, of teachers who made a difference — stories of success and support.

To get the stories flowing takes only a simple prompt line like, "Think about a particularly memorable childhood experience. How did that incident affect you then? How might it continue to influence you now in your role as an adult and teacher?" High school teacher Mark Connelly (1993) responded to this "child in the adult" motif by making a connection between his experience as a five-year-old and his perspective on gender issues as an adult. His story was written following a session on writing for publication presented to the Southcentral Pennsylvania Writers' Workshop.

KINDERGARTEN REBEL
Mark Connelly

"If the girls in the kitchen did not invite you in, gentlemen, then you're not welcome." With this cautionary statement, Mrs. McWilliams left my friend Pat and me and returned to tending to the better disciplined children in our kindergarten class. The two of us exchanged a look and giggled. We were daily visitors to the "thinking box," an area where the most hardened class criminals were forced to sit in isolation and contemplate their misdeeds. Our most exuberant days sometimes called for two or three visits to the kindergarten penitentiary. We knew that we would be permitted to rejoin our classmates as soon as we repented the error of our ways. If the teacher was satisfied that our apologies were sincere, she would release us with a sigh, then say, "I don't know what I'm going to do with you two."

This time it was different. My five-year-old sense of justice told me that somehow my rights had been violated. We were being punished for irreverent behavior at the small kitchen table where the females of the class learned to serve tea and cookies like proper

young ladies. I couldn't accept that we were
wrong. We had simply ventured across into the
simulated, child-sized household to investigate
what was going on. "Pat," I whispered to my
confederate, "we didn't do anything wrong. We
should be able to play there if we want to."
Just then, we heard the authoritative clomp of
Mrs. McWilliams' orthopedic shoes. This was
our moment, and I was prepared to assert my
constitutional rights. "Well, boys," said Mrs.
McWilliams, "I hope you have thought long
and hard about your behavior this morning."
Pat spoke first: "Uh, Mrs. McWilliams? We,
I mean, I, uh . . . " I was mentally urging my
comrade on when he blurted out, "I'm very
sorry about what we did to the girls, and I
promise I'll never do it again." I was crushed.
My partner had lost his revolutionary spirit. As
Pat was released from solitary, I knew that it
was just me against the now even more imposing authority figure. "And you, young man,"
she said, "do you have anything that you would
like to tell me?" I took a deep breath and answered, "Yes. I don't think that it is fair that
boys aren't allowed to play in the kitchen."
Confident that I held the high moral ground,
I awaited a stimulating debate. Instead, a look
of rage swept across my teacher's face as she
spat out, "Young man, I thought that I told
you to come back here and think about your
poor behavior. Apparently, you did no thinking
at all. You will spend the remaining hour of the
morning right here, and I don't want to hear
another word out of your mouth!" As I listened
to Mrs. McWilliams' retreating footsteps, I felt
no remorse. True, I had had an angry confrontation with an adult, but I had won. And,
looking back on it now, I realize what Mrs.

McWilliams gave to me during that hour in the "thinking box"—an opportunity to contemplate my new role in life as a defender of gender equality.

As Mark's tale suggests, story offers an opportunity for self-discovery—in this case, seeing the origins of adult responses to injustice in that kindergarten incident. In fact, childhood influences can be so strong that it would not be an overstatement to suggest that childhood experience is sometimes the origin of a commitment to teaching. The very image that a teacher uses to characterize his or her role can emanate from childhood: Ray, a junior high school teacher, sees school as a "haven," partly because of his childhood experience, prompted by his concern for a student who is trapped in an abusive family (Butt, Raymond, and Yamagishi, 1988). Many of us who pursue careers in teaching can identify with the "haven" image of school. A headmistress in a British elementary school in an economically depressed area, for example, shared the story of a neglected boy named Nigel. Because Nigel lived in a single-parent family and his mother was an alcoholic, he often arrived at school hungry, dirty, and ill-clothed. Once, when they were preparing for a school outing, the headmistress found him a coat and brought him a lunch because she had rightly anticipated that he would have neither. As he bounded off the bus, Nigel paused, walked back slowly toward her and said, "Isn't it funny, Mrs. G., that teachers care about kids' coats and lunches but mums don't?" Due largely to the school's influence, this child grew up to be a teacher. Surely Nigel, like Ray, saw school as a safe haven.

Since many of us in the teaching profession can look back to describe an admired teacher in considerable detail and continue to emulate that role model in numerous ways, it would be fair to say that stories of childhood classroom experience are connected with stories of our lives as adults and teachers.

Stories of Inauguration into the Profession

"I never cared less whether I lived or died than I did my first year of teaching." Whenever we read to others that statement from Garrett Keizer's (1988) book, we see smiles and nods from teachers. Most of us look back on our first year with a mixture of regret for all the mistakes we made and fondness for our idealism and naïveté. During those early experiences, both preservice and in-service, novices use story as a temporary theory about the world of teaching and a scaffold upon which to build expertise (Berliner, 1986). Narratives about the personal and practical issues surrounding teaching can help to orient beginners to the role and introduce them to the reflective stance that is so crucial to masterful teaching. After sharing some "stories of practice" with her cooperating teacher and discussing her journal entries with the university supervisor, a new student teacher made the following comments.

SIMPLE LESSONS
as told to Mary Renck Jalongo

Student teaching has been an adjustment for me. I don't mean this as a criticism of the university, but the past three and a half years were easy. I am comfortable being a student and I didn't have to work that hard to get A's in most of my courses. But after I started student teaching, I felt overwhelmed, even a little sorry for myself because I had to work so hard. Finally, I said to myself, "Get a grip! You're here for the kids, you have to give it your best. For them." I had a long talk with my cooperating teacher — we were here until five o'clock — and it really helped. I realize now that she isn't pushing me just to be tough, she's really trying to get me to learn the most that I can during this experience. I had been making all these elaborate games and staying up late to do a good job, and she said that it just wasn't necessary, that a simpler activity that put more emphasis on the children's responses would actually be better. You had both been telling me

that I needed to show more enthusiasm and I
didn't know what you meant. Then I watched
my videotape and I understood. At times, I am
concentrating so much on what the children are
saying that I look grouchy! I have this bad
habit of resting my chin on my hand. Well actually, I have lots of bad habits. Another thing
is that when I'm back at my apartment planning, I act like I'll have all the time in the
world for discussion and activities but then, just
like today, I lose track of the time and the children missed five minutes of gym class. She
mentioned it to me and I appreciated that, but
I have to start being more aware myself. After
we talked, I just felt better about it. I was reassured that it isn't a matter of passing or failing
student teaching. It's more a matter of coming
to each lesson not only prepared but really enthusiastic. Other people just don't understand.
They think teaching is "Here's your book, do
this." They have no idea. My friends call and
are disappointed when I'm too tired and busy
planning for the next week to go out on the
weekends. For the first time since elementary
school, I actually look forward to being asleep
by 9 on Fridays.

As with this story of a teacher newly inaugurated into the
profession, teachers' exchange of stories about their lives in classrooms provides a collective experience that enables us to discuss common concerns, learn from one another, and lend mutual
support. Paradoxically, this sense of community is best built
when the individuality of its members is emphasized (Rosen,
1988). Harlan Mathers, a field experience student, kept a journal to describe his beginning teaching experience and his initial steps on the journey of professional self-discovery. Although
Harlan's story is individual, we can all identify with the theme
of struggling to become a more effective teacher.

Early Fears
Harlan Mathers

As I began my second field experience, I
had an immense feeling of apprehension. Why?
Because, my first field experience began with a
disaster—no one had really prepared me for
what I was expected to do. I never realized that
I had so much preparation and planning to do
for the lessons that I had to teach. I also did not
deal with the pressure of everyday life along
with the pressures that my initial field experience presented. By the end, I was getting better,
but my confidence in myself had plummeted to
an all-time low. I was at the point where I did
not want to teach or even go to school. This all
changed in my second field experience. At the
beginning, I was scared and afraid of failing. I
wasn't teaching to the standards that my cooperating teacher and my college supervisor expected. Nevertheless, I kept trying and I gradually got better with the support of my field
supervisor. I began to think that I could teach
and be good at it. My teaching got better and
better with more experience and self-confidence.
Next semester, I am doing my student teaching
and I know my success will continue. I can't
wait until I have my own classroom.

Harlan will never forget this story. He now shares it with
other field experience students and it will be told and retold to
student teachers. Through the power of story, he can step back
from experience, gain a better perspective on it, examine it more
carefully, and make it available to others. Thus narrative connects teachers in the circle of stories.

Narrative and Our Ethic of Care

There is yet another basis for connection through story that has
to do with what the ancient Greeks referred to as *telos*—

overriding purpose. From our perspective as teachers, that *telos,* that prime directive, might be described as "care in the service of students' learning." Nel Noddings (1984) writes about the importance of what she calls "an ethic of caring." She contends that a commitment to the care of others is the cornerstone of a helping profession like teaching. We would add that the moment that we compromise that ethic or fail to consider children's learning, we have ceased to teach in the full sense of the word. As we know, teaching is more than telling. The Latin verb from which the word *teacher* originates means "to show" and that is precisely what the best teachers do. They are model learners; they are an embodiment of the concept of care. The consequences of this orientation and ethic are far-reaching and can filter into virtually every aspect of our lives, as it did with Aileen, the subject of Clandinin's (1986) case study: "[Aileen] very quickly decided whether or not she wanted to enter into relationships with people . . . simply put, people were judged as to whether or not they 'liked kids' and whether or not they were interested in 'kids and education.' People were ruled 'out' if Aileen applied her criteria and found them wanting. . . . All children seemed to fall within Aileen's view of people with whom she wanted to establish caring relationships. Their very existence as children seemed to qualify them as people to be included" (p. 65).

Even though Leanne Weigel is only a college sophomore, she too makes a conscious commitment to care in the service of children's learning when she writes this story in her journal.

THE BEST FEELING
Leanne Weigel

This whole field experience has been
something that I'll never forget. Something that
I did not expect has happened to me every day
out in the field and it was hard for me to
choose just one incident.
One thing that I will never forget is
something that occurred at the very beginning
of my experience. It may be something that

does not seem very spectacular to others, but to me it meant a lot.

It was my second day at school and I was sitting at my desk correcting papers when a student came up to me and said, "Miss Weigel, will you help me on my English paragraph?" Many may think this wasn't anything to write about, but at that moment, I got the *best feeling* inside of me. A student was coming to me for help. I've been asking teachers to help me ever since I began school fifteen years ago, and now someone was finally coming to me. When I helped this child and saw that he learned something from me, once again, I got the *best feeling*. To me, this is what teaching is about and ever since that day, I've been getting the best feelings when I see that I've helped a child to learn something or that I've motivated a child to want to learn.

Although she has barely begun to teach, we can read Leanne's narrative and identify with it. In plain, clear language, she has expressed what it means to become a teacher and to accept the ethic of care. Consider how Jyotsna Pattnaik's story about two teaching experiences in India also demonstrates this ethic of care in the service of learning. Pattnaik perceived her first experience as a devastating failure, and the second as an exhilarating triumph.

FAILURE AND SUCCESS
Jyotsna Pattnaik

"Susama's father has arranged a groom for her," my colleague announced to the six teachers in the staff room. "Oh, no!" I nearly shouted. "What's the hurry? She's only thirteen. She's our top student and has a very bright future."

It was my first year of teaching high school in an economically depressed small town in India. Susama, a girl from a low-caste family, entered eighth grade after securing the highest grade in the State Middle School Certificate Examination. This student personified all that her name, "Susama," stands for—she was personable, a leader, outstanding in every field. Bubbling with enthusiasm and confidence, she defied all the stereotypes that high-caste Hindus use to disregard those of inferior status. Susama consistently distinguished herself among the teachers and her peers.

My view of Susama's marriage was a reaction against an outdated, inhuman social system where girls are forced into womanhood and servitude. I tried to stop the marriage in every socially acceptable way. I called her father in hopes of persuading him to reconsider. He argued that, as there were very few educated men in their caste, it would be more difficult to arrange a suitable groom for Susama after she completed her education. Moreover, the dowry would be more than he could afford. My arguments fell on deaf ears. Finally, I asked Susama her opinion. She gave me a vacant look, as if to say, "Who on this earth ever cared for *my* opinion?" After all, she was only a pawn in the traditions of her culture. Within a few days, Susama repeated all the sacred mantras of her marriage without the slightest understanding of those words or the dramatic lifestyle changes that they portended.

Surprisingly, Susama returned to school after some days of marriage, rekindling my hope that she would pursue her studies. But that hope was very short-lived. Teachers complained of her tardiness, repeated absences,

incomplete homework, and low achievement.
Finally, I called Susama to my office. She entered in a cheap cotton *saree,* two knee-long
braids entwined on the back of head, a bunch
of glass bangles covering her tiny wrists, and a
long red powder line parting her hair. Within
only two months, she had been transformed
from an exuberant child into a defeated adult.
"May I come in?" she requested. I was shocked
to hear the timidity in her voice. I nodded.
Susama entered the room and fixed her eyes on
the floor as I reported the complaints of her
teachers. Large tears began to roll down her
cheeks. I was so overcome with emotion that
my throat gave an involuntary sob. With that,
Susama looked at me and then started to tell
her story. She had married into a large family.
Her husband had six brothers and sisters. The
mother had become bedridden and required
constant care. Every day, Susama awakened at
4 A.M. and went to bed at 11 P.M. after doing
all of the household chores. School was her
retreat, but there was never time to even open
her books at home. She was determined to continue her studies, but now she was uncertain
about how to go on. I was an unwilling witness
to the socially sanctioned exploitation of this
child. The family's motives were obvious—a
nurse for the mother, a servant for the household, a caregiver for the younger children, and
Susama was the answer. In reality, the man
did not want a wife, nor the family a daughter-
in-law. Susama's father was free of his obliga-
tions to his daughter now that she was married,
but it would be more accurate to say that this
child had been abandoned.

Suddenly, I blurted out, "Don't get pregnant now." Susama became shy and I was

embarrassed. India is a country where the discussion of sex and marital relations is kept as secret and hidden as possible, so the discussion ended there.

Then one day it happened, what I dreaded most. Susama went home from school with all the symptoms of an early pregnancy. Her attendance grew more irregular and she dropped out of school.

I met her nearly a year later at the market. She called me *didi*, a term of respect for teachers. Then she said, "I wanted to be like you. I still remember the very first day that you came to our class. I was so impressed with you that I tried to imitate you whenever I used to teach my classmates during recess, repeating one of your favorite phrases, 'Do you understand?' *Didi*, believe me, I tried so hard. But I failed through no fault of my own."

Susama could not have known the vision I had for her future. I was the only female teacher among all the male teachers in school, so it was not unusual that she would choose me as her role model. But I had imagined *her* as the role model for her whole community, an individual who could empower her people with knowledge and fight against the caste system, which is still very much a force in rural India.

Ironically, this devastating failure, I believe, became the pillar of my later successes. I arrived at two guiding principles that would serve me well in years to come.

First, *in most situations, the individual child is more important than the dictates of society.* I should have threatened Susama's father with the illegality of the marriage; in India, the marriage of girls below age eighteen is considered illegal. I should have pursued a lawsuit if necessary.

Second, *as an educator, I must go beyond
what is usual or expected in the service of a child.* I
could have kept track of Susama and involved
her in some informal education channel where
she could have pursued her education at any
age rather than giving up.

Six years later, I left high school teaching
to pursue a master's degree in Delhi. One winter,
I was home on vacation languidly enjoying the
sunshine when my sister told me that Hazda had
come to visit. Hazda has a social class background similar to Susama's, but to my unending
joy, he was pursuing his medical degree at a
prestigious school. As I walked into the living
room, Hazda was standing there, strong and
confident. Upon seeing me, he bowed in
respect. I began to cry.

In Hazda's case, I succeeded because I
put the needs of the child before accepted social
practices. The moment I learned that Hazda
had no electricity or windows in his home to
illuminate his after-school work, I immediately
arranged a study room for Hazda in our home.
I ignored the resentment of relatives who were
scandalized by my willingness to let an outcast
child enter our house. My determination and
persistence, learned from my failure with
Susama, ultimately contributed to Hazda's success. I also kept in contact with Hazda, even
after he completed school, and continued to
guide his career.

Many times, I have thought about my
intense emotional reaction to seeing Hazda.
Clearly, the tears I shed were a joyous response
to his success. But intermingled with my tears
for Hazda were my tears of despair for Susama—
an expression of my deep regret for failing to
rescue her from her culture of silence.

In this vignette, Jyotsna communicates powerful emotions and offers her personal interpretation of the experiences with Susama and Hazda. Yet, her purpose is "not to tell readers what to think, but to invite them into her experiential world and draw them into the story to explore its problems and possibilities" (VanMaanen, 1988). Jyotsna's story is embedded in her culture and embodied in her personal view (Clandinin, 1986). It encourages cross-cultural comparisons while highlighting the universal ethic of teacher responsibility—the capacity to care and the will to respond appropriately.

One great advantage of using story, instead of an essay or an article, for the expression of teachers' voices is that narratives speak straight to the heart of what is truly basic about teaching, yet story can also deal in symbols that make abstractions comprehensible. The following story talks about making acceptance of cultural diversity concrete.

DIFFERENT VIEWPOINTS
Mary Renck Jalongo

Several of my student teachers are in a special program that prepares them to teach in a bilingual setting. Our student teachers teach in an immersion program where elementary content is taught in both English and in Spanish. Because there is no immersion program in our region of the country, these students are assigned to a school two states away. Naturally, we cannot observe as often as we would like, and we rely on videotapes and expert cooperating teachers to compensate. On-site visits are often difficult to coordinate because each visit involves a long drive, a two-day commitment, and an overnight stay for the university supervisor. At one point, we were scheduled to observe when the student teacher called to say it was, of all things, "too cold"! Apparently, this school has a high percentage of families who

are newly immigrated to the United States,
most of them from South or Central American
countries. When the temperature drops below
freezing, attendance drops as well, because the
parents have no previous experience with cold
weather and are fearful that their children's
health and safety will be endangered. I asked
my student teacher how other people reacted to
this, and she said that most of the teachers accepted it, but a few teachers and other members of the community were very intolerant and
ridiculed the children's parents for being fool-
ish. The student teacher said that when she
heard disparaging remarks, she tried to help
people to appreciate the parents' viewpoints by
comparing it to a typical New Englander's point
of view of a typical Virginian's response to
snow and cold. Then she remarked, "I guess
I'm having a real multicultural experience."

Access to such stories about "ideas in use" is vital to forging connections, linking us to where we are, where we have been,
and where we are headed professionally. By paying attention,
letting the story's images affect us, and talking about the story,
we make the abstractions more concrete. When we encourage
teachers to exchange stories in this way, we are expressing confidence in the story to do its work (Barton and Booth, 1990).

Conclusion

Narrative is the spark that illuminates our professional lives.
Whether a story of practice occurred last week or a century ago,
whether it happened to us as children or as educators, whether
it was positive or negative, it retains potential for reflection and
growth today. At the conclusion of *The Brothers Karamazov,*
Aloysha explains the importance of memory to his children:
"There is nothing higher and stronger and more wholesome and
useful for life in after years than some good memory, especially

a memory connected with childhood, with home. People talk to you a great deal about your education, but some fine, sacred memory, preserved from childhood, is perhaps the best education. If a man carries many such memories with him into life, he is safe to the end of his days, and if we have only one good memory left in our hearts, even that may some time be the means of saving us." Memory is unquestionably powerful—and what are memories if not accumulated stories? Reflective practitioners need narratives to connect with their childhood pasts, begin their professional journey, and practice their "ethic of care." We also need story to build our individual and collective memories and to actively construct the history of our lives, both as teachers and as learners. Even when the story "belongs" to someone else, we can identify so strongly that it becomes intertwined with our own experience. It is when we are without any story, borrowed or lived, that learning and progress slow down or even stall.

THREE

WHAT STUDENTS
CAN TEACH US

As students learn from teachers, so teachers can use story to learn from — and about — students. The noted psychiatrist Robert Coles (1989) has a message for teachers when he writes how he was moved and educated by his patients' narrative accounts of their lives: "I was urged to let each patient be a teacher: hearing themselves teach you, through their narration, the patients will learn the lessons a good instructor learns only when he becomes a willing student, eager to be taught" (p. 22).

In the following story, a teacher describes the wisdom and candor of a first-grade child.

Jimmy and Miss Renck
Mary Renck Jalongo

It was my second year of teaching first grade and I had saved my money for months to buy contact lenses (this was years ago, so they were the old-fashioned hard type). I purchased them on Saturday, then wore them to school on Monday. One little girl didn't recognize me at first, so I was really convinced they improved

52

my appearance as well as my vision. After
several of the children remarked that I "looked
different," I took the opportunity to explain to
the class about the tiny corrective lenses, how
they floated on the tears in my eye, and so
forth. That afternoon, just as the children were
lining up for recess, one of the lenses popped
out. I let out a cry of "Oh no! I lost my contact
lens!" and twenty-eight first graders started to
run over to help me. All I could think of was
my expensive lens being pulverized by a passel
of small shoes, so I did something I rarely
did—I yelled. 'Stop! Don't anyone move!" But
the effect of my voice soon wore off and a couple of children started to tiptoe over to my side.
"Freeze!" I yelled, "I don't want *anyone to come
anywhere near me!*" Then I sent a child to sum-
mon my colleague across the hall for help. If
she could take them out to recess with her
class, I could begin the search. As it turned
out, the dumb lens was still in my eye and had
just moved off center. I went outdoors to join
my class. Jimmy Fitzgerald walked up and
said, "You know what, Miss Renck? I liked
you better before when you wore glasses."
Looking back on it, he was right. I am a much
better teacher when I put children's needs
ahead of my own.

It is easy to see the effects of the teacher's sudden change
of behavior on her students. The message in this story provokes
discussion about several critical questions: How does a teacher
measure her relationship with students? How do teachers handle emergency situations? What kinds of problem-solving approaches do teachers need for the classroom?

Teacher narratives as shown in the story of Jimmy and
Miss Renck have the power to help teachers learn from their
students and, as a result, understand them better. In this chapter,

we explore how such stories of practice enable teachers to interact more effectively with students as they learn about students, themselves, and diversity.

Placing Narrative in Context

As teachers, we are familiar with the old adage that "teaching is more than telling." There is a corollary to that statement because what we know and experience must often be told in order to be shared, even if it is only to ourselves in the form of reflection. It is the narrative, the teacher's story, that gives form and meaning to practice because stories enable teachers to put into words what they already know (White, 1981). One of the most natural ways to report occurrences is to compose a narrative, to tell a story that recounts the actions and events of interest in some kind of temporal sequence. Such a story, however, does more than simply outline a series of incidents. It places those incidents in a particular narrative context, thereby giving them a particular meaning (Tappan and Brown, 1991).

Just as physicians and attorneys place their clients' stories in a narrative context to better understand their experiences, so do teachers need to share their stories with colleagues who have had similar experiences. It is these professional stories, both autobiographical and those told by others that validate teachers' experiences, help them understand they are not alone, and considerably influence teaching (Schubert and Ayers, 1991; Tappan and Brown, 1991).

Consider this story by one of five classroom teachers in the George Mason University Case Writing Team (1991). These veteran teachers meet quarterly to write cases of children and schooling as a means of wrestling with the recurring dilemmas they face. Excerpts from the case of Jimmy Monroe, a sixth-grade boy who had never been noticed as an exceptional child, symbolize a universal case of human concern for a middle-school child who is experiencing peer rejection and low self-esteem. Jimmy's teacher shares her concerns about Jimmy during a weekly team meeting. "I really have some uneasy feelings about Jimmy Monroe because of the episode that occurred when my students were constructing geometric figures with toothpicks. I noticed that Jimmy had several toothpicks stuffed up his nose and then attempted to insert them into his eyes. When he realized I was nearby, he quickly put all the toothpicks on the table, picked up his direction sheet, and scanned the print. We did not discuss the toothpick incident."

Mr. Perez, another teacher on the team, wondered if this incident occurred on the same day he referred Jimmy to the administration because of a fighting and shoving match. A third teacher who had been listening intently to the stories of Jimmy Monroe added, "That sounds similar to another incident that occurred this morning. Jimmy had a late pass from the office. I quietly told him that we were working on color-coding our maps from the previous day and then would cut them out so they could be mounted and laminated. He seemed slightly out of sorts, but got all of his supplies and quickly settled into work. I noticed, somewhat disturbingly, that Jimmy was vehemently 'erasing' the skin on his arm. I had seen sixth graders do this before, but never with this intensity. In a short period of time, Jimmy had managed to create a raw welt. Having no desire to publicize his action to the class, I pulled a pass from my desk and quietly said to him, 'May I see you in the hall for a moment?' Once outside the classroom, Jimmy put his hands behind his back, concealing the welt against his body. 'May I see your arm, Jimmy?' He surveyed the floor, making small circles with his toe. With his good arm he attempted to wipe the tears now flowing down his cheeks. I handed him the pass saying, 'I think you had better go to the clinic and have that looked at. We'll talk later.'"

Other teachers on the team began to add their "untold" stories about Jimmy Monroe to the ongoing narratives. One teacher spoke up and said, "You know, what's even worse for this kid is the fact that the other students don't like him." Another teacher added, "You know, you're right. Do you remember when Jimmy was running for sixth-grade sergeant-at-arms? There must have been six or seven candidates for that position. Jimmy was the only one booed when he got up to make his campaign speech." And a third teacher added to the mounting concern.

"That same kind of thing happened when the environmental club presented a new update on our closed circuit television show. When Jimmy came on, all sorts of rude comments emerged." When the teacher later asked the other students about the rude comments, the answers were all about the same: "He's just a creep." "He's a jerk." "He's weird." This long list of events brought Jimmy into sharper focus. The team felt that action should be taken.

The case of Jimmy Monroe highlights the importance of the context for understanding students. Teachers who work with sixth-grade students know that the peer group is an important source of validation for sixth graders' emerging identity. They also know that children "learn about who they are by comparing their thoughts and feelings with those of others" (Berns, 1993, p. 284). Whether or not children feel affirmed or rejected by their peers influences their self-esteem. In Jimmy's case, peer group rejection had shattered his self-esteem and underscored his lack of social skills. Sharing Jimmy Monroe's story precipitated careful monitoring of his behaviors by the sixth-grade team and a conference with his parents. The team wanted to refer Jimmy for professional counseling; the parents, however, felt that Jimmy's behavior was only a phase.

Eventually, Jimmy was placed with another team to give him a fresh start. He enrolled in a mentor program with a male teacher. The incidents of self-punishment all but disappeared. He still provoked his peers, but usually by being silly and acting, as he put it, "stupid." He talked freely to his mentor about schoolwork but was reluctant to share any personal feelings.

Individually, each incident with Jimmy did not appear to be particularly serious. Collectively, however, the teachers' stories supplied the context for recounting Jimmy's actions and behaviors sequentially and provided a fuller picture of Jimmy Monroe. The stories brought to light the importance of embedded contexts (that is, parents, peers, teachers, classroom environment) and their influences on students. In this case, stories enabled teachers to attend to several contextual aspects of Jimmy Monroe's world in helping him feel better about himself both as a person and as a sixth grader. Stories provide a way of coherently linking a series of events in time because "the medium in which we communicate is public but the context from which we speak is personal" (Rosen, 1987, p. 14).

Recognizing Children as Resources

Teachers need to know what their students know and what they need to continue learning. Sometimes this may mean that teachers take the lead with a student; other times it may mean that teachers stay on the same level as their students; and other times it may mean that teachers follow their students' lead (Daloz, 1986).

The following story about a third grader demonstrates a teacher's ability to capitalize on a student as a human resource.

JOHNETTA
Mary Renck Jalongo

Johnetta is a third grader who lives in the small town where I teach. On her walk to school each day, she passes the bank where a neighbor works as a teller. On Monday, she realized that she had forgotten lunch money for the week and stopped in the bank after school to get a loan. The teller was amused by her solution to the problem so she loaned her the money herself, but she also decided to use the opportunity for a banking lesson. She told Johnetta that if she borrowed money from the bank, she would have to pay an additional $.10 in interest. Paying interest was an entirely new idea to Johnetta, but she agreed to pay the $.10 extra for the privilege of having the money right away because her single-parent mother would be out of town for the remainder of the week and she didn't want to ask the babysitter. When Johnetta's mother returned from her business trip, she heard the loan story, both

from her daughter and the bank teller. Johnetta
became intrigued by the workings of the bank,
picked up literature about its services, and later
opened a savings account. When I started my
unit on economics, you can be sure that Johnetta
helped me explain some of the basic principles
of banking and found me a guest speaker, too!

Stories like this one provide a forum for teachers to devise
meaningful responses to "what if" questions (Perrone, 1991).
What if this teacher had ignored Johnetta's input into the curriculum? What if teachers do invite children to share their interests, knowledge, and talents along with the teacher? Other
equally probing questions about setting an agenda for learning
can be generated from the stories teachers tell because the significance of story is a paradox — it lies in selectively interpreting
meanings and meaning comes through interpretation (Rosen,
1987).

Ascertaining Children's Special Abilities

Once we recognize students as resources, we are open to the
many times when quick learners challenge us to go beyond where
we ever imagined we could go with a child. Whether we are
able to encourage children to tell us what they need partially
affects whether students will succeed. Personal narratives can
put learners at the heart of teachers' curriculum and teaching
decisions. Teachers who understand students follow Dewey's
(1897) belief that education must begin with "psychological insight into the child's capacities, interests, and habits" (p. 631).
    A preservice teacher writes in her field experience jour-
nal about the challenge one second-grade child presented in
mathematics (DeEulio, 1993). In one of her early experiences,
she discovered how to stretch Chris's abilities with long division. At the same time, she learned to readjust her own notions
of mathematics for second graders.

CHRIS
Dina DeEulia

There is a blue-eyed, rambunctious eight-year-old boy who simply amazes me! Now granted, young children are taught to do things earlier but — *long division in second grade?* I found out one day in my first field experience that Chris was capable of doing just that.

I remember my father helping me learn my times tables when I was in third grade, but even that comes before long division. My long division skills were not sharpened until I was in fourth or fifth grade. Is that because children today are simply taught to think better at an earlier age?

You see, the day I discovered that Chris was mathematically inclined was when the whole class was working on their reading assignments. Chris finished his assignment promptly and accurately, thus leaving him plenty of time to talk or engage in other inappropriate activities. I already had figured out that Chris was an exception in this class from his responses to questions and his grades, but I still thought he would rather create chaos in his "free" time than ask me for extra math problems for practice. He knew addition, subtraction, and multiplication as if they were written on the back of his hand and did not find them challenging. He asked me to give him "really hard division problems." Division? As in long division? Second graders can't do that! They're too young, they haven't been taught yet. But Chris wanted the problems so I gave him a few easy ones to begin, such as 100 divided by 25 or 50 divided by 25. He mastered those instantly. "Give me really

hard ones," he would tell me. Getting really
excited about his progress, I did just that. I
gave him problems like 350 divided by 25 and
1,256 divided by 4. With slightly more time, he
tackled those successfully. Unbelievable! I had a
little more time so I gave him more problems.
As long as they were problems with no remainders, Chris had no difficulty. But when I gave
him problems with remainders, like 235 divided
by 4, Chris said they "didn't make sense!" Aha,
I thought, there *are* limits to the ability of this
eight-year-old, and I found those limits. None-
theless, his mathematical genius shocked me
and I am grateful for having the experience of
working with a child like Chris.

Nurturing Our Affect

We teachers learn from our students in yet another way when
children reach out to adults and lend support and encouragement in times of distress. Here, one teacher tells the following
story from her junior high school experience.

GARY QUIGLEY
Joy Brewer

Does your school give an award for Student of the Month? Mine does. The guidance
department asks the faculty to nominate worthy
students. Although the criteria have never been
clearly specified, I have made assumptions
based on the characteristics of students who
have received the award over the years.
Usually, they have the highest grades and are
active in school and community activities.
"Who did you nominate?" asked a fellow
teacher.

"Gary Quigley," I said.

"Why Gary? He is no one special."

"He is special to me."

Early in the semester, I had laryngitis. Explanations and directions were either written on the board or whispered to a student to pass on. Gary's deep, authoritative voice got the best response. "Get into your response groups and read your draft to one another," he would call out and his classmates obliged.

Still unable to talk, but feeling well enough to pick up a few things at the grocery store, I ran into Gary in the checkout line the next day. "How are you feeling, Mrs. Brewer?" he asked. "Still can't talk," I whispered.

"Hope you're feeling better by Monday!" Off he ran to catch up with his father. Gary pointed at me, evidently explaining to his father that I was his reading teacher. Then we all waved goodbye. On Monday, Gary arrived early as usual and yelled, "How are you today?" I was pleased to report that I was fine and could do my own talking.

One week later my father-in-law died. The following day, my father was admitted to the hospital after having a heart attack. I arrived home to collapse onto the couch with the flu and take care of my ailing mother. Even though I had already missed an entire week, I had to stay home from school. I even had to convey lesson plans over the phone to my substitute. That was an unforgettable week.

After my father-in-law's funeral, my mother and father went home to recuperate, and I got over the flu before going back to work.

"You had a rough week last week, didn't you, Mrs. Brewer?" asked Gary.

"Gary, I hope I never have another week like it for the rest of my life. Thanks for caring."

The next week, my father had another heart attack and was being kept alive on machines. It was unlikely that he would survive, so I explained the situation to my students. Three days later, my father died.

When Gary came into the classroom on my first day back, he did not greet me as usual. All of the children were busy working on a writing activity begun by the substitute the previous day. I passed Gary's desk. He did not say anything. Instead, he handed me a sympathy card. He was the only student to do so. "Thank you," I said quietly and went to my desk to sit down and read it. I was so moved. There was a lump in my throat. I called Gary's home later that night.

"Mrs. Quigley, this is Mrs. Brewer from the junior high."

"What did Gary do wrong?"

"Nothing. I called to tell you how touched I was when I received a sympathy card from Gary. Did you know about it?"

"Yes, I knew because he asked me to get it for you."

"I just wanted you to know I noticed his sensitivity before this episode. I have a son a lot like him, and it is a rare quality in preteenagers. I wished I could have hugged him!"

"It's great to get a positive call from school," Mrs. Quigley said.

Gary is not involved in many extracurricular activities; matter of fact, he likes to go home and play. He is a good student but not an "academic star." Despite my nomination, he

is unlikely to win the Student of the Month
competition. But I will continue to put his
name forward every month that he is enrolled
in junior high school. He is my Student of the
Year.

Exchanging teaching stories with colleagues reveals how
we get more deeply in touch with our affective selves because
of our students. Sharing experiences from teacher to teacher
often helps uncover who we are and who our students are. Stories like Joy Brewer's urge us to be as adept at reading teacher
narratives as we are at reading books (McDonald, 1992) in order
to learn more about ourselves.

Learning Self-Appraisal

It has been said that the best teachers learn from their students.
It is also true that how teachers view their students is inextrica-
bly bound to their own beliefs, values, knowledge, and experience. Here is a story of how Lijun Jin, an experienced teacher
of adults, learned to appraise herself as a professional as a result
of a powerful interaction with a young child.

YIN-YIN
Lijun Jin

About five years ago, I was invited to
teach English to a group of youngsters in a
summer school in China. Because all my previous teaching experiences had been with adults,
I was unsure about what to expect from young
children. A little girl named Yin-Yin was in my
class. She was a very animated, enthusiastic
learner and was always one of the first to raise
her hand to answer a question or to volunteer
to help others. One day when I asked students
to do choral reading, I noticed Yin-Yin didn't
participate. She was preoccupied with drawing

stars in her textbook. Her behavior bothered me. I always expect a good student like Yin-Yin to behave well in class and be a role model for others. So instead of yelling at her in front of the class, which is the common practice for students who are "misbehaving," I went toward her twice and gently tapped on her desk to arouse her attention. But that didn't work. Some students stopped to look at us. In desperation, I took away her textbook. For a second, Yin-Yin looked stunned, then burst into tears and became so hysterical that I had to call her mother. When her mother arrived, Yin-Yin rushed towards her, crying, "Mom, I want to go home. Teacher Jin doesn't want me anymore!" I was shocked. I had never said that I didn't want to see her in my class. When Yin-Yin did not attend class the next day, I was worried. That afternoon her mother came to my office and requested that I return Yin-Yin's textbook. As I gave her the book, I told her that I was still puzzled by her daughter's strong reaction. Yin-Yin's mother explained that her daughter had misunderstood me. The child thought that taking away her book meant that she was no longer allowed to be a student. After I realized how my thoughtless action had hurt the seven-year-old, I decided to go with her mother to their house to return the textbook in person. Yin-Yin came back to the classroom the next day and acted as usual. However, I could sometimes feel that she was distancing herself from me.

I have thought of this story often, perhaps because it made me feel incompetent. Novice as I was in the elementary classroom, I didn't have the repertoire of strategies needed to teach young children. When Yin-Yin mis-

behaved, I felt a sense of helplessness and
reacted without stopping to consider what was
going on in Yin-Yin's mind. If only I hadn't
taken away her textbook so quickly and had
talked to her individually after class, the outcome would have been different. I wouldn't
have hurt the child or lost control of the class.
Whenever someone inquires about why I
changed my major to elementary education,
Yin-Yin's story comes to my mind. Reflecting
on that incident after the fact enabled me to
picture myself more objectively — but it also
helped me to formulate my professional goals. I
felt driven to become a teacher who could
understand and identify with children.

Carl Rogers (1969) once said that "anything which can
be taught to another is relatively inconsequential . . . the only
learning which significantly influences behavior is self-discovered,
self-appropriated learning" (pp. 152–153). Stories of practice like
Lijun Jin's can be a vehicle for helping teachers more readily
heed Rogers's sage advice as they discover who they are from
the children they teach. These kinds of stories often serve as
turning points in teachers' lives because they form the basis for
confronting similar situations with other groups of children, colleagues, and parents (Connelly and Clandinin, 1988).

Learning About Reluctant Students

The opportunities to learn from students are not limited to students who are bright, or to students from other cultures. We can
learn from *all* students. We often hear teachers' stories about children who have difficulty learning, whether it is the inability to read
with fluency or the inability to negotiate a role in a peer group.
Sometimes, these teachers blame students for their own difficul-
ties, calling them lazy, unmotivated, or negative (Melnick, 1992).
A story by Margaret Peterson about her kindergartners
illustrates how teachers learn from reluctant students. In it, we

see how her dinosaur unit provided an unexpected "hook" for capturing the interest of one of her most reluctant students. At the same time, it reveals how stories can be used for reexamining professional roles as a learner about children, content, and pedagogy.

ADRIAN
Margaret Peterson

Adrian was a child who had difficulty adjusting to all aspects of my kindergarten classroom — until the dinosaur unit. One day he yelled excitedly, "Mrs. Peterson! Mrs. Peterson! I can read that. D is for dinosaur! I love dinosaurs; I have lots of dinosaur books and toys. I know about tyrannosaurus rex and brontosaurus."

Imagine my surprise to see Adrian so excited. It was March and the first time he had shown an interest in anything that was happening in the kindergarten. When I asked him where he learned so much about dinosaurs, he said, "There's a dinosaur in my brain!" Soon Adrian began spontaneously talking with other children about dinosaurs.

By this time, Adrian had taken a book on dinosaurs from his backpack and begun to read to the children gathered around him. It was amazing — he never missed a word.

As I watched all of this, I thought back to the beginning of school when Adrian charged into my classroom, so excited and seemingly out of control. Could this be the same little boy who had spent so much time crying in the class and often disrupting activities when he didn't get his way? I was exuberant, but there were still many questions that came to my mind: why hadn't I recognized those signs of potential earlier—the short attention span, the restlessness during circle time, the "I'm bored with this lesson" expression? Why hadn't I learned from my experience last year with Jessica, another child whose star didn't begin to shine brightly until later in the year? Literacy expert Marie Clay reminds us to "expect surprises" and this new Adrian was quite a surprise!

During the next weeks, Adrian continued to surprise us with his ability to read and write stories on many topics. The tears and disruptive behavior disappeared, and his self-esteem improved greatly. Adrian had become a class leader.

Margaret asks herself several questions that challenge her beliefs about students who have difficulty getting interested in learning. "What if I had not had a dinosaur unit? Would I still have been able to tap into Adrian's potential," she says. It's difficult to say because children do not respond to the same spark. For Adrian, it was dinosaurs, for another child it could be art or music. "I'll never forget the day I discovered the wonderful dinosaur in Adrian's brain and was reminded by a child once again to expect surprises" (Peterson, 1994).

Discovering Adrian's interest in dinosaurs provided the energy Peterson needed to appreciate what Adrian already knew and where he needed to grow. We use stories like hers to stimulate teachers' ways of conceptualizing curriculum and establishing positive relationships with children like Adrian.

Realizing Our Own Bias

Teachers' stories have many uses when it comes to learning from our students. For example, they lend themselves to confronting biases held by educators. These biases, often unknown to us, affect our teaching and influence our interactions with students. If we look at different teacher stories from the perspective of bias, we see how story can be used for teachers to discover and face their own prejudices. In the following story, one student teacher confronts her own bias through a shared story of the time she was placed in an elementary school where 90 percent of the children spoke English as a second language and many had special needs.

Vu

Anna Chacko

I prepared myself to reach out and help these little ones. My feelings and attitude were more sympathetic than judgmental. Because of my religious beliefs that all people are equal, I knew I should not discriminate against these children.

Despite these convictions, I found I was not totally immune from bias. There was Vu, a Vietnamese kindergartner in my classroom. I had difficulty getting him to pay attention because of his limited English. Yet, other children in the class also had limited English, and they did not behave like Vu. I found myself constantly asking him to stop disrupting the class! What bothered me the most was the way he sat down. Whether he was sitting on the floor or on the chair, he always sat on his haunches. I constantly reminded him to sit properly (like a pretzel—the way I thought he should sit) but that just didn't happen. He apparently was used to sitting this way and was probably most comfortable.

At another time, I was supervising the cafeteria and Vu and his friend Hong-Phuc were chatting very loudly in Vietnamese; it really did not sound very sophisticated to me. As always, Vu was sitting on his haunches, so I asked him again to sit like a pretzel.

I am now embarrassed to say that I could not help thinking that the part of the world he

came from was really uncivilized. Then I began
to check myself and my thoughts. I realized I
was making judgments that I shouldn't be making about the ways and languages of others. After all, they are human and I am here as a
teacher to teach and to help children learn.
Ever since that incident, I have made a deliberate attempt to confront my own thoughts and
ask myself why I think this way.

This student's story contributed to her recognition of her
own bias. What was in reality a minor behavioral issue became
instead a cultural one. Many teachers find themselves in multicultural classrooms and struggle for ways to reach children of
diverse backgrounds. Reaching all children depends to a great
extent on a teacher's degree of introspection, and stories of practice such as this one enable teachers to confront biases that con-
tradict what they publicly espouse.

We know that to better understand others, teachers first
need to understand themselves, the framework they bring to
their interactions, and how their biases affect their students
(Hidalgo, 1993). Stories of practice such as "Vu" can help; they
make concrete the "isms" (sexism or racism) that influence teachers and provide a valuable opportunity for unlocking teachers'
own cultural issues, understandings, and biases. Analysis of these
stories often uncovers critical prejudices that inform teachers'
practice because "we, as educators, organize our experiences
through stories. We pull together the streams of classroom actions and actors into cohesive events that we imbue with our
own attitudes . . . values [and] perspectives on teaching and
learning" (Dyson, 1990, p. 193). So we can use teachers' stories of their experiences to help both novice and expert teachers
adapt to individual teaching challenges and circumstances.

Using Story for Therapy

Just as stories can be a tool to reveal prejudice, they can be a
tool that helps the teacher to cope with painful situations. As
teachers, we often consider our stories to be merely interesting

or entertaining without delving into their meanings. But narrative helps us make connections between events; it helps to explain and interpret behaviors. Stories not only evoke meaning but can also foster healing. In other fields, narrative has historically been used to help practitioners gain a fuller picture of peoples' behaviors, feelings, and motives because "stories contain reservoirs of wisdom" (Coles, 1989, p. xii). As teachers struggle to interpret children's distressing and troubling behaviors, their stories of practice often become a therapeutic outlet for them.

One junior high school teacher's story of a child vulnerable to school failure became a therapeutic outlet for her when she included it in a class paper written for a child development course. Pat Tarwater has worked with troubled adolescents for years and has watched their desperate struggles. Telling this difficult story—of how she helplessly watched one boy succumb— helped her.

RODNEY

Pat Tarwater

Rodney was a vulnerable adolescent who walked into my classroom a couple of years ago. My heart ached when I learned of his background. From birth, this little boy had had a difficult temperament. His mother, diagnosed as psychotic, did not have the skills necessary to understand Rodney. His father used harsh punishment to handle Rodney's irritability and restlessness. The family was caught in a destructive cycle in which the mother responded to the abuse of Rodney with tears and the father would react by physically and verbally abusing her. Rodney's response to such scenes of family conflict was to verbally abuse his mother and throw household items at his little brother. His father began to inflict physical pain until Rodney could no longer stand it. The boy arrived at school bruised, swollen, and physically ill. He would not eat his lunch nor hardly any food at home. At the school's intervention, the most obvious form of physical abuse ceased, but more subtle types of physical and emotional abuse escalated.

Rodney was forced to stand in a corner, holding weights in the air until he dropped from fatigue. His mother felt helpless and remained silent. I met Rodney for the first time when he entered junior high school. His teachers found him to be unbearable. He failed many courses and seemed to be out of control. I established a behavioral program, pulled him from a couple of courses, and allowed time in my day for one-to-one attention. He seemed to be improving during the seventh and eighth grades. Then, the next summer, Rodney's father died suddenly from cancer. Most of the teaching staff, including myself, felt this might be a blessing in disguise. Yet Rodney returned to the ninth grade withdrawn and depressed. Ironically, now that his father's ever-present physical threat was gone, Rodney identified strongly with his father for the first time in his life. After the grief and sadness, Rodney became aggressive and violent. He talked of killing himself and involved himself with delinquent youth in the school. He stayed out all night and slept all day. His grades dropped dramatically. He was failing ninth grade. I initiated the same methods as previous years to no avail. I gave him my undivided attention and affection. I notified the social worker, guidance counselor, and school psychologist of the severity of this case. They took steps to help Rodney. We were losing him. Rodney was to be placed in an approved private school as soon as possible. I haven't been the same since he slipped away from me.

Pat understands how Rodney's maltreatment made him so vulnerable to life. She can articulate how his long-term neglect contributed to his inability to function in a junior high school setting. Yet, despite all of her heroic efforts to seek help, provide support, and demonstrate alternative methods of discipline, she could not reach Rodney. Her intensely caring story enabled her to sort through her feelings and come to accept that she did everything she possibly could.

Stories like Pat's can be therapeutic to other teachers as well. Because many teachers work with troubled children, they must confront the very tough and complex issue of how best to work with them. Stories of such challenges serve as important tools for working within the complex culture of today's schools and often help teachers recognize that they cannot always reach every child, no matter how hard they try.

It makes sense to use professional stories as a therapeutic outlet for teachers. Interpreting stories about troubled children helps practitioners feel deeply connected to them. In turn, these kinds of stories have the potential to heighten teachers' sensitivity and caring, thereby increasing the students' chances of success.

Learning About Diversity

One area of sensitivity that is very important today, as we discussed earlier in this chapter, is the area of cultural diversity. In his book, *A Different Mirror: A History of Multicultural America* (1993), Ronald Takaki, an Asian American professor of ethnic studies, tells of his taxicab ride en route to a conference on multiculturalism. The cab driver suddenly turned to him and asked how long he had been in this country. The professor replied, "All my life. My grandfather came from Japan over one hundred years ago."

Why didn't the taxi driver view this man as an American? What can teachers learn from this story about constructing their own knowledge with a different mirror, one that reflects the diversity of this country?

Stories such as Ron Takaki's can build teachers' understanding of what it means to teach diverse populations of students. Simultaneously, they can be a catalyst for teachers' construction of knowledge, building new conceptions of teaching, learning, children, and families because teachers' understandings of their world "are neither given nor universal, but social and cultural constructions" (Perry and Fraser, 1993, p. 19). Sharing stories teacher-to-teacher uses teachers' past experiences as raw data to recognize the contradictions between what they think and the realities of children, schools, and families today. Such recognition comes about because narrative is "a central aspect of human existence, based on the premise that we are, by our very nature, 'story-telling animals'—that we understand our actions, and the actions of others, primarily through narrative" (MacIntyre, 1981).

Exploring Personal Beliefs

As we learn from our students, from their experiences and from our own experiences with them, and as we share other teachers' experiences through story, we are continually getting in touch with our own beliefs. This is because the act of writing and reading narratives of teaching contributes to the construction of knowledge, enabling teachers to explore their personal and professional experiences and interpret them as they "form and reform their attitudes, opinions, and experiences within the history of their perceptual beliefs" (Ambrose, 1993, p. 275).

Stories contain a residue of memories that inform the practice of teaching. These memories stimulate teachers' thinking and analysis because "stories not only give meaningful form to experiences we have already lived through, they also provide us a forward glance, helping us to anticipate meaningful shapes for situations even before we enter them, allowing us to envision endings from the very beginning" (Mattingly, 1991, p. 237).

Personal narratives invite teachers to revisit and reinterpret their past. Educators can use their teaching narratives and those of others to connect their experiences with new knowledge; to consider the differences in stories of practice; to understand why there are multiple stories; and to question the unexamined in their own lives (Grumet, 1989).

To illustrate these ideas, we use the story told by Eileen Foulger, beginning her first clinical experience in second grade. She tells of an episode during her nutrition unit in which she realized how much she did not know about other cultures.

BREAKFAST
Eileen Foulger

In my ESL class, children come from
many different cultures. During one of my
nutrition lessons, I asked the children to make
a menu. In our brainstorming, I elicited various types of food we could have for each meal.
Some of the foods mentioned for breakfast were
cereal, fruit, chicken, and rice. I thought that
the child who suggested chicken and rice for
breakfast was confusing mealtimes so I asked,
"Do you eat chicken in the morning before
school?" I thought for sure the child would say,
"No, I meant dinner," but he did not. The
same response occurred for the rice.
   Right then I wanted to say that chicken
and rice were foods for dinner or lunch but I
thought to myself, "Don't say what you think
until you make sure that this information is
correct for this child. Wait with your response."

Eileen's story illustrates her realization that indeed children do eat a variety of foods for breakfast, which made it possible for her to accept this child's answer. Her cultural sensitivity heightened her professional demeanor while at the same time
alerting her to gaps in her own knowledge.
   Part of what we teachers bring to the classroom are our
own personal experiences. Whether conscious or unconscious,
stories help explore what we know, what we still seek to learn,
and what leaves us feeling uncertain. In Maxine Greene's (1988)
words, stories encourage reflection on the diversity of human
experience and in this way help us "to recognize . . . that there

are always multiple perspectives and multiple vantage points . . . to recognize that no accounting, disciplinary or otherwise, can ever be finished or complete . . . " (pp. 128–129).

Narratives and our ways of "reading" and "telling" them also bridge the gap in our professional lives by bringing together a collective knowledge about teaching. Stories of teaching that are read and told cause teachers to "recast, reframe, and reconstruct past understandings . . . and promote careful consideration of teaching's complex nature" (Ambrose, 1993, p. 276).

Conclusion

Teachers of all backgrounds must look both inward and outward, share their voices, listen carefully to their students, and add their own stories to the literature on teaching because what really teaches us about the world of teaching is reflection about the differences among people. We can learn about those differences most poignantly from today's students themselves, who represent so many different cultural and ethnic groups. Stories of experience go beyond fact and deepen teachers' insights into their students. Those differences teach children and teachers. As Robert Coles (1989) so strongly depicts in *The Call of Stories,* stories do not prescribe a way of life. Rather, they evoke reflections of personal experiences that affect our actions.

FOUR

THE PRACTICE
OF REFLECTION

Our discussion thus far leads to a crucial point: that one of the most important decisions a teacher makes is whether or not to become a reflective educator. A reflective teacher is one who really thinks about teaching behaviors, takes responsibility for those actions, and goes about the business of educating children with enthusiasm and openness (Grant and Zeichner, 1984). Reflective teachers do not act blindly on impulse or rely on routine and tradition. Instead, they carefully consider and reconsider their beliefs and practices to reconstruct and reorganize their experience. For only when teachers activate the assumptions underlying their teaching can they begin to interpret their meaning (Greene, 1973). Given the hundreds of classroom interchanges and events that transpire each day, reflective thinking can be applied to incidents during the day, at the end of the day, and at the end of each year.

Sparks-Langer and Colton (1991) identify three elements of teachers' reflections:

1. *Cognitive,* which deals with information processing and decision making

2. *Critical,* which examines the influence of experiences, beliefs, goals, and sociopolitical values
3. *Teacher narratives,* which are teachers' own interpretations of the events that occur within their particular contexts

Engaging in storytelling through teacher narrative is the heart of teacher reflection because narrative is validating. It retrieves and rescues our experience from the realm of a random blur into the realm of meaningful experience. Stories provide teachers with a way of seeing into themselves; they offer good counsel and can be a source of comfort. Through story, teachers can raise profound questions and shape the landscape of their minds for the whole of their lives (Barton and Booth, 1990). Personal narratives help teachers to unlock beliefs, perceptions, and experiences.

Rose Weber, a second-grade teacher, illustrates the *critical* cognitive and narrative elements of teachers' reflection with the following brief story.

LETTERS
Rose Weber

Eighteen years ago, I wrote a personal letter to every child in my classroom and his/her family at the end of the school year. I did not continue the practice with following classes. Recently, I saw a student from that first class. After all these years, the student related to me how much that letter meant to her and her family. I decided to write letters again this year to my second-grade students. I have already received positive feedback from several proud and happy families.

The student's comment caused Weber to reflect and reexamine a past, forgotten practice and critically assess her own behavior. When she shares her story with colleagues, Rose celebrates reinstituting a successful practice as well as encouraging them to experiment with this practice themselves. In this way, both the cognitive and narrative elements of teachers' reflections are addressed. Reflective teachers also use the strength of their stories, their "own products," to acquire insight about values, teaching, children, curriculum, and discipline.

Types of Reflection

Today, classroom teachers are being asked to become more reflective about their teaching, to articulate why they do what they do. Stories of practice offer a vehicle for teachers to become more competent reflective practitioners in three ways (Ross, 1989) by

1. Developing reflective processes such as problem-identification and analysis
2. Developing attitudes necessary to reflection such as open-mindedness and introspection
3. Defining the content of reflection such as what teachers think about

Donald Schön (1987) describes two types of reflective thinking: reflection-in-action and reflection-on-action. Reflection-in-action is the ability to "think on one's feet" when faced with the many surprises or puzzlements in our daily teaching. Reflection-on-action occurs when teachers look back upon their classroom practice.

Reflection-in-Action

For teachers, reflection-in-action makes explicit teachers' tacit knowledge. Central to the ability to think on one's feet is the ability to identify and address a professional problem. Stories of practice, which reconstruct experience, are one way to promote teachers' reflection. Marshann's story illustrates reflection-in-action.

WATER PLAY
Marshann Snyder

Marshann teaches thirty children in a child-care program. She felt comfortable that her program contained enough creative activities to challenge children's thinking. But after reading Selma Wassermann's book, *Serious Players in the Primary Classroom* (1990), she became intrigued with the notion of teaching how to think by providing more investigative play experiences and asking more probing questions. To help children grow as thinkers and experience the process of inquiry sounded exciting to her but hard to implement. Considering the broad age span of her children (kindergarten through sixth grade), she decided to infuse this more investigative approach to learning into water play. Marshann tells about how she used a large rectangular water table that had been used for planting seeds to have children start exploring the scientific principle of conservation. When the table was filled with water, she added different shaped containers (each held two cups), funnels, and two measuring cups that held the same amount of liquid. After watching four children play with the water and the objects, she eagerly asked Aaron, age six, "What did you find out about the amount of water it takes to fill the tall, skinny container and what did you find out about the amount of water it takes to fill the short, fat container?" He replied, "This one, which is the fat one, compared to the tall one . . . [he stopped, paused, and then started again] This fat one looks like it only holds one-half of the tall one but when you pour them together — it's the

same amount!" "Right then," says Marshann,
"I heard myself cut off his own thinking to seek
an answer I was looking for. I knew I had to
ask more open-ended questions and decided to
add a larger variety of containers, measuring
cups, and plastic tubing to elicit more involved
investigative play."

Marshann related that she was neither satisfied nor comfortable with her ability to ask probing questions, so she started
to carry around cards that listed more open-ended questions she
could ask the children. Her story illustrates reflection-in-action
because Marshann reconsidered her questioning techniques *during teaching* and made a conscious decision to make adjustments
to them.

In Marshann's retelling, she used story to become a more
capable reflective practitioner (Ross, 1989). She grappled with
her own reflective process of asking better questions to probe
children's thinking; revealed her own attitudes and understandings to herself first about how she was inhibiting children's thinking; and defined the content of her thinking by focusing on more
inquiry-oriented questions. Interpreting teaching stories in this
way fosters a reflective stance about one's practice that can affect
teachers' thinking by helping us know who we are, who we were,
and who we are becoming (Bruner, 1986).

Reflection-on-Action

Narratives also invite teachers to communicate about and reflect
on their practice after it occurs. Through locating and relocat-
ing their voices within their own world of teaching, teachers gain
insight into what they know, what they think, and who they
are (Noddings, 1991). Reflecting on practice is one way a teacher
gives meaning to teaching.

In telling and writing stories, teachers actually "autho-
rize" their lived experience (Tappan and Packer, 1991), retelling and reliving them to gain insight into their practice and
professional identity. The real potential of narrative for increased

professional understanding however lies in the dialogue, reflection, and analysis of critical teaching issues that are instigated by the story. Only through this type of analysis can teachers forge their personal and professional self-understandings of their own practice.

Consider how the story of one preservice teacher we'll call "Anna" communicates reflection-on-action that prompted her to modify her practice. This excerpt from her journal, kept over a three-month transition period, shows the changes she made as she learned to develop more appropriate first-grade math lessons.

PACKAGED LESSON
"Anna"

I was teaching a prepackaged math lesson on comparison of names. In the lesson, I gave the children a ditto sheet, asked them to write their name on the first line, and then told them to pass their sheet to the next person who would write their name on the second line. This process continued until all six lines on the paper were filled. After all of these tasks, the children were then supposed to count the letters in each of the six names, write the total number of letters in a little circle at the end of each line, determine the longest and the shortest names, and finally, cut and paste the names on another sheet of paper from shortest to longest. From the beginning, the children had problems passing the papers and I had to do it for them. Some had difficulty writing one letter in each box. Most of them could not determine which name was the shortest and longest by just looking at the numbers. Many of them could not even cut! It was soon apparent to me that when the children attempted to order the strips from shortest to longest, their inaccurate cutting

would cause problems. When I realized this, I
abandoned the lesson out of sheer frustration
and sent the group to join others in the ongoing learning centers. I knew this lesson wasn't
working but was too frustrated to figure out
what to do right then.

Anna told her story to her peers as they engaged in their
weekly problem-solving groups. Retelling her story enabled her
to reconstruct her experiences and see the potential of curriculum rather than its constraint. With her peers, she explored ways
to modify the lesson that would enhance first graders' understanding of comparison. In this case, Anna's story stimulated
a group discussion of appropriate ways to make the math lesson more concrete through the use of manipulatives before the
lesson; ordering alphabet blocks from shortest to longest using
a ruler as a concrete measure; and discussing the activity sheet
before distributing it to the children. Anna's story exemplifies
how reconceptualization led to significant changes in her ways
of knowing, thinking, and being. In fact, it facilitated deeper
forms of reflection (Noddings, 1991) on adapting packaged lessons to different groups of children.

Jane Mize also communicates reflection-on-action. Her
story is another good example of a preservice teacher's developing sense of what it means to be an accountable yet creative
teacher. Her voice reveals her frustrating attempts to incorporate
creative, child-centered activities in her unit on "Zoo Animals."
She conveys real concerns and worries in a student teaching
seminar about feeling tied to the objectives of the school division.

It seems that the art objectives for second grade only
deal with the technical aspects of art. There is no
listed objective for creative expression. My principal says I have to use the district's objectives for
all my lessons. How can I infuse creativity into the
lesson when I have to create lessons around these
noncreative objectives? When I tried to tie the lesson to problem solving with authentic materials,

the only objective in the entire curriculum was not
creative at all—it was a math problem-solving objective that dealt with addition and subtraction. I
don't understand what to do!

Jane's comments reveal a common dilemma for preser-
vice teachers. She interprets district objectives literally and feels
limited in what she can do. At the same time, she is beginning
to see herself as a creative, energetic teacher. Through her story,
the class analysis of what she was experiencing and her own
reflections on her evolution as a teacher, Jane identified ways
to infuse creative lessons into her unit while still being accountable to the program objectives. In this case, Jane's communication of her ideas was an effective tool for her growing self-
understanding as a teacher, for communicating about her practice, and for wrestling with the philosophy-reality conflicts that
many teachers face.

Stories and Lived Experience

Over the years, we teachers tell and write many stories about our
work. These stories reveal our experiences, define who we are,
explain ideas, and enable us to pass on traditions (Farwell, 1988).
Not only do narratives help individual teachers make sense of
teaching, they also enable other teachers to connect with the larger
picture. Hence, stories give meaning to our unique lived experiences through reconstructing the past and guiding future decisions (Connelly and Clandinin, 1989; Tappan and Packer, 1991).
Connelly and Clandinin (1988) describe three distinct
characteristics of personal narratives; each has direct applica-
tion to the teaching context.
1. *Voice* enables teachers to communicate meaningfully
with other teachers in a community of learners as well as facilitat-
ing their own understanding about their teaching experiences.
Narrative forms, as journals, storytelling, and biography, enable teachers to reflect alone and "think back" about themselves
and their practice. As teachers come to understand their past,
they express themselves through story in the present.

2.   *Metaphor or image* refers to the teachers' language, actions, and beliefs that inform their daily practice in the classroom. Because teaching is something that is not often discussed, using figurative language to describe it gives teachers an added opportunity to represent their practice to others. The images evoked by common metaphors of teaching, which include teacher as parent, performer, orchestrator, or commander, provide fertile material for analyzing the language used to describe teaching and teachers and the associations conveyed by such images.

3.   *Dialogue* provides the opportunity to make teaching public for others to examine as well as the opportunity for the author to examine his or her own thoughts. Dialogue can occur from teacher to teacher, teacher to student, teacher to parent, or teacher to administrator. These exchanges provide another vehicle for making sense of the practice of teaching.

Choosing a Voice

Hope Brady, a kindergarten teacher and member of a teacher-research group, was struggling with ways to encourage parents' active involvement in their children's reading development at home. Excerpts from her story portray her deep belief in fostering a love of reading by her kindergartners and their parents through the creation of a "read-aloud" program at home and at school. As you read Hope Brady's story, consider how the narrative incorporates the three elements of voice, image, and dialogue.

READING ALOUD
Hope Brady

While reflecting on why I chose to institute this particular type of reading program in kindergarten, my thoughts drifted back to my first teaching experiences in fifth and sixth grades. I really disliked teaching reading. It seemed so boring. I preferred motivating children to think creatively and to enjoy writing.

When I began teaching kindergarten, I finally enjoyed teaching reading and wondered why. The big books were so much more interesting, and the children's attempts at writing reflected their own enthusiasm. Helping to facilitate a love of reading for both children and parents became a major part of my kindergarten program. A "take-home read-aloud" program in my kindergarten class would give me opportunities to encourage parents to read with their children. I want to help parents understand that reading aloud to children at home would foster interested and enthusiastic readers in the years to come. As a parent, I had already seen the positive benefits of such a program with my own daughter. I have always wanted to do this but was never fortunate enough to teach in a school that would support this endeavor.

Hope's *voice* (point of view) of care and commitment to developing lifelong readers as well as her initial frustration and boredom ring true throughout her story. The story depicts her own disposition toward reading; she regards reading as dynamic and engaging. At the same time, it reveals her desire to risk trying something new—a reading program for children and families in which she deeply believes but had never before attempted.

Narratives enable teachers to hear their own voices, so often silenced in the past. Stories of practice can inspire others to contribute their voices to the ongoing professional dialogue and open their minds to change (Jalongo, 1991). Moreover, they bring new perspectives and a sense of connectedness with other teachers experiencing similar struggles.

Creating Images

Teachers' stories also evoke images. Images are the mental pictures we create from others' vivid descriptions, which make complex, abstract aspects of teaching more concrete and personally

meaningful. As another excerpt from Hope Brady's story illustrates, "stories are lived before they are told" (MacIntyre, 1981,
p. 197). Hope's own words enable us as readers and listeners
to envision and thus participate in her experience.

READING ALOUD, *continued*

It was very apparent that the kindergarten children enjoyed reading at home each
night, as did their parents. They seemed to enjoy rereading books they had read at home in
the reading corner, and they discussed books
when they first came to school. I noticed more
children attempting to read and/or successfully
reading easy readers. All of this literacy activity
had occurred before, but now different children
were participating. I was also somewhat embarrassed when I noticed a parent had written,
"He's doing a great job reading each night." I
didn't even know that boy could read, although
I did know he was becoming better at invented
spelling. That morning I sat with him and
asked him to read with me. This incident made
me more aware of providing *all* of the children
with more opportunities to read aloud and/or
encourage them to read to a partner. I am always giving them opportunities to use their invented spelling. Now I need to focus on reading aloud with them individually as well. . . .
       Within the first two weeks, I lost six
books. Some of these were my own personal
books; others belonged to the school. I talked
with my principal and explained my dilemma
about the lost books, wondering if I should
continue this program. The principal's response
of "I don't care if they lose every last one — it
means they are reading!" shocked me. I was so
relieved and thankful for teaching in a school

with a supportive principal who helped me get
back on track. I realize now that I cannot stop
this program just because a few children lost a
few books.

The images in Hope's story are concrete and convincing.
They help readers create mental pictures of children learning
to read. As we envision Hope's struggles to develop positive attitudes toward reading, we can also begin to identify with her
and her situation. An image-rich story made clear the priori-
ties and values she needed to separate a few lost books from
the larger mission of building positive attitudes toward reading.

Through sharing her story about the lost books with her
teacher-research group, Hope solved a minor drawback she first
perceived as major. She invented a check-in and check-out system for the books that enabled the children to assume more
responsibility for their materials. She also validated for herself
the importance she attached to such a program.

Joining in Dialogue

Narrative stimulates dialogue among teachers, which provokes
thought and frequently elicits other stories of practice. Hope's
final comments from her story illustrate one way dialogue can
bring new meanings to teachers' stories.

LISTENING TO TAPES
Hope Brady

Discussions in our teacher-research group
made me aware of how important it is for
fathers to read to their children so that boys do
not view reading as a "female-only" activity.
One preschool teacher in our group asks fathers
to tape a child's favorite story to use in a listening center. I passed this information on to the
children's parents and two fathers asked for and
taped stories for our listening center. Their

children are so proud to go to the listening
center to hear those tapes. I never would have
thought of this on my own.

As Hope's story shows, conversation has the power to
affect the ways teachers think about teaching and learning (Schubert and Ayers, 1992). But until a teacher enters into self-
dialogue — conversation with oneself — participation in the ongoing communication about teaching and learning with colleagues is inhibited. However, public discourse is important for
self-reflection because it enables teachers to think aloud in the
company of colleagues. When Hope recounted her story and
her concern about a "female-only" image of reading, the dialogue and sharing that was a part of the teacher-research group
proved to be a turning point for her and her reading program.
Never before had it occurred to her to explicitly invite fathers
to record books on tape for her listening center.

The voice, image, and dialogue that permeate teachers'
own stories empower them to become more reflective and collegial professionals. Personal narratives legitimize the real-life
experiences of teachers and provide a way for teachers to become researchers into their own practice because "in the telling
of our stories we work out new ways of acting in the future"
(Connelly and Clandinin, 1988, p. xvi).

Narrative as a Context for Examining Practice

Narrative, as we have discussed, serves several functions. It provides us with a dynamic story of human action that differs significantly from the logical, cause/effect, scientific way of knowing (Bruner, 1986). It provides a context for teachers to examine
and interpret their unique professional experiences as they share
them with other teachers, thus acting as a catalyst for change.
It can also validate the fact that teachers are a rich source of
knowledge about practice that, until recently, has been ignored
as a resource worth examining (Yonemura, 1982).

Nancy Lusk, a preschool director, shares her story, which
is a good example of how narrative encourages examination of

practice. Nancy tells how she confronts her struggle to engage
her staff in more appropriate early childhood practice while she
is simultaneously redefining her role as director of a preschool.

ME? A STAFF DEVELOPER? YES!
Nancy Lusk

When I began the job as co-director, I
did not think about staff development as being
part of that job. I was focused on the mechanics
of running the school — filling classes and maintaining the supply closet. Last year, my focus
was to upgrade our administrative functions:
writing policies, creating files, and developing
job descriptions. Ah, I thought, this is what a
director does!

After taking a class in early childhood
curriculum and instruction and as a result of
sharing experiences with directors of other programs, I realized that not everything taking
place in the classrooms in my school was developmentally appropriate. Curriculum changes
needed to be made not only for the children
but also to keep the program competitive in the
community. At the spring 1992 staff meeting, I
announced that beginning with the 1992–93
school year, all the classrooms would be organized into learning centers. I instructed each
teacher to read certain literature and I promised
to set up a workshop in late summer on learning centers. Over the summer, I left the
teachers to their own devices. In late August,
a resource person conducted a workshop on
centers, the first in-service our staff ever had.
The workshop leader explained in simple terms
the purpose of centers, the process of setting
them up, and the teachers' role. As I look back
now, I realize that the in-service contained

an overabundance of new information for the teachers to absorb before they could implement centers.

The classrooms are now set up in centers. But most teachers are not using them as part of an integrated curriculum. Some are slowly slipping back into the "project of the day" mode. One teacher in particular is very resistant to the change. She still wants to sit down with the children one on one and help them do their projects. I have tried to work with her informally to encourage her to give the children choices and to let them do their own work. But she continues to hurry children through meaningless projects.

When I worked with this same teacher last year to create a reading center in her room, she seemed to welcome my assistance. This year, however, the reading center is not being used at all except as a place for children to go while the teacher cleans up after lunch.

I am just now beginning to see that what has happened in my school is resistance and rebellion as a result of my mandating a change to centers. My teachers had no choice and no input. Obviously, one of the teachers did not "buy into" the notion of centers. So, although the rooms will remain organized into centers, I am "stepping back" and not pushing hard for the changes I want. I am now talking with the teachers informally about an appropriate use of centers and hope to begin collaboration with them.

Needless to say, I have felt very frustrated and at times quite annoyed with the teachers because of what I perceived as stubborn resistance. I've had to reevaluate my role as director to include purposeful staff develop-

ment. But I am now beginning to see my role
also as educator. I am beginning to understand
the enormity of the change I mandated and
how threatening that change has been to these
teachers. Our program has operated in a
familiar "rut" so long that, as a first step, I
need to help the teachers see the necessity for
change. I have been far too impatient and want
too many changes at once. I am not hearing
from the teachers about their problems and successes, so the lines of communication have nar-
rowed. I need to reestablish the rapport.
Though I regret what I did in ignorance, I do
not feel guilty.

I am taking a good, hard look at motivation. Who has motivated me? What were their
characteristics? Whomever I think of, I know
they care for me; they believe I can get the job
done; they are resources for me; they give me
freedom to develop at my own pace. I have not
acted in this way as a motivator to my staff. I
never saw that as a primary part of my job.

Nancy's story illustrates her developing ability to examine and change her own practice as a preschool administrator.
She has new understandings of the importance of developing
her own knowledge to support her staff. She also sees the need
for continual learning. In her own words, her story, told and
retold, "has changed my perspective of the job of administering
a preschool and helped me gain confidence about my task. I
believe that much of what an administrator does must be related
to staff development. It certainly is a much broader role than
I ever realized."

Stories such as Nancy's, epitomize how teachers think
about their practice in the context in which they teach. If we
take an anthropological perspective of context, then all behavior
is influenced by the circumstances in which it occurs. Through
stories, teachers can revisit teaching situations over and over

again, providing the context for reflecting and reconsidering circumstances rather than merely recollecting them (Krall, 1988). Moreover, stories of practice enable teachers to give serious examination to a larger context: how their personal values, beliefs, instructional practices, or views of children and families inform their teaching.

Narrative as a Catalyst for Teacher-Research and Curriculum Design

Another way of viewing the importance of teachers' stories is as research. They provide a logical first step for teachers to delve more deeply into their practice. That is because as storytellers, practitioners are already incipient researchers into their own practice. Storytelling is a natural basis for action research because it is something practitioners already do (Mattingly, 1991).

In the wake of school reform, there has been a shift in the role of the classroom teacher. Instead of teacher as technician, the teacher is now considered to be the initiator of curriculum and method. Teacher narratives can be central to this role shift by focusing the teacher's thinking on curriculum design.

Teachers often report that much of their knowledge about teaching comes from being a teacher (Connelly and Clandinin, 1988). As teacher-researchers, many teachers begin to search their minds and hearts to examine their practice. Like a story, in teacher-research, people do things and as a result situations change, or things happen to people and as a result people change.

Liz Klein's story serves as an interesting example for teacher-research in curriculum design because it focuses explicitly on her attempts to incorporate a model for critical thinking into first grade. Moreover, it exemplifies how stories can provoke thinking about teachers as learners and teachers as risk takers as it relates to curricular change.

Liz teaches in a large suburban school. After reading Selma Wassermann's (1990) book, she became fascinated with the notion of empowering children by challenging their thinking, respecting their decisions and choices, and encouraging investigative play.

LIZ'S EXPERIMENT
Liz Klein

"I was training an intern and I thought that maybe I shouldn't try [these] idea[s] right now," said Liz. "Wait until January. No. I would take the risk. We could learn together. I thought I would use the play-debrief-replay model in science. If it worked, I would extend it to other curriculum areas. If I didn't see results, I would leave it and try something else. I knew the hardest part would be the questioning techniques (and it was)!"

Using her weekly teacher-research group meetings as a starting point, Klein began her transition to designing a more experiential curriculum. She wrote down her objectives for her unit on "Falling Leaves" and compared them to those of the school district. She also recorded her observations of the children's behaviors and learnings in a journal. When she felt satisfied that the objectives were congruent, she wrote about the next step—having to examine her beliefs about learning: "I believe in the importance of children working in groups. This means that silence is not golden. Children need to talk and hear each other's ideas. They need to move about the room. I call this business the 'industrial hum.' I also believe in children's play and children's ability to think. After I figured out the objectives and identified my beliefs, I identified the big idea of my science unit, that living things change. Now, I had to weave my activities together so that the children would be challenged by studying how living things change."

As she thought through her ideas with her colleagues, Liz designed a variety of experiential play activities where children could test hypotheses by observing changes in their surroundings (for example, changing colors in the leaves, birds flying in a V formation). The children also took bags onto the playground to collect objects to discover how things change in the fall. Back in the classroom, they talked about their collections in small groups. Klein observed that some of the groups simply explored the leaves, acorns, berries, pods, and seeds that they found. Others classified them into categories. This "hands-on" activity served as the basis for Klein's debriefing sessions with the whole group. She began by asking the children to describe what they observed and to compare their objects by likenesses and differences. She recorded their observations on a chart. In the replay session, they collected more signs of fall and again experienced the debriefing session. Liz recorded the following in her journal:

The children discovered through replay that some leaves have saw-like edges; some have lobes; some leaves are shaped like hearts; nuts and acorns are seeds; tendrils are vines that grow on trees and cling to them. When I finished the lesson, I thought about a lot of things, particularly that child-initiated learning takes time and much of it is interdisciplinary. I was not only teaching science but I was also teaching language arts.

One of the things that I noticed about the children was their level of interest and enthusiasm for investigating on their own long after I had expected. They continued to gather leaves on the playground and ask more questions about the objects they were collecting. I don't think I'll ever bring closure to this unit. In the past, I would always bring closure to a unit, never to open it again. But the debriefing, talking together about their common experiences, ends on a note of unfinished business. If I bring closure, there is no need for replay.

When I gave children permission to find out for themselves, I empowered them. That is what I saw in the replay of my first graders. Some of the children even made their own leaf booklets at home and shared them with the class of their own accord. It is December and they are still working on leaves and finding out new things. I am seeing that children do not develop concepts by having concepts explained. Telling is not the best way to develop understanding.

Liz's story invites questioning and discussion of her role as a curriculum designer. Through the support she gained from her teacher-research group, Liz was able to tread in new territory as she created her own story of curriculum design. Because of the unique nature of narratives, they enable teachers like Liz to delve into their own idiosyncratic and personal storehouse of knowledge (Yonemura, 1986). The story enabled Liz to consolidate her understandings and affirm her beliefs of how children best learn concepts. More importantly, regular reflections of stories of practice help teachers to understand what it means to teach children critical thinking and to respond more confidently to questions raised about play activities. Narrative thus provides a window into classroom events. "To interpret such a narrative demands extensive knowledge of personal, professional, institutional, and cultural paradigms for teaching. By careful reconstruction and reading of these . . . narratives, [we] can thicken our understanding of the quality of particular classroom moments" (McDonald, 1992, p. 27). Such knowledge rises to the level of the conscious mind through teacher-research.

Stories as a Metaphor for Change

While Liz's story reaffirmed her deep-seated beliefs, stories, a compilation of far-reaching experiences, can also offer a unique opportunity to reflect upon and actually begin to change one's practice. Consider the, following story. Martha is a reading specialist who has taught all elementary grades in the same inner-city elementary school for twenty-eight years. In a recent conversation with Joan Isenberg, she was bemoaning her plight as a teacher and despairing about the future of children she was teaching. As I listened uncomfortably to her story, her words evoked unwelcome but vivid images of children doomed to failure by a teacher unable to respond to the teaching situation with anything but a "utilitarian" or "what works" (Goodman, 1984) approach to teaching and learning.

> I'm tired of policing the halls and checking for weapons. You can't possibly know what it's like to be teaching here. These children can't learn. Their parents aren't home, they come to school hungry and dirty, they're really not interested in school. . . . I'm tired of constantly thinking of ways to motivate them. I've come to believe that they are just not smart. Whole language doesn't work with these students, nothing does—nothing. I know from my twenty-eight years at this school what children can and cannot learn and these children cannot learn. I'm convinced.

Although Martha's comments may be a depiction of the harsh realities of the classroom, they could easily be used as an argument for alienated teachers to leave the classroom. Reflecting further on what Martha is saying, we see a teacher who no longer respects children and who does not or will not enhance their learning. We also see a teacher who has concluded that these children are not smart enough to succeed in schools, thereby perpetuating the stereotype of inner-city youth being less capable than their suburban neighbors. Through her own words, we come to see how she defines herself as a teacher and lives her life as a reading specialist. In essence, Martha has "lost her voice" and is bereft of story. Children have become the enemy, teaching has become something to be endured. As teachers we can learn an important lesson from Martha. If we refuse to examine our actions closely and become increasingly defensive, that is the end of our professional development and the beginning of a struggle to merely survive.

Betty, another experienced remedial reading teacher, told a very different story.

BETTY'S NEW APPROACH
Mary Renck Jalongo

Betty enrolled in her first graduate class after many years of teaching in remedial reading programs. After the first class meeting, she came to the professor's office and said, "I guess you know that everything you criticized tonight— phonics, dittos, basal reading programs—is basically what I have been doing for the past ten years in remedial reading. But I have a question for you. There is a second-grade girl, Dorinda, who is in special reading classes because she simply does not read and is not at all interested in learning to read. I have been working with her for two years. We have pretty much ruled out physiological problems or learning disabilities. Based on the whole language approach that you outlined, what would you do?"

The professor replied, "First of all, I would wonder about Dorinda's previous experience with books. Maybe you could begin by investigating the home literacy environment and her background with literature, which is probably limited. Try interviewing her. Ask her what reading material she has at home. Then ask her about some of the most popular children's books for her age: *Clifford, Curious George, Frances.* What does she know about them? And I would begin reading to her. She needs, as Ken Goodman says, 'a reason to read now.'"

After Betty expressed some reservations about temporarily abandoning her skills-dominated approach, the professor remarked,

"Betty, you are far more patient than I would
be. You have given phonics ample opportunity
to work. It's time to use a different strategy."
The next week, Betty arrived at the professor's
office with a chart listing all of the books that
she had read to Dorinda and her responses to
each one. When she asked Dorinda about the
reading materials at home, the child said that
there were none. This seemed unbelievable, but
Betty had little hope for getting the parents in
for a conference, based on their attendance
record thus far. The professor urged her to
make a real effort at personalized communication with the parents, to talk to them and convince them that she wanted to help. Within the
next two weeks, both parents met Betty at
school. They admitted that there were no books
in their home and admitted to their secret — that
they were both illiterate. Even though they
were unable to read or write, they wanted more
for Dorinda and they were counting on Betty to
help. Betty decided to make Dorinda's reading
improvement her class project. She continued
to read to Dorinda and record her responses.
One book in particular, a lift-the-flap book
entitled *Roll Over!* by Mordecai Gerstein, was
Dorinda's favorite. Betty got the idea of
encouraging Dorinda to make her own big
book version of the story. At the culmination
of her project, Betty shared many examples of
Dorinda's work during the semester. She showed
a videotape of Dorinda reading her big book to
her second-grade peers. When Dorinda had
finished, the children burst into spontaneous
applause, and several children rushed up to
congratulate her on the humorous book she had
created. This was a breakthrough for Dorinda,
who began to read at grade level within the year.

Sharing the experience with Dorinda was also a break-through for Betty, her teacher, who learned that children's literature can and should function as the basis for reading programs, even remedial ones. In this story, we see Betty thinking on three different levels. On a descriptive level, Betty shared the methods she used to teach Dorinda to read and the contextual background that Dorinda brought to the classroom. On an analytic level, she began applying her new knowledge of whole language to her work with Dorinda with amazing success. Betty reached a higher level of reflection by choosing to work on Dorinda's reading improvement as her class project, forcing her to make critical judgments about herself as a reading teacher.

One thing we do know about reflective practitioners (Schön, 1983) is that in educational settings "they evaluate and re-evaluate their decisions, examine the situation from various perspectives, and take responsibility for their choices" (Jalongo, 1991, p. 80). In other words, teachers use the "stories of their experience" to adapt and respond to individual challenges and circumstances. Analyzing stories thus facilitates teachers' reflections by uncovering the beliefs and assumptions that form their "practical theories." (Mattingly, 1991).

As Betty's story shows, teachers' stories represent their lived experience, act as a context for examining their traditionally unexamined practice, and play a role in transforming them as professionals. Teachers' stories can be used as a tool for promoting reflective practice because nothing has a greater impact on teacher reflection than the images teachers have of their work and themselves (Schubert and Ayers, 1992).

Narrative as an Insight into Personal Philosophy

The deliberate storying and restorying of one's life is a fundamental method for teachers to represent and examine their evolving philosphy of teaching. When we speak of a personal philosophy, we refer to a "way one thinks about oneself in teaching situations . . . a reconstruction of meaning contained in a teacher's actions and his or her explorations of them in the form of narrative experience" (Connelly and Clandinin, 1988, pp.

66–67). When teachers retell significant teaching events, they see themselves from multiple perspectives. Their own voices help them to reexamine who they are as teachers, to identify their unique needs, and to discover what they care about as they continue to understand the way they think about teaching.

Gail Keller is a former elementary school art teacher who now teaches preschool. Her story, written about experiences that occurred several years ago, is a metaphor for understanding her personal philosophy of teaching.

BELIEF IN ART
Gail Keller

As we were beginning the art activity, Mrs. Z. barged into my art class and demanded to take Randy back to class to finish his mathematics. I was stunned at her abruptness and watched unbelievingly as she marched him out the door. Right then, I vowed this situation would never happen again. Sure enough, the following week Mrs. Z. attempted to extract Randy again, but this time I responded with a simple "no," realizing I would face a later confrontation. In my next conversation, I calmly assured her that I understood her position and time dilemma, but stood firm that Randy was to remain in art class as scheduled. Her sharp retort, "So who cares if somebody knows how to draw a picture?" stunned me. Her misconceptions struck at the very core of my educational beliefs but also enlightened me. Mrs. Z. with all of her experience and degrees had failed to understand two important factors: that art is basic to learning because it helps children make connections between their concepts and reality, and that art celebrates different media. Yes, art is more than "drawing a picture."

Gail's story clearly reflects her views of art in children's lives. It served as a catalyst for connecting her personal beliefs to her current practice by linking her views on art to her infusion of the arts in her present classroom. This kind of connection is what Connelly and Clandinin refer to as "personal philosophy" (1988).

We also see Gail's beliefs take shape as she stands firm on keeping Randy in art class. This response, along with her beliefs and values, comprise a personal philosophy based on both content and experience. Reexamination through story uncovered her fundamental beliefs about the arts and led her to question her current practice. Moreover, it initiated an ongoing dialogue with her teacher-research group that caused others to confront their beliefs and think about ways to reshape their art curriculum.

Gail's story is an example of how narrative provides the impetus for refining a teaching philosophy by "writing about your beliefs and values as experienced biographically, as practiced in your classrooms, and as thought about in your reflections and statements" (Connelly and Clandinin, 1988, p. 70). It illustrates two concepts critical to the practice of reflection: first, the teachers' ability to analyze and articulate the "why's" behind a program, which affects the ability to persuade colleagues, politicians, and families; secondly, an individual teacher's own self-assessment and the ability to see relationships among the stakeholders (Bussis, Chittenden, and Amarel, 1974).

This exploration often helps teachers to identify their own important professional and personal perspectives. Thus, storying often leads to significant change and improved practice.

Conclusion

The heart of teaching and learning lies in how teachers construct meaning (Duckworth, 1986). Teachers' stories legitimize teachers' ways of knowing by taking into account their beliefs and actions and raising their awareness of teaching. Narratives are a way of reorganizing, reassessing, and realigning life experiences and putting ideas and ideals into practice. Teachers' stories document changes not only in the tellers themselves, but also in the listener who appropriates them into his or her reservoir of vicarious classroom experience. In this way, narrative leads to critical reflection on classroom experiences and helps to inform our standards of practice.

FIVE

DILEMMAS
OF TEACHING

Just as personal narratives help us to learn about ourselves and our students, they can also be used to analyze and frame, to formulate and sometimes solve problems. In the words of Alex Haley, author and storyteller, "It helps to talk a story." Whether the teacher is planning a lesson design, responding to a child with difficult life circumstances, establishing classroom rules, organizing the classroom, conducting an assessment, or preparing for parent-teacher conferences, story can help because it looks at teaching dilemmas "from the inside" (Clark and Peterson, 1986) and is an efficient way to organize experience and respond to an event (Rosenblatt, 1983). Personal narratives contain predictable and recognizable patterns, which make them a valuable strategy and obvious source both for addressing practical problems and for assessing responses. In many ways, the neat, linear problem-solving models familiar to us all fall short in the context of a busy classroom. We teachers do not have the luxury of addressing one issue at a time nor can we, as one teacher put it, "Make it all better" for children with profound problems. Rather, we keep confronting multiple dilemmas and find a way to live with them (Lampert, 1985; Elbaz, 1991). A Head Start teacher, for example, described a child whose reaction to the

103

early weeks of school was terrified, violent, and disruptive. The child hid underneath a table and would scream if an adult approached or kick and bite if the adult drew nearer. It must be remembered that while this was going on, there were fourteen other children who were adjusting to the initial school experience. School had to go on. The teacher asked the child's mother, a single parent, to come in for a conference. The mother, who was eighteen years old, could not shed much light on her daughter's aversion to the classroom. When the teacher gently suggested that the child seemed tired and frightened, the mother said, "Well I like those slasher movies like *Friday the 13th,* but I'm scared to watch them by myself, so I make her stay up with me. Do you think there's something wrong with that?" The preschool teacher used this story to characterize the challenges of parent education, but if we put her story in the context of her obligation to maintain a positive classroom learning environment, then we begin to appreciate the complexity of the dilemmas teachers often face. Dealing with the teenage mother's lack of identification and mistreatment of her four-year-old daughter hardly lends itself to simple solutions. The teacher did persuade the mother that the films were totally inappropriate for a preschooler, but she achieved it by building the parent's trust in her rather than criticizing. She proceeded cautiously because she knew that the child's situation would worsen and she could become even more isolated if the mother felt threatened and pulled the child out of school. But even after this issue was resolved, there were many other aspects of the teenager's concept of mothering that became problematic and the child's basic sense of trust in her environment had to be painstakingly rebuilt throughout the school year.

William Pinar (1988) speaks to the ongoing nature of conflict when he writes, "a basic meaning of human life is movement, conflict, resolution, conflict, resolution, each thesis and anti-thesis opposing each other in ways which give birth to a new order of understanding and life. The task is not to control this movement, nor is it to merely portray it. It is to contribute to it . . . in work with ourselves, as well as work with others. It is work which cultivates the specificity of ourselves, the particularity of self and situation. Autobiographical method is one strategy by which this work can be conducted" (p. 151).

Of course, this is not to say that teachers are powerless to solve problems with issues that are more directly under their control. Reflecting upon the following story, written in her journal, guided Shannon Patton, a second-year high school social studies teacher, to resolve what first appeared to be a major problem.

STUDY SESSION
Shannon Patton

Even though I taught a ninth-grade honors social studies class, there were a few misplaced students in each section, students who found the pace and amount of information overwhelming. However, because of the system, placements could not be changed. These students were surely destined for failure. I decided to offer "How to Study/Review" sessions. The meetings were held before school at 7 A.M. or after school. Four students attended the first session. Despite feeling disappointed at the poor attendance, I decided to keep trying. Word-of-mouth must have spread because ten students came to the next session. There were thirty at the final study session. Even students who really did not need the extra help came. Grades were improving and the students were experiencing success in the classroom. The comments were so enthusiastic and confident from the students that I knew I had made a difference in their lives.

We can easily imagine what might have occurred if Shannon had decided to ignore the problem or worse yet to resent the children who were experiencing difficulty in the program. The use of personal narrative became the governing agent that empowered her to reflect, meet a challenge, and grow professionally as a result of her problem-solving efforts. As Shannon's story illustrates, narrative continues to be one of the best ways of obtaining self-initiated feedback.

It is well known that teachers make hundreds of decisions each day and confront a multitude of problems, but how do they go about choosing particular courses of action? In a busy classroom, there is seldom time to stop and ponder every alternative. Rather, we teachers find ourselves making rapid-fire decisions and then debating the effectiveness of our professional judgments afterward. In the remainder of this chapter we examine the role of narrative in decision-making processes and conflict resolution.

Problem-Solving Processes

Considerable attention has been focused on the more superficial aspects of professional problem solving. Who is involved? What occurred? When did it happen? Where did it take place? Less attention has been focused on deeper levels of decision making. How do teachers arrive at decisions? Why do they choose courses of action in a particular situation or with a particular student? How do they respond (or fail to respond) when they realize they were wrong? Why do teachers react differently or similarly to the same situation? It is this last list of questions that remains the most perplexing and unaddressed. Yet, as Cohen (1992) concluded after her in-depth study of five exemplary high school teachers, teachers are seldom asked what they do or why.

Research traditions in education suggest that unless we can find detached, invariant ways of studying a phenomenon, we are unscientific. Yet some of our greatest thinkers and researchers would disagree. Researcher Lee J. Cronbach (1975) observed that educational outcomes are, by their very nature, interactive and that once we accept the individual nature of responses, "we enter a hall of mirrors that extends to infinity" (p. 119). Nearly a decade ago, Cronbach called for research that attends to the exceptions rather than overgeneralizing, research that is sensitive to individual responses rather than torn away from meaningful contexts, research that connects what we feel with what we know rather than attempting to divorce the two. Philosopher John Dewey (1929) argued that a science of education should be liberating and result in the ability to see new problems and devise new procedures, that by seeing more relationships, the teacher would recognize many more opportunities, make better judgments about daily practice, and draw upon a wider range of alternatives when confronted with various situations. Teacher narratives can enrich, expand, and extend insights about the teaching/learning process and as such become an important avenue for confronting dilemmas.

Facing Issues via Story

The stories of many of the most compelling dilemmas in teaching begin with the simple phrase, "There is (or was) a child in my class who . . . " In order to describe the basic steps in teacher decision making, Ross (1989) extended ideas of Schön, Van Maanen, and others to yield the following sequence:

1. Recognize an educational dilemma.
2. Respond by sorting out how it is like other situations and how it differs.
3. Define the dilemma, framing and reframing it.
4. Experiment with the dilemma to consider the consequences and implications of various solutions.
5. Examine both the intended and unintended consequences of an implemented solution.
6. Evaluate the solution by determining whether the final outcome was desirable or not.

As an example of this decision-making process in action, consider the following story, which is also a story within a story, describing a decision reached through connection with a childhood experience.

BOBBY ELLIOT
Mary Renck Jalongo

Bobby Elliot was a second grader who arrived at school feeling ill the day of our class
picnic. The plan was to take a bus to a camping area near Lake Huron about forty minutes
away. Bobby insisted that he would be okay
and that he was feeling better than he did
earlier that morning. Yet, the pattern of his behavior had been etched onto my mind while
still a young child. I had witnessed my older
sister at school, stooped over with pain as we
stood in line waiting for the bus. When my sister told the teacher that she was ill, the teacher
urged her to wait because school would be over
in a couple of hours. I remember standing next
to her, worrying in that wide, sweeping way
that children do because they have such limited
experience in which to ground their concerns.
My sister started to feel better, and I felt encouraged. Later, I was astonished by my calm,
gentle mother's rage at the teacher when my
sister required emergency surgery for a rup-
tured appendix. Back to Bobby. Should we intervene? Evidently, his parents thought he was
well enough to go to school. Based on that
story, my colleagues and I decided to send
Bobby home. We reasoned that if we were
wrong and it turned out to be something relatively minor, Bobby would miss an outing, but
if we were right, and it turned out to be something more serious, Bobby's life could be endangered. As it turned out, we selected the
script that saved Bobby Elliot's young life. He
arrived at the emergency room before peritoni-
tis set in, and we congratulated ourselves later
for having made the right decision. I vividly

recall Bobby's mother stopping by after school while he was still in the hospital. She thanked us profusely, explaining that she had allowed him to go to school against her better judgment, mainly because of the deceptive reduction in his pain after the appendix burst. I still feel panicky when I consider what could have happened if the wrong script had been selected and if Bobby had been in a state park far away from parental permission and medical care with acute appendicitis.

The Bobby Elliot story illustrates all six of the steps in teacher decision making identified by Ross (1989) above. The second-grade teachers and student teachers recognized the dilemma; related the problem to another similar situation; defined, framed, and reframed it; weighed the consequences of various alternatives, and assessed the final outcome.

Narrative and the Exploration of Value Systems

As Kilpatrick (1993) points out, "stories have always been an important way of transmitting values and wisdom" (p. 24). Narrative has moral power because we use the "moral scripts" of stories to guide ethical behavior. The term *values* is used collectively to describe "those principles that one holds dear and that one sees as worth having" (Court, 1991, p. 389). Teachers' values are a theory of the world of teaching, representing the teacher's life goals, and underlying justification for particular courses of action (Taylor, 1961). Teacher narratives often express those values, both implicitly and explicitly.

In some of the situations that teachers confront, the underlying value is clear and solid. Take, for example, health and safety decisions. We know how to respond if a child leaves the playground and dashes out into the street. We know we are right when we insist that a pact between two school friends that involves a pin prick and the exchange of blood is dangerous and must cease. More common and perplexing are situations where the values are unclear or in conflict with existing policies and practices.

Consider how Isabelle Hoag's value system is revealed as she looks back on her early teaching and the decisions she made concerning a particular child in her class. She wrote this story after participating in our conference session on teachers' stories in Geneva, Switzerland.

FLORIDA
Isabelle Hoag

I look back upon my two years of teaching first grade in an all-black school in the deep South by examining bits of memorabilia. Each child beams at me in my photographs, each individual jumps forward as I review work samples, and each personality shines as I remember anecdotes that characterize a particular child. I recall with fondness perfectly normal Annie who staged an epileptic seizure copied expertly from her older sister; Belle, who after we sang a song about animal noises, asked me if I knew the rat sound (I didn't but she taught me and I can make the rat sound to this day); David, whose named was pronounced *Dah-veed,* and his marvelous storytelling abilities (Troll to Billy Goat Gruff: "I'm gonna pull all your bones out through your nose!" Billy Goat Gruff, soft and southern with a sly smile: "Weh-ul . . . "). These children and others push their happy faces in my mind, but there is one whose story I must write, the story of Florida, a seven-year-old who was smaller than the rest.

Florida came to school in Easter Sunday clothes every day; she wore flouncy dresses with ruffles echoed on her ankle socks and her hair was braided into dozens of brightly colored ribbons. The first grader had a surprisingly deep

voice for her frail body and a loud laugh,
which we frequently heard and thoroughly enjoyed. Florida had, as she put it, "the asthma."
The consensus among the other teachers was
that Florida just wanted to get out of school
and used this as an excuse. The school nurse
had told me what to look for and how to deal
with Florida's asthma. When Florida had an attack, she would say, "Miss Hoag, I got the
asthma." Then I would hold her hand, talk
soothingly, coach her on relaxation techniques,
and send her for a drink of water. Sometimes it
worked. If it didn't, I would send her to the
nurse to call home and then visit her when I
could until her mother came to school.

Florida missed many afternoons; if it
wasn't the asthma, then she would have to go
to the doctor for her allergy shots. Her mother
explained that Florida was allergic to practically
everything that was borne in the warm, full
southern air—pollen, grass, the scent of
flowers. The asthma kept Florida indoors.
While the rest of us went outdoors to discover
shadows, fly a kite, or blow soap bubbles, I
would send Florida with a book to one of the
other teachers down the hall. They allowed her
to sit in the back until one of my students
would go to bring her back to the class after
recess. But all the time, the other teachers felt I
was "giving in."

At Christmas time, a young, thin, shy,
African American Santa came to our school.
All the children were arranged by grade level to
sit on his knee, tell him their secrets, and have
their pictures taken. Before first grade had even
lined up, Florida's mother came into the room
with her daughter's coat. They had to leave so
that Florida could get another allergy shot.

It was a tough school full of tough children. They were used to disappointment.
Florida put on her coat without a word because
her mother did not want to wait. I could have
said goodbye, but instead I summoned all the
authority I could, took Florida's hand, led her
past the kindergarten classes, ahead of all the
preschool classes, and onto Santa's knee. She
spoke with Santa and had her picture taken.

The next year, Florida and I were at
different schools, but I kept in touch with the
teachers at my old school. Then I heard the sad
news that Florida had died of the asthma. She
had been staying at her grandmother's farm,
away from doctors but close to nature. I wrote
to Florida's mother and enclosed a photo of her
smiling daughter taken on the first day of
school. Much later, I received a crumpled-up
program from the funeral service. The first line
read, "She is sleep." There was no personal
note from Florida's mother. What would she
have said?

At the time, I had no idea what an important role I would be playing in Florida's life.
She spent one of her seven years in my class. A
friend and colleague tried to comfort me, saying how glad I should be that I was the only
one who took Florida's asthma seriously and
kept her indoors for recess. I wonder about
that.

As Isabelle's narrative so poignantly illustrates, some of
the most prevalent and pressing questions from teachers at every
stage of professional development are "What should I do?" or
alternatively, "Did I do the right thing?" or, as we interact with
colleagues, "What would *you* do?" and "Why?" These inquiries
are at the heart of responsible decision making and therefore
at the heart of many teacher narratives. Isabelle's story reveals

her value system, one in which she consistently put the child's interest first and questioned the effect of even those actions she performed specifically on the child's behalf.

Story as Reevaluation

As we evaluate values, narrative offers a particular advantage — the perspective of the spectator. From this vantage point, teachers can work on their representations of experience and continually modify their theories of the world. The spectator role is characterized by a reflective attitude or approach to experience, something that is crucial to exploring the values that underlie our reasoning (Britton, 1970).

Whether we realize it or not, our actions are frequently evaluated through moral reasoning, posing questions such as, who benefits? Whose interests are being served? With what effects? What is the significance of these effects on children's lives? To what extent do teacher decisions have a limiting or distorting effect on the opportunities open to children? (Tennyson and Strom, 1988).

Our actions as educators reveal what we believe children ought to be and become and what we teachers think schools should do for students (Spodek, 1988). When reflective practitioners arrive at a decision and take action, that action invariably leads to reevaluation. In order to engage in moral reasoning and evaluate decisions, teachers need a commitment to rational thought; an orientation to moral principles such as respect, equity, freedom; an identification with the interests and welfare of others beyond duty or common decency (empathizing with child, parents, administrators); and the motivation to act accordingly (Tennyson and Strom, 1988).

Teachers frequently decide whether their decisions have been good ones in retrospect. They often draw upon their storehouse of stories, using them as a touchstone in evaluating the appropriateness of their actions in particular situations. It is only when teachers' actions are consistent with their personal and professional beliefs and values that their "theories in use" prove successful and provide a certain level of satisfaction (Argyris and

Schön, 1975). Here is one account of decisions surrounding several children and a difficult colleague that were in some ways satisfying and in other ways, dissatisfying. Tonya's story is one that was indelibly imprinted on me during my second year of teaching, an experience that came to mind immediately in response to the theme of reevaluation.

TONYA
Mary Renck Jalongo

Not only was she big for her age, she was older than anyone else in my first-grade class because she had been retained in kindergarten. Her name was Tonya and she put my patience, my professionalism, and my decision making on trial throughout my second year of teaching. Tonya would boss and bully the other children, pilfer items from their desks, or talk them into uneven "trades." Matters worsened when I received a hostile note from a parent. It read, "This is the fourth time that Tommy's snack cake has been taken from his lunch. What are you going to do about it?" What I did was launch an investigation. First, I asked if anyone else was missing items from lunchboxes and discovered that many other children had been affected. Next, I tried to get someone to confess—not in the way that *my* teachers had done it, by sitting in the room until the guilty party or an informant cracked, but simply by asking the perpetrator to leave a note in my classroom mailbox. My classroom was anti-quated, but it included an enclosed hallway, now equipped with coat racks and shelves that led to a restroom. Apparently, while I was preoccupied teaching my lessons, a child was stealing food. Three days later, several other children reported that they had seen Tonya

"messing around people's lunchboxes." I asked
her, but she denied it. At recess, I looked in
her desk and found it littered with empty food
wrappers. Then Tonya and I discussed it again
in private and examined the evidence. I con-
sulted my principal about what to do. He suggested that I punish her severely; a month
without recess seemed warranted, he said. I
thought it might be better to call her mother,
but they had no telephone and the principal assured me that, based on her failure to attend
previous school functions, Tonya's mother
would not come to the school. Then I said I
would write a note and set up a home visit. He
strongly advised against that, telling me that
Tonya's mother had a disease, that the house
was a mess, and that she had a live-in
boyfriend. All these things were true, but I understand them differently now. Tonya's mother
had lupus and was at a debilitating stage of the
disease that prevented her from working, much
less maintaining a spotless home. Tonya's family now consisted of mother, unofficial step-
father (also permanently disabled), and a three-
year-old brother. They lived on a fixed income,
and Tonya qualified for free lunches.

As a first-year teacher, I was reluctant to
go against the principal's wishes, but I did draw
the line at harsh punishment. When I asked
Tonya *why* she took things from the other children's lunches, she simply said, "'Cause I was
hungry." I asked her if she ate breakfast in the
morning and she said, "No. I have to take care
of my little brother before I go to school." I
asked her if having breakfast might solve the
problem and she said, "Yes. My aunt would
help." And so, my first big teaching problem
was solved by an eight-year-old when instead of

foraging for food each morning, Tonya and her brother walked down the block to her unmarried aunt's house before school and ate breakfast.

There was still the matter of repairing Tonya's damaged reputation with the other children, who had accumulated a variety of negative experiences with her and had labeled her as a thief. I stood with my arm around Tonya's shoulder in front of the class and announced that Tonya had agreed not to take things anymore, that she could be trusted, and that all was well. Two weeks later, a child's candy bar was reported missing, and the class was quick to accuse Tonya. I took her aside and inquired about the missing candy bar. "No," she said firmly, "I didn't eat it." As I defended Tonya's innocence to her peers, I noticed how Tonya, the child who had learned to slouch to conceal her size, sat up tall and proud in her seat.

I must confess that I was wondering if Tonya might be lying when Kendra, the child who reported the stolen candy bar, said she was ill and wanted to go home. Then, with a candor only possible from a young child, Kendra said, "I have a stomachache, and you want to know why? Because I just remembered that *I* ate my candy bar on the bus this morning."

Tonya's confidence and competence flourished during the remainder of her first-grade year and throughout second grade. Then, in third grade, she had a teacher who was sarcastic and unfair. When I passed by the third-grade room, I often saw Tonya seated off by herself or washing the walls, desks, or floors as punishment for her misbehavior. She would stop at my first-grade classroom after school,

and when I asked her about it, she said she just
didn't like third grade and wished she could
come back to first grade. Ms. M., Tonya's
third-grade teacher, had the habit of choosing
certain children—always the ones whose parents
were influential and wealthy—for all of the
classroom privileges. One day as I was passing
by her classroom, the third-grade teacher said,
"Alyssa, you have on such a pretty dress today,
why don't you be our messenger? Be sure to
show Mr. B [the principal] how nice you look!"
I caught a glimpse of Tonya's face as she sat
there in her secondhand clothes and felt bitter
tears in my eyes. I hated my colleague for what
she was doing to these children. What to do?
As a novice teacher, I had no idea of how to
respond to or change such blatant insensitivity
from another, more experienced teacher. So I
did the unprofessional thing and complained
about her to others. Naturally, it got back to
her and we had several hostile verbal exchanges
over this and other similar issues. She tried to
retaliate by exerting her authority over my students. There was one incident that now seems
almost funny, having to do with an Easter rabbit she put on her door as a decoration.
Although the rabbit was pictured facing forward, she had attempted to show its furry tail
by drawing a couple of small, curved shapes
between its legs and gluing on two cottonballs.
As two first-grade boys from my class passed
by, one of them pointed to the rabbit and said,
"What's that supposed to be?" and the other replied, "I don't know, must be his balls." She
overheard them and said the two boys had to
stay in from morning, lunch, and afternoon
recess for a month. My professional view was
that a private conversation was hardly grounds

for such punishment. My private view was that
the boys were right; a similar speculation had
crossed my mind when I first saw the rabbit. I
talked with the boys candidly about their "sentence" and told them that I did not agree with
the punishment but that it was out of my
hands. I also cautioned them to be careful
about what they said in school, particularly
around Ms. M.

From these experiences, I arrived at the
basic principle of being as honest as I can with
children, particularly children who have been
wronged in some way. I had the same kind of
heart-to-heart talk with Tonya and I think it
helped her through a difficult year for both of
us. I also learned to be more diplomatic and
direct, even with inept and callous colleagues.
Clearly, my complaints and confrontations did
neither of us any good and, even more importantly, it made matters worse for the children.
To my great relief, Ms. M. got married and
moved away a year later.

Throughout this series of events, the teacher attempted
to act in ways consistent with her value-oriented beliefs. She
also learned from her mistakes.

Narrative and Case Study Research

Narratives also offer a way of conducting research, particularly
through the case study method. Consider, for example, the research goal of exploring relationships with colleagues. Colleagues
are people who are responsible for themselves, yet dedicated
to mutual improvement (Bonstingl, 1992). Supportive colleagues
always see room for improvement in themselves and can generally recognize the good in others. Research suggests that the
supportive colleague recognizes efforts, cooperates to solve problems, builds self-esteem, listens with a nonjudgmental ear, and

invites others "into the fold" by functioning as a role model (Applegate, Flora, and Lasely, 1980). Laurie Stamp relates this story about an admired colleague who worked with her in child day care, a story first told and later written at our request.

Ms. Violet
Laurie Nicholson Stamp

Jennifer had recently joined our toddler class. She was almost walking, standing and holding onto everyone and everything. Jennifer's mother often expressed guilt and sadness over leaving her baby day after day and confided in the other member of our teaching team, Ms. Violet, that she was "afraid of missing Jennifer's first steps." Sure enough, on that very day, Jennifer began to walk at day care. I worried that Jennifer's mother would be heartbroken when she heard the news. When the mother arrived, Ms. Violet said, "I think that if you spend some time tonight holding out your hands to her a little bit, she'll walk right to you." The next day, Jennifer's mother was thrilled as she reported that Ms. Violet had been right—Jennifer *did* take her first steps! I marveled at Ms. Violet's sensitivity to that young mother's needs and resolved to always put families first, just as my colleague had done.

Of course, co-workers can also be nonsupportive or attempt to socialize others, particularly novices, in negative ways. Research characterizes nonsupportive co-workers as those who instigate conflict, create obstacles, instill self-doubt, criticize teaching methods, and reject or exclude others (Applegate, Flora, and Lasely, 1980). The following scenario about nonsupportive co-workers was developed by the Case Study Writing Team at George Mason University, 1992. The case is a real-life experience of an elementary school teacher in the group.

WHEN YOU'VE TAUGHT A LITTLE LONGER
George Mason University Case Study Writing Team

Susan felt her throat constrict and her
eyes fill with tears. She wondered if Laura had
spoken outside her door deliberately so that she
could overhear those cutting words. Moving
about her room mechanically, Susan put books
in order and erased the chalkboard, trying not
to think, yet not able to erase Laura's words
from her mind: "When she's more mature, had
had more experience, then she'll know she's
wrong. There's no way she can make a wise
choice now."

After finishing her master's degree in education the previous spring, it had been hard going for Susan as she began teaching. She loved
the culturally diverse student population and
loved teaching, but finding her place among her
fellow teachers had been a struggle from the
very beginning. Susan found that two teachers
on her five-member team formed a strong alli-
ance. Laura and Hope, the team leader, were a
negative force within the faculty as a whole. If
Susan happened to walk by Laura and Hope in
the hall, they would stop their conversation,
leaving Susan with the uncomfortable feeling
that they were talking about her. At lunchtime,
Laura and Hope were openly critical of practically everyone—the children, the parents, the
principal, even the custodian. Outspoken as
they were, they dominated the conversation.
Those who attempted to change the subject
were stifled by disapproving looks and telling
silences from the two. Laura and Hope spread
negativity in their wake and dealing with them
became an ongoing challenge for Susan. When
the school district prepared a special in-service

on multiculturalism, Laura and Hope refused to attend at first. Finally, they went begrudgingly, with Laura remarking, "What a waste of time!" and Hope agreeing wholeheartedly.

Situations like these kept coming up and Susan knew there was no permanent solution in the offing. She was grateful that her own professional self-esteem did not depend upon Laura's and Hope's approval, but she also wished that her work environment could be a more positive one.

And now this! It had all started with the reading series adoption process. Each team in the school had been asked to choose one of the newly adopted reading series to be used in their grade level for the next several years. As Susan read over the materials, she and two of her teammates became very excited about the series that took a whole language approach and was, according to the grapevine, the preference of the school system and the principal. But not so for Laura and Hope. They firmly believed that "children can't learn to read with the whole language approach, especially when English is their second language. They need more basic skills." Laura and Hope became very vocal about their opinions regarding the reading series. Susan wondered if this would be another time when keeping team peace would prevail over responsible decision making.

And then Laura's words from the hallway, "When she's more mature . . . When she's had more experience . . . She can't possibly make a wise choice."

Susan became angry. "Am I not entitled to an opinion? Am I not entitled to respect? What should I do about the reading series and about the team itself?"

As a followup, the case writing team formulated questions such as, with whom do you identify and why? Why do Laura and Hope act as they do? What are Susan's thoughts and feelings? How can children be served best in this situation?

Role play was the next step in this case study, with two suggested scenarios: (1) Susan goes out in the hall to confront Laura and Hope talking about her, and (2) a team meeting is held to discuss the textbook adoption process. The George Mason University Case Study Writing Team then distributed the following one-page document.

When You've Taught a Little Longer
(AND NOW FOR THE REST OF THE CASE . . .)
George Mason University Case Study Writing Team

There is no definitive solution for this case. Every school has its Hopes and Lauras, as individuals, in pairs, or in groups. The dynamics and situations involved are ongoing and seem uncontrollable. Working together as adults, however, requires dealing with human nature and resolving conflict.

Particular to this case, Susan and two other team members decided to stand firm behind the Blue Series [whole language]. The administration allowed the team to split their choice, so three chose the Blue Series while Laura and Hope chose the Green [traditional]. During the following year, Susan continued to appreciate her choice as her children, including the ESL students, flourished with it. She noticed that Hope and Laura had gone all the way back to using the school's old basal series instead of the Green Series they fought to keep. On several occasions, she overheard explanations such as, "The stories in this new series are just too hard for beginning readers."

Susan and the two other team members

slowly began to bond as a group within the
team. As trust developed among them, they
were able to provide strength and support for
one another, emotionally and in decision making. Susan and one other teacher spoke with
the principal about their concerns for the team
and its unity. The principal was supportive but
expected the team, as professionals, to solve
their own problems.

We can only imagine how professional dialogue and work
with case studies such as this one might prepare novices for the
philosophical differences they confront as they interact with colleagues. The case study so clearly demonstrates that narrative
can be a tool for conducting research into our own practice and
examining various courses of professional action. When we
shared this case study with a group of our own graduate students, they felt inspired to write their own case studies, based
upon their own real-life experiences. Next year, the case studies
the group developed will be used by a classroom teacher who
leads a group of colleagues in monthly discussions, a college
faculty member who works with undergraduates, and a principal who plans to institute some voluntary faculty meetings that
focus on the meaningful discussion of pertinent issues. (Some
excellent published sources for additional case studies include
Child Advocacy for Early Childhood Educators (Fennimore, 1989) and
Case Studies for Teaching Special Needs and At-Risk Students (Buzzell
and Piazza, 1994).)

Narratives and the Long-Term Consequences of Decisions

In some cases, as in the story of Chad, below, we have no case
studies to rely on and we need to create them.

Each of us has a personal philosophy, a reconstruction
of meaning based in classroom actions and expressed through
stories of practice, as well as a value system, a coherent statement
of beliefs, values, and action preferences, often contextualized

in terms of classroom events (Connelly and Clandinin, 1988). When unfamiliar, difficult situations arise, a personal philosophy and values system is sometimes the only support available. Naturally, for novice teachers, many more incidents that are new and challenging arise. Yet even the most expert among us confronts for the first time emerging questions of our historical era, such as, what do I do about the learning problems of a drug-exposed child? How do I meet the educational needs of a ten-year-old girl who is pregnant? How should I respond to the legal, ethical, and health issues surrounding a child who has contracted the AIDS virus? Questions like these were hardly raised before they demanded immediate answers. They leave us struggling not only because they have profound implications for the quality of children's lives but also because our collective case literature, our stories of practice, are so limited on these issues.

The dilemmas of teaching pose new levels of conundrum when they focus on social and ethical issues. Here the paths to follow are not well marked; here chaos and uncertainty reign. Decisions are sometimes delayed or avoided altogether, or, if they are reached, it often becomes painfully obvious that they were ineffective. Even more troubling is the knowledge that we did not trust ourselves to make the right decision and therefore made an unsatisfactory one. Preservice teacher Kathryn Chaumont shares her experience in her student teaching journal.

CHAD
Kathryn Chaumont

Chad is a first grader who already has a bad reputation at school. He lives with his mother and younger sister. Chad's father is in the state prison. According to my cooperating teacher, Chad has only mentioned his father once. She did not bring up the topic after that, something I became aware of while teaching a unit on the family.

After three days of talking about families, Chad came up and whispered in my ear that he

had written a letter to his father. He wanted to
know if we could mail it to him. Chad said that
he missed his father and wanted to send him a
pair of sunglasses as a present. This was a side
of Chad I had never seen before. His actions
that day belied his reputation. He never
whispered. He never hid things. Usually, Chad
was at the center of attention, wanting all the
other students to see what he was doing. His
demeanor and concern surprised me. I had
never seen Chad grow quiet and sad as he
talked, nor had I ever heard him reveal his
feelings. My cooperating teacher obtained the
address of the prison, and Chad became very
excited about writing the letter. He said it was
the first time he had ever written to his father.
He asked me repeatedly if I thought his father
would like the sunglasses. I told Chad that I
was sure his father would be thrilled to receive
the letter and the gift from him. In his letter,
Chad wrote: "I love you, Dad. I miss you. I
play football. I am the safety. I love you.
Chad." It was a short letter but a touching one.

Two weeks later, the package was
returned to school unopened with a "denied"
stamp across it. After looking into the situation,
it was discovered that Chad's father violated
some prison rules and as a result had his mail
privileges revoked. My cooperating teacher
brought the package back to the classroom to
show me. We decided not to tell Chad about its
return because he had been so excited about
contacting his father and the returned package
would be such a disappointment.

The more I thought about this situation,
the more I have regretted our decision not to
tell Chad. It seemed reasonable at that moment, but as time goes on, Chad will surely be

disappointed that his father did not send him a
letter in return. Yet, if Chad were told that his
father was not permitted to receive mail, he
would realize his father was behaving badly,
even by prison standards. It is not just that
they are living apart, it is that his father did
something seriously wrong and is being
punished for it. Is this too much to tell a seven-
year-old boy about his father? How much will
he really understand about the situation? And,
if he does understand, how will that affect his
relationship with his father? His view of himself?

     I need to understand more about children
with parents in prison. I do not know how the
parents deal with this situation, how much the
children can be expected to understand, or
what we as teachers should say or do. I need to
know the feelings that children have about these
things. I need to feel more confident about my
decision not to tell Chad that the package was
returned. Right now, I have debated the issue
both ways. Since I am the student teacher, I
went with the advice of my cooperating teacher
and did not tell Chad. She seemed very confident of this decision. I hope it was the right
one to make. I hope it was in Chad's best interest.

When this story was shared with other educators, they
disagreed with the classroom teacher's decision. One pointed
out that the teacher could have spoken with the warden about
making an exception in this case. Another wondered why the
teacher didn't try to mail the package again, because mail
privileges must have been reinstated at some point. Everyone
agreed that the teacher had given up too easily and that the child
might infer that his father had rejected, not only the gift or even
the letter, but also his son.

Conclusion

As we have seen, teachers must act on their instincts and intuitions because there is little time to ponder in the midst of a hectic classroom. Times of reflection and discussions with colleagues are frequently the sole opportunities to examine decisions based on immediate, practical concerns and their underlying rationales as well (Court, 1991). It is common to ask a newly certified applicant for a teaching position, "What is your philosophy of teaching?" but the question is seldom posed again. We educators treat a teaching philosophy as if it were fully formed on graduation day, when we know full well that it is continually evolving. We must stop treating a teacher's philosophy, values, and nonacademic decisions as if they were abstract. In fact, they are made concrete and tangible not through some survey of opinions but through daily classroom practice. As teachers listen, read, write, and discuss professional narratives, they articulate their personal philosophies, explore their values, and evaluate their decisions, not in a detached way, but out of the experience of their practice (Connelly and Clandinin, 1988). It is the ability to build and use this "wisdom of practice" that is the hallmark of masterful teaching.

SIX

PROFESSIONAL
DEVELOPMENT

The narratives in this book reveal that teachers use their stories of practice and their reflections upon them to address significant teaching and learning issues not only for their students but also for themselves. We believe that respect for these teacher narratives is an important step in elevating the status of the teaching profession and in fostering professional development. To look more closely at how teachers can use their stories for professional development, we look first at forms of professional inquiry, then examine career themes, and finally discuss orientations to the teaching role. We conclude with specific ways that story can be used to foster professional growth.

Professional Inquiry

According to Michael Huberman (1994), throughout the course of teachers' professional lives, it is important to ask some significant questions:

Portions of this chapter originally appeared in Jalongo, M. R. (1992) "Teachers' stories: Our ways of knowing." *Educational Leadership, 49*(7), 68–73. Reprinted with permission of the Association for Supervision and Curriculum Development. Copyright 1992 by ASCD. All rights reserved.

- What do teachers find satisfying (and dissatisfying) about their chosen career?
- How does commitment wax and wane and what influences help it to regenerate?
- How do teachers' private lives and professional lives interact?
- Are there some typical "trajectories" in the teaching career?
- Do teachers change the ways in which they interact with colleagues and students over the years?
- Why do some teachers become more skillful and others less so with additional experience?

Without question, many teachers have learned to address these questions, and as a result some have managed to function at much higher levels of professionalism than others. We contend that reflective practice is one significant way that teachers attain the hallmarks of a profession, acquiring more specialized knowledge, gaining greater insights about responsible practice, learning to function as decision makers, and earning more prestige in the larger community. We further contend that narrative study can offer insights into what motivates a teacher's actions and an appreciation for the complexity of teachers' everyday lives, provide many detailed cases of teaching dilemmas and events, and give practitioners the professional insight that results from self-inquiry (Sparks-Langer and Colton, 1991).

Of course, no one can expect that large numbers of classroom teachers attain these achievements as soon as they receive initial certification. Rather, they progress through various developmental themes and stages and over time learn to seek out those influences that nurture professionalism. At the same time, expert teachers grow more astute about avoiding or counteracting the forces that diminish their professionalism.

Career Themes

What, then, are these various themes that represent a teacher's career? Theory and research has identified specific career development stages of teachers (Ryan, 1986; Swick and Hanes, 1987). To begin with, many preservice teachers are still in the process of making their career decision about teaching. They usually have the idealism characteristic of their age, but they are also fearful of failure. Then, as they move into their first "survival" year, new teachers are generally shocked by several things: the stamina required of the job, the amount of paperwork, the range and intensity of students' needs, the parents who lack confidence in them, and the lack of support for their efforts within the school and district (Ryan, 1986).

Karen Liard addresses the self/survival theme directly when she looks back on her student teaching experience and writes in her journal:

SURVIVAL STRATEGIES
Karen Liard

As I have shared in class, my curriculum is driven by the school district's program of studies, and I was assigned to teach a specific unit and lessons during my student teaching. During a meeting, the principal and site coordinator revealed the extent to which teaching interns would have to document any lessons that they created (i.e., anything not part of the canned curriculum), and I decided to play it safe. If I could stretch a "canned lesson" to include some aspect of creativity, I did, but these lessons were not creative in and of themselves. I find that it is more difficult to take dry lessons and make them creative than it is to design lessons from scratch. Although I survived my semester of student teaching, I was not proud of my unit. As everyone shared their units during our final seminar, I felt a knot in my stomach because I realized that I had not mastered the art of "creatively cheating" with the planned curriculum. I had decided to take the path of least resistance and now, faced with the prospect of being held to account by my peers, I regretted it.

My most creative lessons were those dealing with Native Americans. I had to delete them to make room for the least creative teaching experience — making pilgrim hats. This activity was perhaps the biggest waste of time I have ever witnessed. I was told that the kindergarteners were incapable of producing these hats without help. One might ask, "Why do it then?" but that would make too much sense. They *had* to be able to choose between Indian headdresses and pilgrim hats for the feast, silly! The kindergarteners' third-grade buddy readers traced the patterns onto paper and the kindergarteners cut along the lines. Three teachers busily stapled and folded the hats. One child cried because he could not cut out his buckle for the hat as well as the sample presented. This episode says something about me as a creative teacher. I am less creative in a tightly controlled environment. My inclination is to do what is necessary to survive even though I may not believe that what I am doing is best for children. Until I can break through that barrier, I will not be a creative teacher.

Kane (1992) chronicles similar decisions and incidents, both serious and humorous, in her book entitled *The First Year of Teaching: Real World Stories from American Teachers,* a collection of twenty-five essays by first-year teachers. Their experiences highlight what all experienced teachers have come to accept: "Teaching is a complex, situation-specific, and dilemma-ridden behavior" (Sparks-Langer and Colton, 1991, p. 37). The book *Reflective Teaching: The Preparation of Students of Teaching* (Cruickshank, 1987) proposes a series of questions that are designed to encourage reflective thought, even at this early career stage.

After student teachers have had a teaching experience, the author recommends that novices ask themselves these questions:

- What happened?
- What did I do and why?
- Did learning take place?
- What got in the way of learning?
- What might I have learned?
- What other ways might the experience have been organized?

After most teachers have survived the initial year or two, their role is more clearly defined, and they begin to focus on the task — the consolidation and refinement of their teaching strategies. If they are to become expert teachers, this stage is characterized by experimentation and an expansion of the teaching repertoire rather than clinging desperately to whatever enabled them to survive. Often, they begin to question generally accepted practices. This emphasis on task, on improving performance, is described by Shawneen Peterson as she analyzes her innovativeness and planning roles in her field experience journal.

CREATIVE PLANNING
Shawneen Peterson

When I taught, I would put out materials and let the children do whatever they wanted with them. I gave them little or no direction, believing that this was "creative teaching." Now I understand that instead of just putting out open-ended materials, I need to guide and enhance children's creativity by giving them an interesting problem (e.g., creating a paper mosaic) to solve, having them brainstorm or discuss ahead of time the many different ways of using and inventing with the materials, allowing them choice in developing their ideas, and then providing opportunities for children to explain and share their work with others.

With these purposes in mind, I began to
plan more thoughtfully. This also helped me a
great deal in formulating more open-ended
questions and statements that fostered children's
divergent thinking ("Picture something that you
have never actually seen before. Draw it and
write about [it].") and having children make
connections to either their experiences in the
classroom ("Remember the story about . . . ")
or in their personal lives ("Tell me about a
favorite harvest food your family likes to eat.").
By considering what I was going to say ahead
of time, I also found it easier to implement the
activities in the classroom and make on-the-spot
changes as I taught the lesson.

I was impressed with the results of this
thoughtful planning approach to teaching. Children came up with varied and interesting
responses and ideas. Additionally, having children share and talk about their learning with
each other and me was not only revealing for
me as a teacher in assessing how children think
and respond, but it was also helpful in inspiring the children's classmates. Children were interested in what each other had to say and at
times incorporated and adapted their peers'
ideas into their own work. This was especially
helpful to children who did not speak very
much English. I found creative experiences
helped to foster in all children positive self-
esteem or a sense of "I can" because these experiences allowed all children to participate and
succeed.

This attention to developing children's
creative thinking was difficult but rewarding. It
was difficult because it meant a change in my
way of thinking about what constitutes a creative experience. Creative teaching is more

than teachers using clever activities in the classroom; it is a commitment to engaging children
in interesting and meaningful problems that
could be explored in a variety of ways (Isenberg and Jalongo, 1993).

   I now believe this to be true because I
found when evaluating the children's work using the above criteria, there was not only a
multitude of different responses but a great deal
of enthusiasm displayed while working as well.
For one art experience, after a discussion of
texture, the children were given a box of different textured items and invited to create a texture collage. I found the results fascinating.
How the children planned and used their space,
created pictures with the items, or explained
the reasons for their choices gave me great insight into children's thinking and language development. Lessons like this one and others I
developed affirmed that my attitudinal change
had been instrumental in my growth toward
becoming a more creative teacher.

Good teachers who have accumulated four or more years
of experience usually begin to reappraise their situation, seek
renewal, and wonder about the long-term consequences of the
learning experiences they provide. For Donna Witherspoon, her
son's struggles in first grade became the impetus to take stock
of her teaching methods and take charge of her own professional
development. She wrote this narrative as a story on literacy in
a graduate course.

My Son, My Teaching
Donna Witherspoon

   As I greet them at the door, their faces
share a common expression. It's familiar to me
by now: a mixture of wariness and expectation.

Although they haven't been in the system long, these first graders come to me with histories. Frankie doesn't know his letters yet; Ian "fools around" a lot; Carla has a short attention span; already many have been found to be lacking in some way. Yet, I know that each one of my first graders is ready to learn something about reading and writing. I also know that how I teach them will have a tremendous impact on how they come to view themselves as learners and literate beings.

For as long as I can remember, I have been aware of the misalignment that exists between what is espoused and what is commonly practiced in primary classrooms. The vague and discomforting sense of incongruity I felt from the beginning of my teaching career became more sharply defined when my son, Dan, entered school.

Beginning in first grade, children in Dan's school were ability grouped for reading and math and changed rooms and teachers for these subjects. As a first grader, Dan moved daily among four or five teachers. Initially he was placed in "average" reading and math classes, which were overflowing with close to thirty students each. After several months, he was moved to a much smaller "low" reading class but didn't seem to fit there either. That year he was moved between these two classes a total of four times, something he remembered vividly ten years later.

The second week of first grade, Dan brought home a list of thirty words to memorize. Soon after, math fact flash cards came home for study. First graders were not permitted to use anything concrete when solving addition and subtraction problems and any backwards

numbers were marked wrong right from the
start. Much of the day was spent doing seat-
work packets that the teacher dutifully checked
and graded. As unseemly as it sounds, Dan's
first-grade experience was not atypical. As a
result of his experience, I came to consider it a
personal mission to advocate for appropriate
primary programs.

Even the most casual observer recognizes
that, under normal conditions, young children
are active, social beings. Yet in primary classrooms, isolated learners sitting silently with
workbooks and worksheets comprise a familiar
scene. We find young children being sorted, labeled, and switched for instruction in settings
that look and feel like high school for the
primary grades.

At the core of the issue are institutional
goals of efficiency, consistency, and continuity
that often overlook developmental considera-
tions of young children. The underlying message is that what's good for a twelve-year-old is
also good for a six-year-old.

Scattered throughout our schools, however, are primary classrooms where teachers are
cognizant of the whole child and regard learning as an active, social process. They are safe
places where ideas are valued and where children share in the decision making and are encouraged to take risks. Reading and writing are
viewed as developmental, language learning at
school is an extension of the natural language
that occurs during the preschool years.
Teachers model an enthusiasm and love for
literature and reading. Instruction is informal
and interactive as children learn together.

These are the classrooms of teachers who
have discovered what they believe and can ar-

ticulate those beliefs, even in uncomfortable situations. These are the teachers who have made
a conscious decision to break out of what is
sometimes self-imposed isolation to share
professional knowledge with one another (Reunzel, 1993). My personal journey toward this
end grew out of my frustration professionally
and as a parent.

I began by examining my beliefs about
language and learning. I read widely and became immersed in whole language philosophy.
The integrated, learner-centered approach to
curriculum that is central to whole language
confirmed what my experience, reason, and intuition told me about how learning happens. I
assessed my teaching and began to increase
those practices that were consistent with my
philosophy.

My next step was to seek out friends. I
teamed up with interested and like-minded colleagues, joined a local literacy council, and became more active in other professional associations. When I queried teachers in my building
about forming a primary share group, I was
surprised, both by the number of respondents
and the enthusiasm of the response.

The purpose of our group is to share
ideas and information about whole language
learning and literature from the particular perspective of teachers of primary-age children.
We meet regularly and have carried out several
districtwide evening in-service programs involv-
ing administrators and board members. We
have expanded our professional knowledge and
developed a new sense of connectedness and
common purpose.

By speaking as one voice, our share
group prevented the implementation of a dis-

trictwide ability grouping policy in the primary
grades. We make sure that all district policy-
making committees contain a representative
number of primary teachers, and I volunteer
personally when possible. During my involvement in the grading committee last year, I successfully argued against competitive grading
systems for primary-age children.

    Teachers of young children are in the
best possible position to influence administrators, school boards, parents, and others who
share in the planning and implementing of
primary programs. Productive changes are possible to the extent that we are willing and able
to articulate a clear, realistic understanding of
what is needed. As Phillip Schelechty (1990)
has asserted, when every teacher becomes a
leader, every child will be a success.

Clearly, Donna's story is one of reappraisal, renewal, and
a major shift in her role as a master teacher.

    The final stage in teacher development is disengagement,
a time when teachers prepare for retirement and review their
lives in classrooms. In Erik Erikson's (1963) terms, the crisis
to be resolved is "integrity versus despair." A life well spent builds
integrity, while wasted human potential elicits feelings of frustration and despair. We have all seen teachers who manage to
remain enthusiastic and effective until their last day in the classroom. As educators, we need to examine the lives of these individuals more carefully and ask, "Here you are, ready to retire
without the slightest sign of teacher burnout—how did you do
it?" We have posed that question to teachers we admire over
the years. In virtually every case, their answers were some var-
iation on the theme of "never stop learning." One teacher said,
"Look in my cabinet and you'll find reams of old lesson plans
and teaching ideas. I could 'coast' for years on what I've accumulated. Instead, I make it a point to keep reading and to try something new every day. If I get bored doing the same things over

and over again, how can I expect my students to be enthusiastic?" To a person, these teachers whose performance is consistently superior across the career span possess the self-knowledge
to meet their own needs for professional growth and institutional
savvy to avoid negative drains on their energy.

Orientations to the Teaching Role

Perhaps these model teachers have found a way to define their
role that helps them to meet their goals. One useful way of conceptualizing different orientations to the teaching role is to
categorize them in three ways: public servant, professional, and
role model. Teachers who regard themselves as public servants
emphasize obedience to authority and lay claim to expertise
through the possession of a body of information. Attempts to
change that information or go against the "powers that be" are
perceived as a threat to job security. With a public servant outlook, the goal is simply to deliver information to students, the
assumption being that some will understand and/or appreciate
it while others will not.

Teachers with a professional career orientation have a
much different outlook. Although they too recognize the importance of complying with institutional requirements, they see
it as cooperation rather than oppression. Even more importantly,
they have moved beyond mastering the academic content to seek
improvement in instructional techniques.

The third and highest level of teacher functioning is that
of role model, in which the teacher goes beyond what is expected
to become an advocate for children and insist upon the best possible educational experience, even if this means opposing current practices. In the role model orientation, concern is not
limited to academic content or even to pedagogy. Rather, the
role model orientation has higher purposes, often altruistic, that
consider learners as complete persons who are highly individual. Because the role model teacher does not feel as bound by
authority, tradition, or majority rule, the need to be in complete control of children's behavior and learning is also reduced.
Role model teachers see learning as emulative, hence they function

as learners throughout life, while remaining flexible and open to experience. In the classroom, they are more experienced learners and colearners but learners nevertheless. A concrete example of the distinction among the three can be applied to education in three statements. Each of these statements has underlying implications for power and care:

1. *Public service orientation:* "I'm just a teacher." Implications: lack of power, carelessness, teachers' stories deteriorate into teachers' lounge complaints.
2. *Professional career orientation:* "I am a teacher." Implications: power primarily conferred through recognition by others, focus on masterful teaching techniques, teachers' stories recognized but not particularly valued.
3. *Role model orientation:* "I'm becoming a more child-centered teacher, a whole language teacher, etc." Implications: teacher empowered and sufficiently confident to challenge authority, improving teaching/learning as a life project, children's needs put first, teachers' stories central to the goal of becoming more reflective practitioners.

It is when we teachers embrace not just a job or even a career but move forward to becoming a role model that we take the thoughtful stance so crucial to meaningful, continuous examination of the stories of our professional lives.

Influences That Enhance or Diminish Professional Development

Ayers (1993) argues that becoming an outstanding teacher is dependent upon three things:

1. *Really seeing the students and what they can do.* Teachers must become students of students. The master teacher realizes that authentic education is not about labeling, not about deficits, and not about fixing things. Effective teachers have high efficacy beliefs; they are convinced that they can make a difference in children's lives. Rather than focusing on what children cannot do, they work diligently to find out what a heavily labeled student *can* do.

2. *Creating an environment, a laboratory that nurtures and challenges.* Selma Wassermann (1990) says we need to develop a "can do" environment for all children, classrooms that focus on problem solving and teamwork. This educates children for the future rather than for the past.

As Linda Darling-Hammond asserts,

> . . . there is little room in today's society for those who cannot manage complexity, find and use resources, and continually learn new technologies, approaches, and occupations. In contrast to low-skilled work on assembly lines, which was designed from above and implemented by means of routine procedures from below, tomorrow's work sites will require employees to frame problems, design their own tasks, plan, construct, evaluate outcomes, and cooperate in finding novel solutions to problems. Increasing social complexity also demands citizens who can understand and evaluate multidimensional problems and alternatives and who can manage ever more demanding social systems.
>
> These changes signal a new mission for education — one that requires schools not merely to "deliver instructional services" but to ensure that all students learn at high levels. In turn, the teacher's job is no longer to "cover the curriculum" but to enable diverse learners to construct their own knowledge and to develop their talents in effective and powerful ways [Darling-Hammond, 1993, pp. 753-754].

3. *Building bridges from the known to deeper and wider ways of knowing.* Good teachers know how to make connections, how to tap into students' prior knowledge, how to enlarge and enrich their students' learning as well as their own. The research on this aspect of professionalism is clear: the best teachers are the most avid learners. As one teacher who was interviewed for a case study put it, "Teaching, like learning in life, is ongoing.

I hope that as I teach and keep moving through my life, I continue to learn too. Teachers must be learners. If you are not a learner yourself, how can you teach children to be learners?" (Isenberg, 1992).

The converse of each of these three elements becomes a prescription for disaster: teachers who feel powerless to help children learn, who create negative environments that threaten and frustrate learners, who "cover" material but never *dis*cover or connect isolated bits of information for children or for themselves.

Stanislavski, the famous Russian director, said that there are three major flaws in actors, which Ayers (1993) relates to teaching:

1.   The failure to draw on life, on autobiography and experience
2.   The notion that acting (or teaching) is primarily technique
3.   The goal and expectation that you will one day "get it" when in fact the project is you and is therefore never finished

The Story Is You

Susan Ohanian (1989, p. 542) once observed, "The more I teach, the more I realize that we teachers are nothing but our anecdotes, our reflections on experience." As teachers, we *become* the stories we choose to tell. If our personal narratives are primarily celebrations of student learning, we have high expectations for students; if the stories we choose to tell about teaching are little more than petty complaints, we have grown dull and apathetic; or if our personal narratives are mainly tales of despair, we are in desperate need of renewal. This happens because personal narratives are a way of "structuring experience itself, laying down routes into memory, for not only guiding the life narrative up to the present but directing it into the future . . . a life as led is inseparable from a life as told . . . a life is not 'how it was' but how it is interpreted, told, and retold" (Bruner, 1988, p. 528). Stories about teaching enable us to organize, articulate, and communicate what we believe about teaching and to reveal, in narrative style, what we have become as educators.

How Teacher Narratives
Contribute to Professional Growth

Professional growth is more like finding our way through a tropical rain forest than driving down a freeway; each of us must work to discover a personal path to professional fulfillment. Often, as Fuhler (1992) concludes, it is teacher narrative that shows us the way: "Not long ago a young salesman rang my front doorbell. During our conversation he questioned me about my preference in advertising. What type of advertising had the greatest effect on me? My immediate response was, 'Word-of-mouth from someone I respect.' A personal endorsement from someone whose judgment I have confidence in far outweighs glitz, razz-ma-tazz, or frivolous insults to my intelligence. I apply that same response within my professional career as well. When I'm stymied, I turn to trusted colleagues and query, 'What works for you? Why do you think it works?' Their ideas are sought . . . because I value their educational judgment" (p. 411).

Teacher stories contribute to teachers' process of self-discovery and growth in five significant ways (Jalongo, 1992):

1. *Teachers' stories invite reflective practice.* One thing that differentiates reflective practice from routine practice is the quantity, richness, and flexibility of the "scripts" teachers bring to the classroom setting (Schön, 1983; 1987; 1991). Those scripts, remembered in narrative style, enable expert teachers to "use richly elaborated conditional knowledge to interpret situations, bring a variety of information and procedures to bear on the case, and reflect constructively on their experience. . . . Although experts' procedures and patterns of thinking are often routinized or even automatic, their methods are not formulaic. Rather, they can adapt flexibly to a wide variety of standard and novel circumstances in their domain of expertise" (Carter and Doyle, 1989, p. 61).

As teacher educators, we sometimes hear veteran teachers complain that novice teachers "just don't have common sense." Professional educators' common sense derives not from rote memorization of many precise pieces of information but from the stories used to make all those bits of information cohesive and relevant. Reflective practitioners have "common sense" precisely because they have a storehouse of stories that organize, apply, and interpret what they know about teaching (Shafer, 1981).

2. *Teachers' stories chronicle growth and change.* Stories are not crystallized; they are fluid. As stories evolve, they sometimes seem to "take on a life of their own. New revelations of meaning open out of their images and patterns continually, stirred into reach by our own growth and changing circumstances" (Hughes, 1988, p. 35). As an illustration of the dynamic quality of narratives, consider this story about Krista, a preservice teacher.

MAKING JUDGMENTS
Mary Renck Jalongo

After her initial meeting with a small group of first graders, Krista said, "I am really going to have problems. I was handing out construction paper and giving them their choice of color and this child shouted, 'I want black. Black is superior. Black is always superior.'"

"What part of the situation was problematic," I asked, "the shouting?"

"No, I just never thought people had those racial attitudes so *young*."

"Oh, the child was African American. Would you have made the same inferences if a white child had said 'I want white. White is always superior'?"

"Maybe not," Krista admitted, "maybe he just wants attention."

The next morning, Krista said, "I'm just going to go in there right off the bat and say 'Hi! I'm so glad to see you again.' If it's attention he wants, I'll give it to him for good behavior rather than for acting out." Several weeks later, Krista had a different viewpoint.

She announced to the class, "I have to share
this because I was, you know, complaining
about a behavior problem in my group. Yesterday, I was teaching a lesson on the concept of
celebrations. At the end, I asked the children to
draw a picture and tell a story about a celebration they had experienced. The child I told you
about just sat there and said 'I can't think of
anything.' When I tried to persuade him, he
said 'No! There ain't no celebrations at my
house since my baby sister died.' Then the
other children started to explain, saying that his
sister who was 'just two years old' had been
'real sick' and 'in the hospital lots of times.' I
talked to the teacher later and found out that
the boy's sister had died of leukemia." There
was silence in the room for a moment, then
Krista said, "Next time, I won't be so quick to
judge. I'll learn to focus more on the child and
less on my own problems."

When that story was told to another group of students
who were preparing for their first field experience, some were
quick to judge Krista. Rose remarked, "I'll bet she felt ashamed."
But when Rose had a personal experience with misinterpreting
a child's behavior, she quickly recognized the similarities. Rose
told the group about a child who came into her summer school
class the first day, slumped in his chair, folded his arms across
his chest, and mumbled obscenities. She took him aside and
the cursing stopped, but he remained uncooperative for several
days. Later, the child confided that he was going to have "a really
mean" teacher next year in third grade. He thought that summer school "would be the same" and evidently began by defend-
ing himself. Rose realized that "just like the story you told about
the boy whose sister died, I was worrying about what I was going to do instead of wondering *why,* why is this kid behaving
this way?"

Notice how the same story was interpreted and reinterpreted. For Krista, what began as a "racial incident story" ended as a "becoming a more child-centered teacher story." For Rose, it was a vicarious story about a mistake she could not imagine herself making, yet later she realized that the issue was the same one she faced.

When Krista's story was told to a group of teacher educators at a conference, one remarked, "Yes, that is precisely the thing that I have been trying to teach *my* students — to identify with the child. I *say* it to students, but [Krista's story] *showed* it to students."

The same story, told and retold, can become a metaphor for change, a timed-release change capsule. It not only reveals the transitions made by those directly involved but also transcends the boundaries of time and space when it is shared with others. That is because "a story is something happening to someone you have been led to care about . . . whatever its subject matter, every story is about change" (Shulevitz, 1985, pp. 7, 47).

3. *Teachers' stories promote the "ethic of caring."* "What is the worst thing anyone could say about a teacher?" I [Mary Renck Jalongo] asked a group of preservice and in-service teachers one day. One said, "That I am incompetent," another said, "That I am unfair." "No, the worst thing they can say is that I don't care." Then Teri said, "There's something I worry about. Maybe this sounds funny, but I worry about caring *too* much, about children's problems getting to me." Teri's comments prompted me to share the following story about a child I happened to observe in a kindergarten classroom.

TAKING ACTION
Mary Renck Jalongo

The first child I noticed in that class was
April. She looked terribly neglected and seemed
desperate for approval. I had seen April's
teenage mother pick her up at school once, but
April's maternal grandparents, who were openly
resentful about her imposition on their retirement years, appeared to be in charge. I was in

the classroom one day as the children were getting ready for "quiet time," a rest period when
they would lie down on carpets or blankets. A
child asked sarcastically, "Hey April, where's
your rug?" and another answered, "She probably
doesn't even *have* one." April responded in what
was becoming a characteristic way: she acted
silly. She made a funny face and danced
around wildly to distract her critics. When the
derisive laughter faded, April walked over to
the sink and pulled a handful of paper towels
from the holder. I wondered what she was doing. Then April unfolded the paper towels,
spread them out on the tile floor, and curled up
on top of them in an awkward fetal position. I
couldn't stand it. I started to cry. I had no idea
why April didn't have a carpet of her own or
how long this had been going on. April's
teacher was oblivious to this dramatic Friday
afternoon event. That weekend, I discussed the
incident with my family. I wanted to take action, but I didn't want to cause an incident.
My nieces, who were in elementary school at
the time, instantly recognized what had to be
done. Almost before the story ended, they were
rummaging through the linen closet. They
thrust a small carpet into my hands and said,
"Here. Take this to school and give it to her.
If you're worried that the teacher will get mad,
don't let her see you." I took their advice.
Recently, I saw Teri, the student who worried
about caring too much, and she said, "Your
class was wonderful. I'll never forget the story
you told. It really helped me to feel it's okay to
be sensitive and it's reasonable to take action."

April's story was a better response to Teri's concern than
any other I could formulate. It was better because it underscores

the ethic of caring that must dominate our profession. (Noddings, 1984; Witherell and Noddings, 1991) When I shared the story with experienced teachers, they spoke — many of them for the first time in their professional lives — about "unrevealed kindnesses," things that they had done for children without any expectations of reward or recognition. That ethic of care and stories about it remind us of the reasons we went into teaching in the first place — because we care and because we believe that we can help students learn.

4. *Personal narratives help teachers to find their "voice."* Shirlene was a four foot eleven inch college student who had just graduated. When I asked her how it felt to have her master's degree, she said, "I feel taller! No, seriously, I was at a party last night, and my husband proposed a toast to my achievement. Later, I noticed that people were listening more closely to what I had to say, really *hearing* me." This is a good example of a teacher "finding her voice." I like the singing voice metaphor for several reasons. First of all, it implies that we are being heard. Second, it reminds us of our singing voices, our vocal range, that place where the voice neither bottoms out on the low note nor squeaks to hit a high note. It is that place where our voices do not quaver, where they ring out loud and strong. A third reason why the analogy of voice works so well is that, through practice, a person can extend her or his vocal range. It is in fact the extent of the range and the versatility within it that contribute to a vocalist's talent. Fourth, as with the singing voice, our teacher's voice is developmental. Just as a young child begins with a vocal range of about five notes, novice teachers begin with a very limited repertoire. By the time teachers become experts, their versatility is comparable to a "trained" singing voice. Fifth, a voice is something within you, and developing it is an inside-out operation. No one can bequeath a voice to you or improve it for you. Rather, they can listen and encourage, offer suggestions, guide your practice, or function as role models. But you are always the one controlling your own voice. Sixth, and finally, what enables anyone to sing gloriously is a combination of talent, confidence, experience, and persistence. It helps if you have mentors, appreciative audiences, and fellow musi-

cians; it helps if you feel like a member of the choir (Jalongo, 1991).

In *Finding Our Own Way,* Marian Anderson (1990, p. 73) describes finding her voice as a teacher.

> In situations where I followed my intuition, letting myself respond to the person, I felt confirmed, validated, liberated. When I did what was expected of me and reacted only to the situation, I felt a disloyalty to students. I wondered why I had continued to respond in ways that clearly did neither me nor the students any good. The more I thought about it, the more I saw that my reluctance to respond on a more personal level was based on fear. My inability to go with my feelings lay with my fear that I would not be considered a good teacher if I did not meet certain expectations. . . . Isn't it our fear that children will fail the system that accounts for many of the practices we institute in the classroom?

Personal narratives enable us to express our authentic voices as teachers at every stage in our professional development.

5. *Teachers' stories can enhance cross-cultural understandings.* Sun, a visiting scholar and doctoral student, used metaphor and story to make this interesting comparison. "In America, you have an expression, 'You can lead a horse to water, but you cannot make him drink.' I think that this expression characterizes American attitudes about teaching children as well. You say to the child, in effect, 'Here is some very nice water. Wouldn't you like to drink some?' You trust the child to drink when he is ready. In China, we think we know much better than the child what he needs. We put the water, the learning, in front of him and say, 'This is water. Drink it.'"

Sun's narrative style shone like a beacon on the issue of cross-cultural contrasts. Up until the time that she shared that story, I knew that the other students were struggling with feeling a bit smug and more enlightened than their Chinese counterparts. This story helped them to appreciate the philosophical differences between our two cultures rather than assuming American ways are always right or better. But Sun did not limit her use of story to educating us. She also used narrative style to illustrate to her people what she had learned in America about placing undue pressure on the very young.

> Once there was a farmer who was impatient for his crops to mature. When the first shoots appeared, he tugged on them every day in an effort to hasten the growth process. He expected his plants to flourish with this treatment, but instead, all of the plants died.
>
> Even those who are unfamiliar with this Chinese fable know the moral of the story: that you cannot accomplish a project that takes many months in just a few days. We immediately recognize the farmer's folly, yet the same error is not as apparent where children's growth and learning processes are concerned. Not only in China but also in America, we are, in the word coined by psychologist David Elkind, "miseducating" young children.

Sun used story as a bridge between the Chinese and American cultures. Narratives play a key role in developing multicultural sensibilities: "Stories open you up to the stories of others, as common and as singular as your own. That remains the best way we storytelling animals have found to . . . develop compassion and create community. Indeed, if the unique stories of individuals are not cherished, a group of people may become a mass, or a collective, but never a healing community" (Keen, 1988, pp. 46–47).

Conclusion

Personal narratives can develop cross-cultural understanding, help teachers to be heard, reveal the nurturing dimension of the teaching role, characterize important changes in our professional lives, and encourage more reflective practice. All of these benefits have a direct impact upon professional growth: "Our lives are made of stories. Such stories allow us to explore our lives, to try out alternative possible ways of acting and being in the world, and indeed to help shape our future actions" (Kazemek, 1985, p. 211). Personal narratives are not superfluous features of teachers' lives, they are the foundations of our growth in professionalism. Ultimately, "The world we know is the world we make in words, and all we have after years of work and struggle is the story" (Rouse, 1978, p. 187).

SEVEN

FROM NARRATIVE TO INSIGHT

Stories of course require both a teller and a listener. It is interesting to note how much of our self-respect is connected with being heard. In law, we speak of a fair hearing; in writing, we speak of a readership; in personal relationships, we speak of communication. Similar parallels exist for our lives as teachers. When we find our professional voices through story, we have the opportunity to enter into conversation with other educators regardless of time and place boundaries. This is because narrative has an uncanny power to present, analyze, and weigh experience for us (Rosen, 1988).

Story is an indispensable part of the educational dialogue. It encourages teachers to talk, to exchange beliefs, to share experiences with colleagues, and to wrestle with the dilemmas associated with teaching. However, opportunities to talk about teaching are seldom a planned part of teachers' daily lives. More often than not, they occur "on the run" in the hallway or in a family setting, where a colleague or a devoted family member hears and responds to a teacher's story of practice. In fact, the virtual absence of meaningful professional dialogue in the school setting prompts many of the best teachers to return to the university year after year, frequently at their own expense, often pursuing

152

advanced degrees or professional development with little extrinsic reinforcement other than a small monetary increment on the salary schedule. One reason that professionally aware teachers pursue learning is that they discover hope and strength through listening, telling, reading, writing, and thinking about stories in the classroom. The power and energy gained from the rich exchange of experiences increases teachers' knowledge, affirms their learnings and beliefs, internalizes the special vocabulary of teaching, and frees teachers from the academic isolation of the classroom (Perrone, 1991). These dialogues are not mindless chatter about teaching, nor are they merely occasions to vent frustrations. Rather, they are an important arena for teachers to activate their unstated theories of teaching, their beliefs, and their practices. These teacher-to-teacher conversations or practice-centered discourses thus become an avenue for exploring critical issues in teachers' lives.

Professional Conversations

Teacher-to-teacher dialogue about classroom life is an important form of communication. These serious conversations contribute to the dialogue unique to teaching in several ways:

- By offering teachers an opportunity to reflect upon the practice of teaching
- By providing an appropriate outlet for teachers' job-related tensions, feelings, and frustrations
- By enabling professionally aware teachers to examine the consistency between their stated beliefs about teaching and their actual practice (Yonemura, 1982)

Narrative provides a natural vehicle for teachers to listen to each other and to themselves. Oral or written, story enhances the ongoing dialogue about teaching. When teachers tell a story, they can choose whether to or how to respond to questions. At the same time, the narrative enables both the storyteller and the listener to broaden their perspectives about the meanings of teaching and learning.

The following story was told by a college instructor teaching a developmental reading course to freshmen. *Developmental reading* is the current terminology for courses designed to improve "at-risk" college students' reading. Expectations for these students are generally low and many faculty assume that what these students need is a heavier dose of practice in basic skills. To teach students of any age who are expected to fail is challenging for even the best and most caring teacher.

KURT'S STORY
Mary Renck Jalongo

This year will be my third year of teaching what unenlightened colleagues refer to as "the dregs" of the college population, the course they still refer to as "bonehead English." Of the seventy-eight students I've worked with in this course, Kurt is the most memorable. He was a twenty-year-old from Philadelphia who had learned to cope with insults to his intelligence by being charming and athletic. Once, when Kurt was the leader of a small group of his classmates, they were struggling to understand the main idea of a pithy quotation from Gandhi: "As human beings, our greatness lies not so much in being able to remake the world . . . as in being able to remake ourselves."

Monica: I have no idea, no idea at all. I don't have a clue.

Glennys: I can't think that hard. It's giving me a headache.

Me: See if you can figure out one part of it.

Kurt straightened up in his chair. "I think he's saying that if you try to change the whole world, you'll probably give up because it's too big of a job. But if you try to improve yourself, then you might really make a difference. Sort of like the Michael Jackson song, 'Man in the Mirror'." I cannot describe how exhilarating it was to see the "lights go on" in Kurt's head. Up until that small incident, he had been using disinterest as a defense. This was the first time he had shown any enthusiasm for a learning experience in class and it had been a very challenging assignment. As if to confirm my intuition, Kurt passed by my desk and said in a half-whisper, "I really liked that today. It made us think."

During the fifth week of a seven-week course, Kurt was absent several times and failed a test. His study partner told me that Kurt had moved back to Philadelphia. She also said that Kurt had a child and that she had tried to encourage him to talk to me about salvaging his grade in the course. Immediately after summer session was over, I left for the beach for vacation. When I came home, my mother, who had been watching the house, said a young man had called, wouldn't leave a message or his name. I knew that it was Kurt and my heart sank. Now I wonder about him. What is his life like now? I could have given him a grade of incomplete if he was having family problems. Maybe he had a reading disability that went undiagnosed for years. I'm not sure. He was undeniably functioning at a very low level of reading proficiency, and I suspect that he would have floundered in other college-level courses with the heavy reading load. I question the morality of giving a student a false hope. Even if Kurt had managed to struggle through college with barely a 2.0, would that really give him the opportunities he had been led to expect from a college degree? I see Kurt as a metaphor for the dilemmas I face as a developmental reading instructor.

Clearly, conversation about this teacher's story provides an appropriate outlet for her tensions, frustrations, and ethical dilemmas associated with her teaching (Yonemura, 1982). It also opens the door for others to describe their concerns about hard-to-reach students and to devise strategies to help them.

Teachers who plow deeply into the writings of published experts in the field are often surprised and delighted to discover views and practices similar to their own. As one student recently stated, "A faculty member recommended this article to me written by Frank Smith. Until I read it, I had no idea how smart he is. He agrees with *me!*" "Yes," another student added, "This happens to me, too. I read things written by somebody famous and I say to myself, 'That's the way I think." But, then, nobody ever asks *me!*" Story is a way of inviting teachers into the conversation of teaching.

Entering the Educational Dialogue

The great advantage of asking a teacher for a story to share instead of an essay or an article is that narratives speak straight to the heart of what is really basic about teaching. Paradoxically, stories can also deal in symbols that make abstractions comprehensible. Story is a simple but powerful way of entering into the educational dialogue; it provides a significant forum for "talking shop" (Koerner, 1992).

Lori DeLuca shares an intergenerational story of teacher "shop talk" when she tells how a conversation with an experienced colleague and a later talk with her mother, also an experienced teacher, helped her to reaffirm her emerging teaching philosophy.

HAVING FUN
Lori DeLuca

When I think of how my view of literacy
has changed, I recall my first job with low-
achieving fifth graders. As a new teacher, I was
assigned to a very regimented veteran teacher
who dismissed the ideas I learned in college
and stressed instead phonics and vocabulary

memorization. I was eager to follow her advice because she had a reputation in the district for getting results and improving her students' reading skills. I began my first year with phonics workbooks and vocabulary notebooks. I also imitated her strict discipline, even though I found it burdensome. By the end of the first month, I was overwhelmed, frustrated, and exhausted. It required so much energy to get my bored students to complete all their wearying work. I did read aloud chapter books and poems, but only after all the work was finished. When I expressed my discontent to the teacher I had emulated, she said, "These kids are tough. You've got to be tough to light a fire under them."

After another month of this, I decided that I was just not equal to the task of working with these students. I expressed my insecurities to my mother, a teacher in a different district. She encouraged me to have fun, to "do my own thing." She said I needed to trust my own ability and discover my own style of teaching. I decided to take her advice to heart, and my classroom changed dramatically. I abandoned many of our workbook pages and encouraged children to respond to literature in a variety of creative ways. We read chapter books, researched topics of interest at the library, discussed books by favorite authors, used the computer to compose original stories, read picture books to the first graders, and went on a poetry picnic. To my surprise, when doing these supposedly less structured activities, I had fewer discipline problems and more on-task behavior from my students. I enjoyed my job much more, and my students enjoyed reading much more. My sober, teacher-controlled classroom took on more of a workshop atmosphere as stu-

dents grew motivated to become literate. My
current teaching methods are based on that enlightening first year of teaching. I base my role
as a teacher on one simple idea: I want my
classroom to be a place where children learn to
love learning.

As Lori's experience illustrates, "shop talk" can help educators learn to trust their voice because it is an honest account of
what we do and why we do it. School districts offer workshops
in the latest educational ideas, in which the dialogue is often
one-way, information transmitted from "experts" to teachers.
Unless teachers have the opportunity to interact, to discuss the
content and apply it to their particular situations, these efforts at
improvement will be unsuccessful. What many leaders fail to
recognize is that teachers must have a time to tell their own stories about their past experiences before new ideas can become a
meaningful part of the organization. Utilizing teachers' stories
of their experience as a central part of the discussion contributes
to "teachers' renewed enthusiasm for learning and renewed confidence in their capacity to make decisions" (Perrone, 1991, p. 96).

In many enlightened school districts and schools of education, prospective and practicing teachers have the option of
visiting exemplary classrooms as part of their coursework. Teachers welcome these opportunities because they permit useful shop
talk and initiate a dialogue between the members of the profession. A teacher who visits another teacher's classroom for the
purpose of professional development asks, in effect, "So, what's
the story?" Access to stories about "ideas in use" is vital to the
ongoing dialogue about our own professional awareness. A visit
with an outstanding colleague provides the opportunity to use
narrative—attending to the story, letting its images pour through,
and talking about it—as an agent for change.

Telling Stories of Teaching

Conversation and professional dialogue is inevitably a result of
the stories teachers tell, in which we share our teaching successes and failures, enlist support from our colleagues, illustrate

how students learn, affirm our instructional decisions, or seek comfort in difficult interactions. Perhaps we even tell our teaching stories because they validate our experiences and make them concrete (Gomez and Tabachnik, 1992). Yet, these stories of practice are rarely used as the context for unlayering the purposeful actions associated with the complexities of teaching.

Telling stories of practice is one way for teachers to gain insight into their actions and behaviors in the classroom, to explore common issues, and to address concerns particular to teachers' experience. As teachers analyze their stories, they "bring their intuitive knowledge to consciousness for critical evaluation" (Yonemura, 1982, p. 240), enabling them to examine teaching from multiple perspectives (for example, students', parents', colleagues', student teachers'), identify their teaching strengths, and seek ways to improve specific practices. Talking about their stories helps teachers understand themselves as professionals, their relationships with families and colleagues, and their responsibility to their students. It also helps them raise questions about the how, what, why, and when of teaching.

The support that teachers find through dialogue about stories often illuminates their own unarticulated guiding principles of practice. It also gives new meaning to the complex relationships and levels of negotiation that constantly challenge teachers (Gomez and Tabachnik, 1992). Think about how the following story contributes to the dialogue about learning to teach. Jane Mize had just completed an intensive one-year teacher preparation program in a professional development school. When her professor asked her to highlight aspects of her experience and offer some practical advice to the incoming group of students, Jane chose to tell her story about substituting for her clinical faculty after about a month by reading excerpts from her journal kept throughout her year-long experience.

JANE'S STORY
Jane Mize

I was excited because I would have the
second-grade class all to myself for the day. It
was harder than I thought keeping children focused.

According to the schedule, I was juggling a lot
of balls, and I dropped more than one. We did
an experiment to time how long it would take
for the children's worms to crawl from the top
of the dirt to beneath the wall. Well, we all
started when I said, "Go." Some worms took
two minutes and some fifteen to twenty minutes
later were still crawling. One even died! The
pair of girls who lost their worm went immediately into mourning and started crying. Help!
This wasn't in the lesson plan. Today I learned
that being flexible and adaptable is a must for
teachers. P. S. We buried the worm ceremoni-
ously at recess.

When Jane told her story to her fellow students, she had
a new opportunity to look back on her own practice. She revisited
the challenges of dealing with the unexpected—in this case, a
dead worm. Jane's story provides real grist for questioning and
grappling with the realities of substitute teaching. In this informal retelling of an experience, Jane shared with the new students her thoughts about one of the real dilemmas teachers
face—the unexpected critical teaching moment. A story like
Jane's provides a relevant vehicle for considering the broader
issues of learning to teach, such as flexibility in the schedule,
the teachable moment, or thinking on one's feet. For those students preparing to enter the profession, Jane's story provides
a context for examining a variety of perspectives on such questions as "How does a teacher respond to children's public dis-
play of emotion over a worm?" or "What kinds of planning must
occur to accommodate children working at different rates?" or
"What does it mean to be a flexible teacher?"

Shevon (not her real name) tells her story as a kindergarten student teacher who has been in the classroom for three
weeks. As part of a weekly student teaching seminar, students
share and analyze a story in small groups. During this particular week, Shevon talked about assuming responsibility for the
kindergarten's opening activities.

GROUNDHOG DAY
"Shevon"

The students arrived from the bus, put
their jackets and backpacks away, and came to
sit on the rug in a circle. I took attendance and
then asked the calendar person to put the day
and date on the calendar. I forgot that the
calendar person then decides when the class
should start counting the days that have passed
in the month. Instead, I asked the color date
person to color in the date on the calendar and
the weather person to fix the weather calendar.
The current event person went to the mailbox
and brought me the mail. Since it was Febru-
ary 2nd, the information was on Groundhog
Day. So, I started a little discussion about
Groundhog Day, but I really didn't know very
much. Suddenly, I looked up and there was my
cooperating teacher with her hand over her
heart. She was subtly reminding me that I had
forgotten to do the pledge. So, I had the class
stand up and do the pledge and sent them on
to small group work. . . . It was obvious to me
that I was unprepared for the opening activities. I had watched my teacher do them for
over a week and they seemed so simple! I
should have made a list of the activities that
take place so I could refer to it if needed. I also
stumbled when trying to have a discussion on
the current events of the day. I tried to wing it
with the discussion of the groundhog, but I
should have thought through what I was going
to say. I know the children didn't get very
much from our discussion. . . . This experience
taught me that I cannot take things for
granted. I must be prepared and know what I
am going to do. I have been told by others that

student teachers need to overprepare, but I was
sure that it did not apply to something as easy
as opening activities. Much to my chagrin, I
found out it applies to everything. In the future, my preparation may not work out as
planned, but I will be prepared.

When Shevon retold her story to her peers, it became the
basis for considering the role of planning and preparation in
teaching. It also initiated a group discussion on alternative ways
to face those inevitable, unexpected teaching moments. Telling stories of practice opens teachers' minds rather than offering easy solutions to the real dilemmas we face as teachers. In
the process of preparing future teachers, teacher educators must
guard against simply providing a list of quick fixes. Instead,
we need to promote student teachers' autonomous thinking about
such dilemmas. Story offers teachers a safe and nonjudgmental
support system for sharing the emotional stresses and isolating
experiences in the classroom (Yonemura, 1982).

In Jane's and Shevon's stories, we see two prospective
teachers take control of their professional development. The opportunity to engage in dialogue about critical teaching incidents
in their experience enables all teachers to interpret "learning how
to teach stories" as real concerns of student teachers.

Using the retold story as source material for peer-listeners
requires that teachers first examine the role they played that led
to their particular teaching story. Analyzing this role is critical
to finding the meaning of the story. If prospective teachers are
expected to think for themselves, then their conversations about
teaching must help them interpret the meanings of their own
stories rather than having others clarify their experiences for
them.

Stories of teaching also enable prospective teachers to get
more in touch with themselves as professionals. The teacher
storyteller is in a unique position to select which story elements
to retell, and, through interaction with others to shape the story
and give it special meaning by recreating critical teaching incidents (Gomez and Tabachnik, 1992).

Writing Teaching Stories

Writing teaching stories offers another way for teachers to contribute to the continuing dialogue about teaching. Like telling, writing enables teachers to rethink events, to understand experiences, to perceive themselves in new ways, to uncover tacit questions, fears, values, or beliefs, and to make better sense of teaching (Smith, 1991; Wassermann, 1993). Writing also provides a safe vehicle for clarifying confusing feelings and is thus "a primary vehicle for self-understanding" (Wassermann, 1993, p. 195).

In the following story by Harriet Houghland, a veteran kindergarten teacher, writing revealed new insights into her own art program. Houghland teaches in a low-socio-economic, culturally diverse school. The children, who speak seven different languages, attend a half-day program. As a member of a teacher-research group, Harriet was charged by her faculty advisor with the task of writing about the changes in her curriculum that she truly wanted to make but simply never had. After lengthy discussions with her colleagues about a number of possibilities, she decided to modify her art program because "it did not offer a sufficient selection of materials and the limited choices inhibited the children's creative expression." It wasn't until she overheard one child say to another, "If we choose art, we don't have to get the stuff out and clean up afterward. Mrs. Butner [the aide] has to do it" that she realized that she was also dissatisfied with the physical arrangement because it did not encourage children to work independently. Here's what she wrote:

Art Program
Harriet Houghland

After confronting the realities of my art program, I made plans to develop a new art area that would encourage children to be self-sufficient with materials, with enough time to explore the process of art. These changes have been designed to foster creativity, exploration, experimentation, open expressiveness, and independence . . . I noticed so many changes in the children's involvement with people and materials even though the time allotted for centers remained the same. The first notable difference that occurred was the children's increased enthusiasm and interest. Prior to all the new visible choices of materials, only two or three children would choose art. Now we have a maximum limit in the area—eight children. The children want to try out everything on the shelves. Some try out the collage box and glue materials; others get out a tomato basket and weave ribbon, yarn, and narrow strips of gift wrap in and out of the holes. There is now opportunity to explore the materials. . . . Secondly, there is a great diversity of art being produced in my classroom. When I was observing the children creating with art materials, I saw one child wadding up tissues and using paper and ribbon from the collage box to make a "pretend present" and another using the same materials to make a birthday card for his sister. And thirdly, the new art facility has allowed children more independence. No longer do the children have to wait for an adult to set up the area and no longer are adults doing the clean-up. This self-sufficiency affords the children opportunity to develop responsibility for materials and frees the other adults for more important tasks. . . .

My own awareness of the possibilities for engaging art activities, stimulated by my weekly conversations in my teacher-research group, has resulted in significant changes in my classroom. One evening as I drove into my driveway, the sight of all the empty boxes from my kitchen renovation gave me a great idea. Children love to play with boxes. Boxes are fun

to decorate. I'll take them to school. The next
day I held a brainstorming session with my
children to decide what to do with the boxes.
One child's idea that the refrigerator box could
be an apartment house led us to the idea of
making different kinds of city buildings — a
project that lasted all day long. . . . What I
realize as I write this long story of the past two
months is that a day-long project of creating
our own city could never have happened had I
not focused on changing one aspect of my
room. I learned how excited I can get about
teaching and how easy and natural it is to integrate learning from children's interests and
ideas. Both the children and I are excited about
the changes our art play has brought to the
classroom. Art is play and play is fun. Fun is
the best part of my one-word educational
philosophy — *fun*damental. Art is truly fundamental.

Harriet's story reflects both her intended meanings (describing the changes she made in her art program) and her
unintended meanings (how much responsibility children can
assume for their own learning with the appropriate learning
environment and opportunities). Through writing her story,
she increased her understanding of how children learn through
art and grew immeasurably as a professional. She also contributed a substantive story that portrays teaching as a "dynamic profession carried out by teachers who are continuing
learners rather than simply managers of others' plans" (Perrone,
1991, p. 117). Writing stories about teaching enables teachers to explore both intended and unintended meaning because
"the medium in which we communicate is public but the context from which we speak is personal" (Smith, 1991, p. 117).
In other words, writing helps us search for the deeper meanings
woven throughout our stories of practice as we take control of
the dialogue.

Dialogue as a Means to
Confront Difficult Teaching Situations

Whether we write or tell our stories, they are a more important tool now than ever before. Recent demographics indicate an increase in child abuse, divorce, and childhood deaths; an increase in the number of children destined for school failure because of poverty, neglect, and lack of adult protection; and an increase in homeless children (Hodgkinson, 1991). How do teachers with little or no experience in such situations gain the confidence and competence to deal with them professionally? Stories of practice help teachers to explore the difficult situations that challenge their very teaching ability and to find alternative ways to manage them.

Kathryn's story of a dirty first-grade child is an example of how story can be used to examine assumptions and to broaden perspectives on difficult teaching situations.

MARIA
Kathryn Chaumont

Maria is a child like no other I have taught. On my first day of student teaching in kindergarten, Maria came over to hug me at least four times. The first time this happened, I hugged her as I had hugged all of the other children. But she was different from the others. She was very dirty and had a strange odor about her. For the rest of the day, I tried to avoid contact with her. I almost had to hold my breath when she was near because of her smell. I noticed that the other children avoided Maria as well and that she played alone both inside and on the playground. When children did approach her, they teased and ridiculed her.

I asked my cooperating teacher about the situation. She said that Maria always came to school that way, dirty and smelling of cat urine. Her family has fourteen cats in the house, who frequently urinate on Maria's backpack and clothing that she keeps on the floor of her bedroom. Maria's clothes are usually soiled with dirt and food and are generally too large for her. It is not unusual for her to come to school with food matted in her tangled hair that covers her eyes. In addition to all of these problems, Maria has a speech defect. She deletes both beginning and ending sounds and has difficulty enunciating some words.

Despite all of these problems, Maria appears to be a happy child. She almost always is smiling, laughing, singing, or dancing. She loves to read to others and to be read to and does not seem bothered by her clothing. As I watched her on my first day I wondered how I would be able to teach this child for the next eight weeks.

As I sat at home thinking about my first day of student teaching, I thought about my reaction to Maria. I was upset with myself with actually pushing her away when she came near me. How could I have reacted to a child this way? Maria is only six years old. Could she be expected to bathe herself? Should she know she needs a bath? How could she wash her own clothes or cut her own hair? Were her table manners her fault? Did anyone ever teach her how to eat without getting food on herself? Was she taught how to keep clean? These were just a few of the many questions that raced through my head. The more I thought about the situation, the more upset I became. Why weren't her parents taking care of her? Why didn't the school look out for this child? All of the things that upset me about Maria's situation were not

the child's fault. She deserved to be treated like
all of the other children. She was a six-year-old
child needing to be cared for and to be taught
how to care for herself.

From my experience with Maria, I have
learned a lot about myself. I thought that I
could be accepting of all children in the same
way. I was shocked when I thought about the
way I treated Maria on the first day I met her.
I was just as cruel to her as the other children
were. I treated her differently from them. Soon
I began to treat Maria as I did the others. I
hugged her when she wanted a hug. I read stories to her and listened to her sing songs. Even
though her appearance and odor did not
change, I changed my attitude and actions.
Whenever I started to pull away from her, I
reminded myself that this was a six-year-old
child who needed as much love and attention as
all of the other children in the classroom.

There are probably children like Maria in
every school. I may have a student similar to
Maria in the near future and I must always
remember to treat the children with the same
respect regardless of how unaccustomed I am to
responding to this type of child.

When Kathryn retold this story to her fellow students,
their eyes were glued to her, the room was silent, and they
listened empathetically. Following a long silence, the teacher
asked small groups to discuss the questions Kathryn herself
raised as she retold her story. How do you teach children whom
you naturally want to avoid? What are realistic expectations of
parents? Who is responsible for teaching children appropriate
social behaviors? Stories like Kathryn's motivate others to share
their own stories of difficult teaching experiences. Some of these
stories are rarely communicated because there is no appropriate arena for sharing them. Yet, the issues are ones which
teachers must understand.

Kathryn communicated amazement at her assumptions about parental expectations, physical appearance, and her own needs in responding to children like Maria. Sharing her story provided Kathryn with an important opportunity to reinterpret her behaviors. It also produced a meaningful outlet for sorting out her emotional responses, figuring out alternative ways to respond to children such as Maria, and analyzing her coping mechanisms. For others, it can become an arena for examining the realities of teaching that must be shared. Clearly, stories like Kathryn's illustrate the challenges regularly facing teachers. They are powerful teaching tools "because they relate the kinds of events [teachers hope] they never would encounter" (McLean, 1993, p. 266) and act as exemplars for learning how to cope vicariously with such realities.

Dialogue as an Interpretive Tool

The process of telling and retelling stories helps teachers to find the subtext, or underlying meanings. Stories of practice facilitate teachers' understanding because they make abstractions concrete by demonstrating how and why certain actions happened, a strategy that Aristotle, in the *Poetics*, described as imitative (Mattingly, 1991).

Of the many stories we have been told by teachers themselves, Charlotte Jaeger's story of a first-grade child she believed was lying illustrates how a personal frame of reference can influence interactions with students. Asked to share a story with other teachers in training, Charlotte wrote this one.

RAMEY
Charlotte Jaeger

Ramey is the oldest of three children and has a sister with severe disabilities. His dad left the family when the pressure of continuous care became too great for him to handle. His mother works and spends all of her spare time caring for Ramey's sister. When I see Ramey and his mother together, there is real affection and bonding between them.

My problem with Ramey is that I don't believe what he says. During my first days in the classroom, I thought I had found a child who could help me "learn the ropes" because he seemed so eager to tell me anything I needed to know. Initially, I was delighted to have such an enthusiastic helper. I soon learned though that what he told me often was not accurate. For example, when there was a question about the schedule for the day, he volunteered information that I later discovered to be untrue. It wasn't long before I knew that nearly everything he told me was fabricated. Once, when I approached him at a computer and he was sitting with two others, I said, "Excuse me, but there are only two allowed at the computer at a time." Ramey said, "Uh, uh. Four can be at the computer." There happened to be a list of four names taped to the computer, but I knew that the list meant that for this particular assignment those four children would rotate on the computer. Ramey pointed to the four people and said, "See? There are four names." I told him that the list was there only for this particular assignment and that they were meant to rotate but really only two children were allowed at the computer at the same time. He still insisted that four were allowed. I then said, "Ramey, you are not telling me the truth" and reported the incident to my cooperating teacher. She suggested that I speak to him about the incident in a private conversation. In that conversation, I said, "Ramey, it hurts me that you will not tell me the truth. Do you know what happens when you continually lie to people? Those people begin not to ever believe you, even when you are telling the truth." Ramey just stared at me and nodded.

Thinking back on my time with Ramey, I realize that I did not handle my interactions with him in the most appropriate way. In my conversation with my peers, I have come to understand that Ramey's "lying" was a code for "Please notice me" and my responses to his behavior may have contributed to or even perpetuated his efforts to gain my attention. I am struggling to better understand the influence of Ramey's home situation on Ramey. My interactions with Ramey failed, but I learned from the questions posed to me as I retold my story that a child of six does not lie for the sake of lying. That child is most often reaching out for help. Next time I will be more sensitive to what children's behavior is really saying and plan my responses in a more thoughtful way.

When Charlotte told her story, it was a memorable moment that generated many questions relating to her view of students. By representing her experience through story (Bruner, 1986), Charlotte was able to explore the *why* behind her practice — the values, beliefs, motives, and concerns that lead her to make certain kinds of decisions. In her eagerness to find out about classroom routines and procedures, she responded quickly to a child whom she thought would help her "learn the ropes," an optimistic judgment of what a first grader could be expected to do. "Professional growth, however, implies more than 'learning the ropes' and becoming 'street wise' in the world of teaching" (Dollas, 1992, p. 148). The more she verbalized, the more she and her peers developed shared understandings of age-appropriate expectations as well as a common language for suggested strategies for interacting with children such as Ramey. Having to articulate our unique experiences in the classroom creates a common understanding of our teaching concerns. Story helps us critically evaluate and make sense of our professional experiences.

Charlotte's story can continue to be a model for her teaching in the future because it acts as a mirror of the power she holds in her interactions with students. Stories such as Charlotte's "function as arguments in which we learn something essentially human by understanding an actual life or community as lived" (Connelly and Clandinin, 1990, p. 2).

Action-Centered Discourse

Stories, as living artifacts to self-inquiry, conceptualize the whole category of human behavior as "enacted narratives" (Tappan, 1991, p. 9). When we view behavior in this way, stories can be used to examine professional practice, to study the benefits or costs of completed or anticipated actions, or to try to understand the actions of self and others. No longer do teachers have to await the research team, the statistical analysis, or the final report. Discourse centered on their actions, their enacted narratives, enables educators to research and amend their practice in a different and equally valid way. Rosemary Burton's story illustrates how an administrator's story can become a tool for discussing practice.

Rosemary directs and supervises four child-care centers. In the past, when evaluating teacher performance, she conducted general observations in which she tried to summarize teachers' overall behaviors. Recently, she decided to focus her informal observations and conferences with teachers at various centers. The focus she selected was questioning — teachers' questions posed to children and children's questions posed to teachers or peers. Rosemary emphasized teachers' observed questioning strategies at her postobservation conference. Her story exemplifies the power of narrative to generate professional dialogue on such critical issues as teacher performance, the role of questioning, supervisory conferences, and personal growth and development.

POSTOBSERVATION CONFERENCE
Rosemary Burton

This shift in orientation for conferences
with teachers probably reflects my personal

progress toward more child-oriented thinking, a
deeper interest in children's theories about the
world, how they think, and how they learn language. I conducted many of the other postobservation conferences this semester using this
"new" technique. Two notable successes include . . . a four-year-old classroom with walls
covered with children's words and stories when
before the walls were relatively bare, and
teachers who are less likely to try to explain
why they are doing what they are doing when I
enter their classrooms. I feel I have only just
begun to consider the issues addressed here.
Talk to me a year from now and I might have
a more integrated model in place for making
effective change in teacher behavior.

Rosemary's story enables us to see how one director took
risks in observing and conferring with her teachers in an unusual way. Her story revealed her decisions and experiences to
her colleagues, but most important, it helped to increase her
understandings about postobservation conferences. Revisiting
her experiences through collegial conversations helped her become more self-critical and begin to make better sense of teacher
evaluation. When challenged about the reasons for her "new
focus," Rosemary began to feel more comfortable with her decisions and more confident in explaining her reasons to her staff.
Rosemary's ongoing narrative demonstrates the reciprocity
inherent in professional dialogue. As so aptly illustrated by Mattingly (1991), narratives are more than a listing of events: they
are coherent, organized "dynamic accounts where people do
things [and] the motives and intentions of particular actors are
a focal point of concern" (p. 242).

Conclusion

Stories provide a mechanism for sharing our classroom experiences. Planning to share a story helps us view our experiences

in new ways because as we plan, we must first "talk" to ourselves about what happened in the classroom, so we come to our own understanding first. The process of storymaking itself offers the opportunity to look at ourselves from two viewpoints: as a participant in the experience and as a participant in the story. These perspectives allow us to "look over our own shoulders" or watch ourselves (as others might see us) teaching (Gomez and Tabachnik, 1992). Stories are both mirrors of our own practice and windows on the practice of others.

EIGHT

STRATEGIES FOR GENERATING NARRATIVE

When we say that a story is "told," what we really mean is that a story is "shared," even though the verb *told* is sometimes taken to mean "said," sometimes to mean "read," and sometimes to mean "written." In every case, the common element is communication. As we relate our stories of practice, we forge connections between listeners and tellers, between writers and readers. In our work with classroom teachers we have found, mainly through trial and error and partly through the writings of others, that certain strategies are useful in getting teachers to think about the stories that are already within them (McLean, 1993; Cooper, 1991). We are not endorsing "recipes" — formulaic, arbitrary assignments that limit creative expression through narrative. Rather, we have discovered a variety of strategies that support teachers in their struggles to portray and study the stories of their professional lives. Rosenshine and Meister (1992) differentiate between a "strategy" and a "formula" when they write, "A strategy is not a direct procedure; it is not an algorithm. Rather a strategy is a heuristic that supports or facilitates the learner as he or she learns to perform the higher-level operations. . . . These cognitive strategies are more like supports or suggestions than actual step-by-step directives" (p. 26).

175

A good strategy should help teachers to realize how many stories they have to tell rather than prescribe or make them feel that their square peg story fails to fit the proverbial round hole. Strategies for generating teacher narratives should be like collections of materials used in constructing a collage rather than a paint-by-the-numbers picture kit.

In our efforts to encourage teachers to chronicle and examine their stories of practice, we have uncovered, adapted, and invented strategies for generating teacher narratives. A good example is a format that we have used successfully with prospective teachers as a reflective summary on their student teaching logs and professional portfolios. It includes four components: I learned, I wonder, I wish, and I need. For most students, this is clearer than simply instructing them to reflect upon their experiences. Those four components help students to frame their thoughts and yield more insightful commentary than an ordinary summary statement, as the following example from Gail V. Ritchie illustrates. She begins with an overview of what she has learned during the experience, then moving into the nagging questions that remain (I wonder), next describes her goals (I wish), and concludes with a strong statement about her role as a professional (I need).

> *I wonder* about where to draw the line between artistic freedom for the children and requiring them to take time and care with their work. I do not feel comfortable making children go back to a table and "fix" something they've made, yet I see other teachers require this daily. *I wonder* how this affects children's self-esteem.
> Concerning the habits and practices of other teachers, *I wish* I knew what to do when someone, usually an experienced teacher, gives me unsolicited advice with which I disagree. *I wish* I knew an effective alternative to behavior modifications for relating to a disruptive child.
> In my portfolio, I have included a copy of Me-

gan's smiley face behavior modification sheet, a chart I developed at the teacher's request to reinforce Megan's positive behavior and send home as a report on her progress each day. I am not at all comfortable with the concept of behavior modification; I feel as if I'm "bribing" the child. However, in Megan's case, the system *does work*. *I wish* I knew whether it was the system itself, or the additional one-on-one attention she gets that is causing her improvement. If I knew for sure that it was the latter, I'd be happy to throw out the sheets and just give her the needed extra attention.

Lastly, as I look over my portfolio — the materials I've created, the lessons and activities I've planned, the centers I've helped create — *I need* more than ever the opportunity to try all these things in my own classroom. *I need* to teach in my own style. *I need* to be free to interact with the children as I see fit. I feel that the contents of this portfolio accurately reflect my development, what I have accomplished and what I can do as an educator. All *I need* is the opportunity.

As Gail's use of the "I learned, I wonder, I wish, I need" strategy exemplifies, a simple tool can yield impressive results and urge teachers to examine more closely their responses to particular situations. Clearly, the reflective practitioners of whom Schön (1983) speaks do not spring into being from the second that students are admitted to colleges of education. Even four or five years later, it is obvious that becoming a teacher is a lifelong project, not a short-term goal. Just as preservice teachers need practice with lesson plans or practice in working with groups of students, so do they require practice in analyzing thoughts, words, actions, and ethical issues. Composing teacher narratives is one important way of obtaining that needed practice.

Story Elements

What, then, are the essential components of a story? In their research with children and adults, Mandler and Johnson (1977) have identified six major story elements: (1) setting, (2) beginning, (3) reaction, (4) attempt, (5) outcome, and (6) ending. These elements are equally applicable to teacher narratives. The absence of any one component would diminish the power of the story as whole. As educators begin to generate teacher narratives, they should strive to include these six elements in their stories of practice. Yet, these elements should never be used rigidly as a recipe or even a sequence, because every good story also contains elements of surprise and suspense. A storyteller might choose to describe three attempts and reactions rather than just one (see "Unrevealed Kindness" below) or might deliberately begin with the reaction (see "Personal Letter" below). By using the elements, but using them flexibly, teachers can create stories that communicate more effectively and powerfully. We hope that this compilation of suggestions will stimulate your thinking, telling, writing, and discussing stories.

Recently, educational philosophers and curriculum theorists have been discussing how writing a story creates a sort of freeze frame that pulls experience out of the continuum (Grumet, 1987). Sometimes the "finished" quality of a written story will cause us to return to it later with the feeling that it is no longer about us. True, a biographical or even an autobiographical account of a teacher's life might feel like notes separated from a melody, but that is no reason to discourage the consummate form of self-report, the teacher narrative, for if teachers do not write their own stories, many will remain entirely untold. Other stories will be reported by those who know little about the rich contexts of teachers' lives or by those who would further depersonalize the teacher into an anonymous written comment or a survey statistic.

Advantages of Written Narratives

Writing teacher narratives can be beneficial in several important ways. The written narrative can document experiences, supply a perspective, enable us to share in the authority that comes with authorship, and elevate autobiography to an aesthetic object.

Preservation of Experiences

Of course, a teacher narrative can be told and discussed, but if it is written, it can be returned to again and responded to by an audience that extends beyond the sound of the teacher's own voice. Too often, teachers feel isolated and disconnected from the larger community of teachers. A written story can transcend the place-bound nature of teachers' jobs, can put them in contact with teachers in contexts much different from their own. We can read Ann Marie Low's (1984) *Dust Bowl Diary* today and relate to her experiences as a teacher even though she lived in the 1930s. We can read Sylvia Ashton-Warner's *Teacher* and glimpse what it is like to teach Maori children or read Jaime Escalante's story (Matthews, 1988) and imagine the challenges he faced in Los Angeles. Not only books but also articles in professional publications enrich our perspective on teaching by taking us into a fellow teacher's classroom in another place (see Appendix A). Paradoxically, the many written and/or published teachers' stories we encounter show us what is unique about the contexts of teaching while simultaneously reminding us of what is universal.

As long as the story is recorded, we can keep it, return to it later, and give it away. A child being interviewed about why people write once said, "You write so you can keep it." Through the writing of personal/professional narratives, experiences can be transformed into keepsakes. Conversely, story can allow us to share an experience with others or put it behind us. As children's book author Gail Haley (1970) puts it in the context of an African folktale: "A story, a story/Let it come/Let it go."

Supplying a Useful Perspective

It is a common misconception that we know all about something before we write. If this were true, writing would be little more than an essay exam. Talks with real writers suggest that just the opposite is true, for they say that they write in order to find out. Authors write, as Donald Murray (1990) argues, to discover what they have to say. Among the most surprising things that writers say, Murray includes:

- We surprise ourselves by what we write. Writing is thinking, not thought recorded.
- We discover how much we know rather than how little we know by writing.
- The text will teach us how it should be written if we learn how to listen to the evolving draft.
- Our voice on the page reveals what we think and how we feel.

Writing the teacher narrative is an act of professional discovery that gives us a new vantage point on our classroom experiences. Through narrative, we can step away and examine our experiences from the spectator stance or, conversely, look closely beneath the surface. This is one reason writing can serve a therapeutic function. We can use the same story at one time to distance ourselves from whatever is unpleasant or painful, at another time to examine underlying meanings, and at yet another, to discover how we have managed to transform a negative experience into positive action.

Sharing in the Authority That Comes with Authorship

In our society, something that is engraved upon paper by pencil, pen, or word processor is regarded as enduring and official. The same holds true for writing our stories of professional practice. If we commit them to print, they become indelible records of our teaching experiences. But the role of authorship exacts a price. It is accompanied by responsibility for what we write; authors are not only the originators and creators of their stories, they are also responsible and accountable for their thoughts, feelings, and actions in the world: "Human beings can be held to account for that of which they are the authors" (MacIntyre, 1981, p. 195). Somehow, it is less culpable to embellish a real-life spoken story than a written account that is presented as factual. We could modify the oral report to please the audience and perhaps do no harm; we could even protest, if challenged about a point, "But that isn't what I mean." Written words on the other hand are frozen in time and place, can be scrutinized by virtually anyone who takes the trouble to read them, and can be checked for accuracy against various standards and sources. This is why "The writer . . . is careful of what he reads, for that is what he will write. He is careful of what he learns, because that is what he will know" (Dillard, 1989, p. 68).

A teacher's story is nothing if it is not true or does not ring true. This is not to suggest that narrative is infallible, only that it be candid. We can look back on something we have written and interpret it differently as we become enlightened, but the story must be honest at the time. All things considered, writing rather than (or in addition to) telling is a more powerful way of documenting our professional lives.

Story as an Aesthetic Object

Another distinct advantage to written teacher autobiographies is the chance to revise and refine them, keeping them honest but fashioning the words into a thing of beauty, crafting our stories of practicing our craft. In ethnographic study, researchers are obligated to give verbatim accounts—the awkwardly phrased sentences, the pauses, the thinking out loud. But when story is turned over to the teacher, the author has creative control and is free to apply every skill to elegant self-expression.

Picasso's (1971) observations about the artist's relationship to a painting are equally applicable to teacher's relationship with narrative and teaching.

> When I paint, my object is to show what I have found and not what I am looking for. In art intentions are not sufficient. . . . What one does is what counts and not what one had the intention of doing. . . . A picture is not thought out and settled beforehand. While it is being done, it changes as one's

thoughts change. And when it is finished, it still
goes on changing according to the state of mind of
whoever is looking at it. A picture lives a life like
a creature, undergoing changes imposed on us by
our life from day to day. This is natural enough,
as the picture lives only through the man who is
looking at it [p. 262, 268].

Based upon the advantages of written teacher narratives —
the permanence, the perspectives, the authorship, the artistry —
we urge you to tell, write, and share your stories of professional
practice.

Strategies for Writing Teacher Narratives

Telling or writing stories of practice is a way for teachers to make
their tacit knowledge of teaching more explicit. Because a teacher
narrative is a creative act, it must meet two basic conditions
for creative growth (Rogers, 1954). The first is psychological
freedom, which has to do with how we see ourselves. Do teachers
believe that their work is significant? Do they think they are
capable of giving a voice to their professional lives? The second
is psychological safety, which has to do with external forces. Does
the environment make teachers feel secure so that they can try
something new and accept the accompanying risks? Ultimately,
teachers who write their stories of practice will pose some of the
same questions as their students: What stories do I have to tell?
Why would anyone be interested in what I have to say? What
if the story I choose to tell or write isn't good enough? Will it
be safe to reveal myself to others through story?

Here are some strategies we have used successfully to
generate teacher stories (Jalongo, 1992). Strategies like these can
lead to brainstorming by an individual or in groups, help teachers
to see the possibilities, and build a sense of community among
the participants. Do not think of these techniques as prescrip-
tions or limitations. Instead, experiment with the strategies, adapt
them to suit writers' purposes, and invent your own strategies
for successfully tapping into teachers' professional lives.

These strategies and examples can be used in a variety of ways. We suggest that you re-read the strategies periodically, because original stories have a way of resurfacing in unpredictable ways. You might think that you have no story for the Unrevealed Kindnesses strategy on first reading, for example, and later realize that you have more than one. Our list of strategies, then, can be used as a mental checklist. As you scan through it, a story that occurred so recently that it is only half-formulated may emerge and, at another time, a story that you had not thought about for years will suddenly be resurrected. As you read other types of autobiographical material written by teachers (such as that contained in Appendix A), this too will stimulate your imagination and elicit stories of your own.

For the individual teacher who is interested in writing, we suggest keeping a journal about teaching experiences that you can dip into again and again as a reservoir for narrative. The journal need not be like a diary with lengthy entries. It can take an average of no more than three minutes per day with a notation like: "Nadia's return to school after her auto accident," or anything that is sufficient to trigger your memory. You may want to supply more details and collect some artifacts, such as copies of children's work, copies of correspondence, or verbatim transcripts of dialogue. For an excellent example of this, see "Dear Ms. Gillion" in Judith Newman's *Finding Our Own Way* (1988). Don't make the journal a chore; be flexible with it. If you have nothing to write about, save your three minutes for another day when there is much to say.

The support of at least one trusted colleague can really contribute to the quality of the narratives produced. With someone to read and respond—in person, in the mail, on e-mail— you receive rapid feedback and encouragement. As a first year teacher, for example, you might find that another new teacher, a friend who shares the ride back and forth to your student teaching site, is a better person to respond to your mutual first year concerns than an experienced teacher.

From a teacher educator's perspective, perhaps the ideal situation is to work with a small community of writers, such as a group of student teachers, a group of interested in-service teachers at a workshop, or graduate students in a seminar class. These situations that bring together diverse groups of teachers are well-suited to the production of narrative. Many master teachers find that a workshop or course taken during the summer is a good way to become energized for the fall. We recommend incorporating some type of autobiographical writing for teachers in virtually all teaching methods and professional development courses. It is a way to respect teachers' experience, a way to invite teachers into writing for professional publication, and a way for teacher educators to know their students.

After you have generated a story using any of the suggestions we have just outlined or any of the strategies we will now present, you may want to consider whether or not to share it with a wider audience. To assist you in the process of publishing teacher narratives, we have assembled an array of resources in Appendix B.

Reflections on an Episode of Teaching Improvement (Chism, 1989)

The professional development of teachers depends upon growth and change. It also depends upon "response-ability," the willingness to reflect upon our actions and evaluate the impact of the changes that we make. Identify a significant change that took place in your teaching, what precipitated that change, and your evaluation of the change using the following three sentence stems as a guide. To better illustrate different types of responses to the same strategy by teachers at different levels we offer two examples for this first strategy, one written by a student teacher, and another written by an experienced teacher.

The change I made:

What prompted the change:

The impact of that change and how I assessed it:

Here is how Pamela Nelson described the transformation she underwent as a creative teacher.

I believe that I am a better guide/facilitator now than I was at the beginning of the

year. I began with the mistaken impression that
to encourage creativity, I had to accept everything the children said without question. I
thought this was respecting them. What I have
learned is that I can question them carefully
and thereby challenge their thinking. I am
respecting them and their opinions by discussing their ideas and not just quickly correcting
them. They are capable of having their own
ideas and adjusting those ideas as more information is presented. They can be prompted to
question their own thinking and refine their
judgments. . . . I have also tried to make use of
"wait time" phrases like "Tell me more," "Can
you explain what you mean?" or "Give me an
example of that." These questions help the children to clarify what they mean for themselves,
the other children, and the teachers.

The impact of the change has been better
class discussions and better personal interactions with the children individually. The children have appreciated the "wait time." . . . The
questions have given me a better understanding
of what the child means and what he or she is
thinking and learning.

In assessing myself on the success of this
change, my clinical faculty noted improvement.
I also felt it was better based on the children's
responses. They feel freer to say, "I changed
my mind" after thinking it over or listening to
someone else's explanations. This will be an
area that I want to continue to focus on, but I
am pleased with the improvements this
semester. I believe this will foster creative
growth in my students by making them less dependent on me for answers and more confident
of their own abilities.

Here is an example of how an experienced teacher used the strategy:

> The change I made in my teaching of first grade was to include music in the daily curriculum. We have a music teacher who is a specialist in this area. Because I always doubted my musical abilities, I was more than happy to turn this responsibility over to her. But one day, one of my students asked "Why don't we ever sing?" and I started to re-examine my assumption that 30 minutes per week of music was sufficient. So really, the change was prompted by a child's candid question. After that, I took advantage of every professional development opportunity in music. I attended a workshop on teaching children to read through music and participated in several "music for nonmusician" conference sessions. I am working toward permanent certification, so in the fall, I enrolled in a graduate course entitled "Creative Activities for the Elementary School Child." I selected music as the focus for my paper and project and, in the process, I discovered many useful ideas in the professional literature about how to integrate the arts throughout the first grade curriculum. As a result of all these experiences, I quit focusing on what I cannot do (sing beautifully, play a musical instrument) and started to focus instead on sharing my enthusiasm for music with children and focusing on what *they* can do with music. I believe that my efforts to include more music in the curriculum have contributed significantly to the quality of children's learning experiences in my classroom and to my own enjoyment of teaching.

The Personal Letter (adapted from Cooper, 1991)

Select a person from your professional life. Imagine all of the things that you would like to say to that person and write them in letter form. After you have written the letter, make a decision about whether you want to mail it or not. An unsent letter can have a cathartic effect and serve as an outlet for powerful emotions. It allows you to express those feelings without jeopardizing your career or causing interpersonal conflict in the workplace. College students who are enrolled in a class together, for example, can share a particularly troubling experience through the unsent letter. They can profit from the multiple perspectives of trusted classmates and, in doing so, gain a clearer perspective on the issue. The advantage of the unsent letter is its anonymity. Like the situation in which a person says to a counselor or psychologist, "I have a friend who . . . ," the unsent letter allows the writer to step back from the experience and examine it in a more detached way.

Here is an example of an unsent letter written to a former principal.

> Dear Mr. Carlton:
> Why did you pressure me into attending the ceremony? I know that it was a social obligation from your point of view — I was his teacher, you were his principal. But I told you that I do not deal well with funerals. All I had to do was look at that closed, child-sized coffin, imagining how badly he had been burned, and I fell apart. When his mother walked in, I thought about the newspaper story — how he and his brother had been playing with matches upstairs while she was running the vacuum cleaner in the basement, how something in the boys' bedroom had ignited and how she had struggled in vain to reach them. His mother walked as if in a nightmare, her hands wreathed in gauze dressings, guided by her husband to the church pew. I imagined the "if

only . . . " thinking that would seep into her mind
after the tranquilizers wore off and then embarrassed
myself and you with loud sobbing. We stood in the
church vestibule together, principal and teacher, and
you told me to go home instead of finishing the
school day. I wish that you had not insisted that I
go and trusted my judgment, for my presence did
nothing to comfort that grieving family.

A Metaphor for Myself (adapted from Cooper, 1991)

A metaphor is an abstract symbol, something that stands for
something else. The metaphors we choose reveal underlying beliefs, values, and attitudes. Some metaphors are so pervasive
that they have become trite, such as using sports metaphors to
describe education — the faculty becomes a "team," the principal
a "coach" to the teachers, the students' test scores the school's
"track record," and so forth. But there are more original, more
powerful images that can be used to capture the essence of a
person and the role he or she assumes. Karen D'Angelo Brom-
ley, a teacher and teacher educator with whom we have worked,
once described her writing relationship with Mary Renck Jalongo using this metaphor: "You're the balloon and I am the
string. You have all of these great ideas and are capable of soar-
ing, even sailing away with enthusiasm. I keep you anchored,
connected to the earth."

Think about what best symbolizes you as a teacher. What
are the features that unite you and the symbol you selected?
Write your narrative using your own metaphor.

Here is an example of a "metaphor for myself," described
by Rose, a former student.

When I was five and lived in New York
City, my mother and I were in an auto accident. I was okay, but they took my mother
away and because she was seriously injured, I
was not permitted to see her for a long time.

While my mother was recuperating at the hospital, she crocheted a poncho for me. It became a tangible reminder of our relationship. In kindergarten, I invented a game called "Guardian Angel" where those who were being pursued by evil forces would find sanctuary behind the "wings" created as I raised my arms beneath the poncho. I see the echoes of this experience in my career choice and orientation today. I still want to nurture children, to defend children, and to be an advocate for the very young. However outdated that sixties poncho might be, it is a metaphor for me.

At Least (adapted from Cooper, 1991)

Generate a series of statements about making the best of a bad situation in your professional life (for example, "Our district may be in a budget crunch, but at least I . . . "). Choose one item from your list and elaborate upon it.

Joyful Moments (adapted from Cooper, 1991)

Make a list of the most joyful moments in your professional life. Share your list with someone else, then select one item from your list to use as the basis for a teacher narrative. Here are some examples of joyful moments:

When Evelyn, a child who lived in an abandoned school bus with her family, brought me a present wrapped in a piece of newspaper. The package contained a coloring book with all of the pictures carefully colored and each page was signed, "Love, Evelyn." I treasured that gift more than any I ever received.

When tough-guy Todd, a second grader, listened to the chapter where Charlotte dies in *Charlotte's Web* and said, with tears in his eyes, "If I wasn't a boy, I'd be cryin' right now."

When the migrant children in my preschool classroom insisted that my name could not be Mary because I was too "simpatica" (good, nice) to have an American name. When I told them my name was Maria in Spanish, they smiled and nodded their approval.

When I asked Angie, a first grader, why she was wandering around the room and she said, "I want to see where you sleep."

Colleague Appreciation

When we work closely day after day with others, we sometimes begin to overlook the strengths of our colleagues. If we can learn to work with one another's strengths we can have a far-reaching effect on the quality of the workplace, because without colleagues and community, our lives as professionals are dissatisfying. Here is one maturing teacher's account of her struggle to become a better colleague:

> I attended a professional conference with another female colleague and friend and we shared a room together. One night as we were talking and she said, "How do you deal with the envy?" I was totally taken aback by this question, so she went on, "Have you ever thought about what you have that other people want?"
>
> "Well," I admitted, "I do feel like I'm a hard-working teacher and that I have a good reputation. I also sense resentment from some teachers when I am held up as an example of the model teacher. Sometimes, I feel those disapproving looks. It reminds me of when I was in seventh grade and went all-out to make a creative cover for my book report and the other kids were complaining about it. Is that what you mean?"
>
> "I think there are some things you are

really overlooking here," my friend went on,
"You're young, healthy, and you have a high
energy level. The majority of your co-workers
aren't and don't. What about the fact that you
have a happy marriage? Many of your co-
workers have marital problems. Also, you are
very knowledgeable and persuasive, so few people will take you on in an argument — even the
principal. If we weren't friends, I would probably feel intimidated by you. I'm not sure that
you always realize that many other teachers
don't want to work as hard as you do. That's
what I mean."

 After we had this conversation, I thought
about it several times, not in the sense of "poor
me" or with the intent of dismissing others
with, "You're just jealous!" but in the sense of
being more sensitive to situations that might
make my colleagues feel threatened. After careful consideration, I guess that the real answer
to my friend's question was that I used to just
ignore envy. But after our talk, I mellowed. I
quit expecting everyone to be like me. Now I
try to treat my colleagues as resource people
and work to their strengths. If someone's only
claim to fame is that they are very neat, I try
to get them involved, if only at a minor task on
that level. It's interesting that my friend's conversation had such an impact. I think it did because I knew she was trying, in her own way,
to keep me from alienating others and becoming isolated in my own school.

What do other teachers have that you want? It could be
something tangible, like computers purchased with a grant. It
could be a professional skill, such as expertise in classroom management. Or, it could be a personal skill, such as poise in social
situations. It could even be a physical characteristic, like the

young teacher's high energy level in the preceding example. Now try to think in terms of what you have that is admirable, even enviable, from the perspective of others. Ask others who know you well to identify what they appreciate most about you — you may be surprised at how others see you.

A new principal we know adapted this strategy to form an exercise he called a "Search for Strengths." He instructed everyone to be constructive, then distributed a list of characteristics with instructions that read: "What materials, skills, knowledge, and personal characteristics on this list are your greatest assets? What materials, skills, knowledge, and personal characteristics on this list do you value most about your colleagues?" He then compiled a custom list for each person that contained the person's own appraisal, followed by a compilation of the assets identified by all of that person's colleagues. He got to know the teachers better, found that they felt more appreciated, and referred to the lists when meeting with individual teachers to discuss their personal goals for the year.

Critical Incident

Write about a "turning the corner experience," a critical incident that caused you to abruptly see yourself in a different relationship with your professional world.

Here is an example of a turning the corner experience written by student teacher Jane Mize.

> During my unit on zoo animals, each child adopted a zoo animal for a "pet." The children then spent quite a few days doing research and addressing questions we thought should be answered in a pet-care manual. Having worked hard on gathering information about their animals, I believed it was important for every child to have the opportunity to share with the group. This would also help the other children to learn about a wide variety of animals instead of just the one each had

"adopted." My concern was how to do this in an appropriate way.

During a previous unit on insects, I had used whole group sessions. Each child came before the entire class and presented information about the insect he or she had researched. It was agony for all of us. The children were nervous, often did not know what to say, and I was constantly prompting them and repeating what they said so everyone could hear. It also seemed to go on forever and I really felt the children learned very little. They were definitely not actively engaged in learning. I did not want a repeat of that.

What I decided to do this time was to have the children take charge of their own learning. I designed an animal chart for each child to complete. It asked the children to gather facts about other animals, including a description, what they eat, where they live, and a surprising fact. I then divided the children into two groups, "animal experts" and "fact finders." The experts were positioned around the room with their pet manuals while the fact finders interviewed the experts about their animals and recorded the information on their animal charts. After the fact finders learned about three animals, everyone switched roles. It was so exciting to see this unfold. The children had a wonderful time, took their jobs seriously, and also had a chance to excel. We did this as a culminating activity for three days and not one time did I have to step in for discipline. I did help with some questions, and also visited some experts myself, but there was no doubt that they were enthusiastically learning from each other. I cannot tell you how excited I was. I cite this example because I think it was significant in my growth as a teacher.

One more experienced teacher wrote about a particular opening day of school. One of her colleagues was making arrangements for lunch and when she asked about inviting the new teachers, her friend said, "I think the young teachers want to go out together." Until that moment, she had never really thought of herself as the "old guard," but suddenly, she realized that with eighteen years of experience, she *was* one of the veterans. At first, she felt depressed about it. But gradually during the course of the year, she began to enjoy her mentoring role and found that working with the younger teachers was a gratifying experience.

What does your choice of critical incident reveal about you and your individual process of professional growth? After that "turning the corner" experience, what new direction did your life take? In what ways was it irrevocably changed? How does your critical incident compare or contrast with those of other teachers? Are there any recurring themes? Professional association journals often publish accounts of teachers' success stories—narratives that describe the struggles and rewards of instituting innovative practices, such as making the transition to a whole language classroom or teaching for multiple intelligences.

Unrevealed Kindnesses

Write about a situation where you went above and beyond the call of duty to help a child in distress.

Here is an example of an "unrevealed kindness" story written about one of our teaching colleagues.

One of my team teaching partners saw that a second grader who was a recent immigrant from Mexico was without gloves or a hat on a bitter cold Michigan day. Over the weekend, Sharon knitted a matching pair of mittens and a warm hat, then gave them to Juanita at recess. The next day, it was colder still, and Juanita arrived at school without her new hat or her mittens. "What happened to the ones I made for you?" the teacher asked. "I lost them," Juanita replied. So the teacher set to work again and knitted another pair. Within a couple of days, this set disappeared as well. Once again, the child said that she had lost them. The third time, the teacher put the mittens on a string that pulled through the sleeves of Juanita's coat, but the next day, the mittens were gone, and the hat disappeared within the week. At this point, the teacher was becoming frustrated with the second grader's apparent inability to keep track of her possessions. Then the teacher had bus duty, glanced around the playground, and recognized her handiwork on several other children's heads and hands — children who just happened to be three of Juanita's six siblings. On the way home that evening, she stopped at the mall. "Now that I know I am knitting for a crowd," the teacher reasoned, "I'll definitely need more yarn!"

Share your unrevealed kindnesses with other teachers. It is an affirmation of the practice of our ethic of care and can be an exhilarating experience. A new principal we know and admire used this strategy to get to know his staff and discovered in the process just how dedicated they were.

Mentors

Write about a role model or mentor who had a positive influence on your decision to become a teacher.

I was a student teacher and this was my first experience with parent-teacher conferences. Mrs. Reilly, the regular classroom teacher for this group of second graders, was modeling the process. We had prepared folders for each child and now we were hoping that Crystal's parents

would appear as scheduled. Even before the
nurse had gotten around to completing the routine vision exam, it had become apparent that
Crystal needed glasses. We also knew that her
father was unemployed, that her mother
worked as a waitress, and that the ten-member
family was desperately poor but fiercely proud.
Our primary objective in meeting with the parents was to secure their permission for the local
Lions club to provide the second grader with
glasses. About ten minutes after the appointed
time, a huge man in bib overalls appeared in
the doorway. He began by saying that his wife
had been called into work and that the only
reason he was at school was because she would
kill him if he didn't go in her place. Crystal's
father had been drinking and began to weave a
bit. I looked on with admiration as my supervising teacher calmly offered him a chair and
then went to work on persuading him to agree
to the glasses for Crystal. Through that single
incident, Mrs. Reilly taught me three important things about working with parents: first,
always put children first; second, empathize
with parents' circumstances rather than judge;
and third, remain calm in a crisis.

You may want to send your profile to the role model or
mentor as a tribute to his or her influence on your professional
life. Very often, these significant people are surprised to learn
that they were so influential.

Childhood Incident

Reflect upon your own experience as a child at school. Write
about an incident from your childhood that has enabled you
to develop greater empathy for the children you now teach. Here
is an example written by us.

Mrs. Stevers was my fifth-grade teacher when my father got transferred to West Virginia. The school was overcrowded, so my classroom was a large, temporary building set up on the playground. When my mother took me to meet my teacher and my class, Mrs. Stevers never got up from behind her desk. Little did I realize at the time that was how she would be for the rest of the year, unless it was time for recess or lunch! Whenever I asked Mrs. Stevers a question, she would compliment me, tell me to look it up, and then assign a written report for the next day. Maybe a smarter child would have stopped asking questions, but I persisted, undaunted because I really wanted to know the answer. My fifth-grade year with Mrs. Stevers cured me forever of becoming a "sit at the desk" teacher. I also became determined to really encourage children's questions and respond honestly rather than silencing them with homework.

Abandoning Teaching

Describe an incident that nearly caused you to abandon the teaching profession. Looking back on it, why was this such a critical incident? If you could (or had to) change occupations tomorrow with a snap of your fingers, what occupation would you choose? Does this interest affect your style of teaching in any way?

I nearly quit teaching the day Andrew was assigned to my first grade class. Andrew was heard long before he was seen, because he was screaming so loudly that everyone in our elementary school was aware of his arrival. We had already been informed that the next new student would be assigned to me, so the other

teachers were saying things like "Good luck —
you'll need it," "Forget this team teaching
stuff — I'll stay with my own class!" and
"Shouldn't you be putting on your riot gear?"
They seemed particularly pleased to be closing
their doors when the first bell rang and I was
left feeling abandoned and vulnerable. When
the principal knocked on my door, I stepped
outside to see Andrew crouched underneath a
tall television cart, pelting the principal with
items from his lunch — an apple, a sandwich, a
juice box. When the principal reached underneath to gently lead him out from under the
cart, Andrew bit him and then started to kick.
His middle-aged mother stood by and watched
and the principal made a hasty exit. I found
myself wishing that my classroom had a back
door so that I could leave quietly before my inability to teach this child became painfully apparent to my colleagues. Not knowing what to
do, I sent the other children to recess early
with another teacher and left the mortified
mother to talk quietly with her son. I said that
I wanted Andrew to come into my room and
show him all the interesting things inside, including our guinea pig, but that he needed to
calm down and walk in all by himself. Then I
went inside my classroom, closed the door, and
waited. I started thinking how sad it was going
to be to abandon my teaching career after the
seven years I had invested — four years in college and three years of classroom teaching — and
how humiliating it would be to just quit. Then
I thought, "It's him or me," and tried to think
of ways to survive. About five minutes later,
Andrew and his mother came in. I invited him
to sit down for a moment because he looked so
distraught, but I was very firm with him

because I was so fearful that his violent behavior would "infect" my entire class. Then Andrew proceeded to urinate on the floor. At that
moment, I realized that Andrew was just as
terrified of me as I was of him. We got him
cleaned up, found a change of clothes, and after that, everything was fine between us. Ironically, he was, if anything, a sweet, shy, quiet
child rather than an aggressive one. I never
really got to know him that well because his
family was reputed to relocate often to avoid
the landlord and they moved away five weeks
later. But I did learn a valuable lesson from
Andrew. He taught me to identify with a child
emotionally, to put my personal worries aside,
and to realize that much of the inappropriate
behavior we see in children is an act of panic
rather than an act of aggression.

After you have written your story about nearly abandoning teaching, try to analyze it in terms of what it reveals about
your dominant concerns. In the example above, for instance,
this teacher seemed to lack confidence in her ability to deal with
disruptive behavior until she made the transition from focusing on how others would evaluate her and began to emphasize
the child's needs. Many stories about nearly abandoning teaching
have to do with a teacher's professional reputation among peers.
Why is this so important? What does it say about how we are
socialized as teachers? How we are evaluated by parents, colleagues, and supervisory personnel? We know that many teachers actually do leave teaching. Why might one teacher persist
in the same situation that drives another teacher away? Some
might conclude that those who leave teaching simply were not
meant to become teachers in the first place. Do you agree? Do you
know any good teachers who have left the field? Might some teachers remain in teaching simply because they feel they have no other
acceptable options? Do some outstanding teachers leave the field
because they crave respect, autonomy, and professionalism that

was not forthcoming? Explore these issues and any others that seem relevant to gaining insight about authentic commitments to teaching.

Learning Experiences

Write about your most and/or least successful learning experiences. How would you characterize them? Here is an example of a least successful learning experience:

> My least successful learning experience was learning how to drive. I enrolled in a driver education course in high school. The first thing they showed us was a movie of horrible accidents where a dead baby was under the car seat—just what I needed to watch, considering that I was nervous about driving already. I did very well on the book learning part of the class, but then the actual driving instruction began. There were two other students in my car, both boys who already knew how to drive and had been driving on a learner's permit for a year. Their only reason for taking the class was to get lower auto insurance rates. For me, on the other hand, it was the first time I had ever sat behind the wheel. On day three, my instructor took me out to a busy intersection and told me to merge with the ongoing traffic. I nearly panicked, but refused to give the boys the satisfaction of seeing me break down, so I just floored it and frightened them all. It was pure torture to have three men laughing at me every time I took the wheel, which I did often because the two boys didn't really need any practice. I felt inept, embarrassed, and wanted desperately to quit but my parents wouldn't let me. Now, whenever I teach writing to students, I have this little voice

that says, "Remember driver training!" It reminds me how frustrating a learning experience
can be.

Here is a most successful learning experience:

My best learning experience was a Spanish conversation course at the University of
Detroit. Dr. Delfina Paccetti, a professor from
Cuba, was my teacher. Unlike some other
courses I took, this class immersed us in Spanish. We were required to speak only in Spanish
once we passed through the threshold of Professor Paccetti's classroom. We conversed in class
about real situations, invented and performed
ad-lib plays, went to a Mexican restaurant
together, watched a movie at the Spanish
theater downtown, and planned a celebration
for native speakers of Spanish that included a
piñata at the student union. On the last day of
class, we visited the professor's home for a
party and saw so many beautiful things from
her native land. It was rumored that she had
once been a professional dancer, although none
of us felt comfortable asking her directly. At
the party, she played music and demonstrated
some of the folk dances she knew. She was so
alive, so energetic, so enthusiastic that everyone
in the class admired her greatly. A simple comment that she wrote on one of my papers—
"You should consider becoming a Spanish
major, María!"—was a driving force in my decision to pursue a double major in English and
Spanish. When I try to identify the features of
that learning experience that made it so
memorable and successful for me, I think about
how our efforts were encouraged and accepted,
how Spanish was truly a living language, how

we learned to appreciate the rich cultural
heritage of the language we sought to master,
and how she worked to give us something that
was much more than the course description
could ever convey. I try to emulate her passion
for teaching in my own teaching and try to
give my students opportunities for more active
learning as a result of that satisfying learning
experience as a Spanish student.

We have found that, after teachers write one positive and
negative example of a learning experience, they are better able
to step back and say, "This is what I believe about the best conditions for learning," or, conversely, "Learning is impeded or
stalled when . . . " The best learning experience becomes an ex-
emplar; the worst, a constant reminder of what we want to avoid.

Teacher Profile

Profile the best and/or worst teacher you ever had. Here is an
example written by a college freshman.

The worst teacher I know is a college
professor. On the first day of class, he very
seriously told us that he "hates teenagers"
(which most of us are, since we are freshmen)
and that he "grades on the curve," so a certain
number of students have to fail. I am preparing
to become a teacher, and I can't think of a
worse way to start a class than by telling students you despise them and don't expect them
to succeed. When he handed out the guidelines
for our major course assignment, it started like
this:
Put your name and social security number in the upper right hand corner. If you do
not put your name and social security number
in the upper right hand corner, you get an F.

In the center of the cover sheet, type the name of your paper. If you do not put the title of your paper in the center, you get an F.

Type the course title, section number, and date in the lower right hand corner. If you do not type the course title, section number, and date in the lower right hand corner, you get an F.

The instructions went on like that for two pages! I put up with this tyrant for most of the semester. Then, during the last two weeks while people were presenting their papers, he fell asleep in the back of the room — and not just once, either. By this time, I had had it. I organized a group of disgruntled students and went to see the dean of the college. The professor evidently found out that I was the "ringleader" and I ended up failing the course even though I went into the final with a B. By this time, I was really angry. I made an appointment to see him and tried to remain calm and professional. He told me the reason for my failure was a low score on the final, but if it was only 20 percent of the grade, I argued, I still would not have failed the course. I asked to see my test paper and as he flipped through the stack, I could see that there wasn't a mark on them. So, I ended up going through the grade appeals policy. When it started, there were six students who said they would meet with the panel (composed of professors and administrators), but when it came down to it, only four followed through. I am so glad that I pursued this because I was treated with respect, given a fair hearing, and asked good questions. The professor was supposed to be there too but he never showed up. He was asked to produce a copy of the syllabus that included the grading policy and copies of my papers to document his grading, but he didn't have a syllabus (only the "guidelines") and I doubt that he graded my final. Based on all of this, I had the F removed from my record and my B was reinstated based on the copies of work I had kept. He was the most uncaring, incompetent teacher I have ever known.

Suitcase

If you were invited to teach overseas and knew that your teaching resources would be very limited, what would you pack in your suitcase? Compare/contrast our choices with those of other teachers. What do your choices reveal about you as a teacher? This narrative provides an example.

For me, this wasn't just an exercise, it was something I actually had to do because I participated in an exchange program that enabled me to teach in Mexico during the summer. At first, I started thinking that I should take along specific materials that I had developed in various teaching methods courses, but that was close to impossible due to the size and amount of materials to choose from. Besides, I had no idea whether the teaching theme I developed on health and safety would translate well or whether there would be any equipment available to play the videotapes I had made in my media course. I knew that I would be teaching children to speak English, so I decided to go for "high density" material, resources that had multiple uses. First, I made an audiotape of popular children's folk songs and the lyrics to accompany each one and packed a small cassette player. Then, I went through my collection of paperback books and chose ones that I

thought would have universal appeal. Armed
with those materials, I was able to plan many
interesting activities that the children enjoyed
and learned from. This experience taught me
how much I value children's literature as a
resource for the classroom. It revealed that I
see the arts as a basic, rather than as a curricular frill. Interestingly, my favorite classes during my teacher preparation program were children's literature and creative expression. In
analyzing why that was the case, I concluded
that it was because I want to be a creative
teacher and because the instructors for those
courses were very enthusiastic and a bit
unorthodox — they weren't the least bit offended
if a student told them they were crazy, or zany,
or eccentric. I want to be that kind of teacher,
one who breaks out of the pack and develops a
personal style instead of just following the
teacher's manual.

Interview

Contact a former teacher you admired and interview him or her.
What insights did you gain about the teacher? about yourself?
Some basic guidelines for conducting the interview include:

1. Share your reason for selecting this teacher to interview.
   You could say, for example, "I would like to interview you
   because you are the person who had the greatest influence
   on my decision to become a teacher."
2. Arrange the interview conveniently for both of you. Select
   a time when you can have your admired teacher's undivided
   attention. Agree also on the type of interview that the interviewee prefers — written, telephone, face-to-face.
3. Plan questions in advance and send them to the interviewee
   ahead of time. This permits time for reflection and encourages more in-depth responses.

4.   Make plans about how to record the interview and obtain permission to do so. Reach an agreement with your admired teacher on whether you will use written notes, audiotape, videotape, and so forth.

5.   Design thought-provoking questions, ones that get to the heart of the matter. Try to avoid questions with yes/no answers and focus instead on those that lead to elaboration. Asking, "What influences and experiences caused you to choose teaching as a career?" will get a more interesting response than asking, "Do you like teaching?" Even though you should plan thoroughly, this does not mean that you cannot respond spontaneously, genuinely, and conversationally—"That answer really surprised me!" Nor should planning prevent you from delving deeper into the topic by asking a probing question—"Could you tell me a little more about that?" At times you may want to recap and make a smooth transition to the next question—"You seem to be saying that . . . I wonder why, then, that so many teachers . . . " Also, be certain to conclude your interview rather than just stop. By that, we mean that you should ask the interviewee to sum up the theme of the interview in her or his own words—"If you had to give one piece of advice to all new teachers that would have a lasting, positive effect on their careers, what would it be?"

6.   Follow up the interview with personal communication. After an admired teacher has given so freely of his or her time, you will want to thank him or her in some way. You could send a personal note or bouquet of flowers, or make a telephone call.

7.   Obtain permission to use the interview. If, for any reason, you want to quote the teacher you interviewed in a published work, be certain to obtain permission and find out if that person wants to be recognized, and, if so, how.

The Child Who Still Haunts Me

Write about an unresolved issue surrounding a child from your class. Why do your concerns about this child continue to resurface?

Here is an example.

> With her wispy blonde hair and pale complexion, first grader Kim had the look of a waif. At times, her speech immaturities, such as saying "foots" rather than "feet" or "goed" for "went" really surprised me. She tried so hard to please everyone and was sensitive to the smallest slight. Years later, when Kim was in junior high school, I learned through a friend who is now in central administration that Kim was still in the district and it was discovered that she was being sexually abused by her mother's current boyfriend. Now the worry began. I wondered when the abuse started and if I, in my naïveté, had overlooked the signs early on when Kim was in my first-grade class. I will never know and because of that uncertainty, Kim's earnest, trusting face still haunts me.

100 Things

Generate a list of "100 Things You'll Never Learn in a College Course" (Ayers, 1993). Select one of those things, explain it, and persuade someone else of its importance by relating a story. These are a few of the "100 Things" student teachers have come up with.

> "Nobody ever tells you how hard it is and how tired you'll be."
> "Why didn't somebody tell me that teaching is such a frenzied activity? There are constant interruptions, frequent distractions, competing demands. I feel overwhelmed!"
> "I had no idea that collecting lunch money promptly and tallying it accurately was such a big deal. If you get in trouble with the secretary and the cafeteria staff, you're in big trouble."
> "When a drug-exposed child was assigned to my class with his full-time personal tutor as part of the school's inclusion

program, I had to make adaptations in the curriculum. A situation like this was not discussed in my university classes."

Student teachers might want to compile their lists and edit them into some advice for new teachers. Meeting with a group of college students who have not yet begun their student teaching assignments to share these insights is a worthwhile activity for both groups. Those who are finishing student teaching can use the list to reflect upon what they have learned; those who are just beginning can avoid some of the most troublesome mistakes.

Horror Story

Write a "horror story," a teaching disaster that occurred or that was barely averted (McLean, 1993).

Here is a student teacher's horror story written by Stacey Sanders.

> Just when I thought I had made it through student teaching unscathed, my last day was a day of humiliation.
> I was extremely nervous because I was teaching back-to-back lessons all day for the first time in my life. That morning, I was in the midst of presenting a math lesson and using the overhead projector. The cord wrapped around my foot and I fell to the floor, and my paper flew up in the air—along with my skirt. I was mortified, but I got up, regained my composure, and completed the lesson.
> Then it was time for lunch. One child was screaming at the end of the table, and as I leaned back in my seat to quiet her, my chair tipped over. For the second time in one day, I was on the floor. My first graders were laughing so hard they could barely finish their lunches.

> To top off my day, one of my students
> saw my first name on some of my lesson plans.
> When I sat down next to her, she remarked,
> "Stacey, you are having a bad hair day!"
>   Fortunately, the second half of the day
> went smoothly. I realized that my students did
> learn something from me because they said that
> *Alexander and the Terrible, Horrible, No Good, Very
> Bad Day* should have been written for me. Iron-
> ically, that was the book that I had read to
> them that very morning.

Vianne McLean's (1993) research with beginning teachers suggested that this was one of the most compelling types of narratives for novices in the field of education. Perhaps this is because these horror stories remind teachers that educators at all levels make mistakes, survive them, and even become better teachers as a result of them. It is sometimes especially reassuring for novices to hear the stories of veteran teachers and see that, even though the incident they recount was a disaster, it did not lead to the termination of an entire career. Stories of overcoming very difficult situations and emerging as a more competent and caring teacher are a source of hope. Horror stories also offer the advantage of instantly contributing to teachers' storehouses of available plans of action for what to do in a crisis.

Teaching Fantasy/Teaching Reality

Write about a time when your expectations for a teaching experience deviated dramatically from the reality.

Here is an example written by Jane Mize.

> I had a lot of information I needed to
> "teach" to the children. I envisioned them, eyes
> glued, listening to me intently. In reality, I
> kept having to stop during the lesson to refocus
> the children or attend to behavioral problems,
> sometimes losing my calm demeanor. After one
> particular lesson that had not gone well, I just

stopped and sent the children back to their
seats early. I realized that I was getting more
and more frustrated. At first, I thought it was
the children. The more I thought about it and
analyzed my teaching methods, the more I realized that I had to make some changes in my
approach.

Within the next several days, I had my
"pet invention lesson" (where the children were
to create imaginary pets out of cloth and other
materials). I kept my focus on the children's
literature that I selected to go along with the
lesson and tried to concentrate on giving clear
instructions to the children about the accompanying activities. Then off the children went,
and for the rest of the morning I helped with
the materials, observed children eagerly learning, and listened to them tell me excitedly
about what they had made. This lesson was the
beginning of the change in my approach to
teaching. I realized that I had been keeping the
children in their seats too long and doing most
of the talking instead of engaging them in good
dialogue, not only with me, but also with each
other. Also, I realized that in my old approach,
I was getting responses from the same children
while others were sitting there squirming or
tuning me out. I was not using the time I had
with the children to the best advantage.

I decided to try and revise my approach.
We still came together as a group, but not as
often and not as long. I tried doing more in
small groups or pairs, having the children share
information with each other. I hoped that this
would encourage some of the more reticent
children to become involved and gain confidence with their ideas. When we did come
together as a group, I read good literature. I

also attempted to improve my divergent questions and tried to encourage more children to
participate.

When discussing these teaching fantasy/reality stories, it
is often helpful to think in terms of how we can bring the real
and ideal closer together. In Jane's story, for example, she imagined rapt attention from her students and then, by changing
her teaching, came very close to achieving it. If your fantasy
is for a group of sixth graders to be excited about writing, you
might make that into an action plan by restating it as an achiev-
able goal: "This year, my students will produce a high-quality
class newspaper." From there, you can take the necessary steps
to make it a reality, such as surrounding them with sterling examples of journalism, arranging for them to visit a newspaper
office, conducting and transcribing interviews, and learning to
use a new piece of computer software.

Professional Discussions

Sometimes, our professional discussions or readings elicit a
teacher narrative. Tell or write a story of practice that occurred
to you as a result of the things you read or talked about with
other professionals.

Here is an example written after a discussion of child
advocacy.

When I read Marian Wright Edelman's
(1992) *The Measure of Our Success: A Letter to My
Children and Yours,* it brought to mind some
teaching experiences that I have been wanting
to share for a long time. Edelman says, "We
need to stop punishing children because we
don't like their parents. The truth is we are
punishing ourselves in escalating welfare,
crime, and lost workers and productivity by
failing to value, invest in, and protect all of our
children" (pp. 45–46). Her words reminded me

of a situation where teachers quit caring about a student because of the child's father.

During my third year of teaching, several of my colleagues argued against a nine-year-old boy because of his father's reputation. We were in a faculty meeting, deciding upon a family to "adopt" for Christmas. When one family's name came up, several teachers were quick to dismiss it. They argued that the fourth grader's father was an alcoholic who sat on the front porch all day and contended that if the family received gifts of food or money, the father would probably just trade the items for whiskey. I was furious that the child would be penalized in yet another way by the circumstances of his birth and said so. This was the first time that I really got angry during a faculty meeting, and the other teachers were startled I think by my impassioned plea for fairness to the child. We voted to support the family in question and those who were on the other side of the argument tried to save face by trivializing the matter. One teacher chided me for being so "defensive," another attributed my reaction to "having a bad day," and a third added insult to injury by alluding to my Italian heritage as the reason for my emotional outburst.

That one sentence from Edelman, "We need to stop punishing children because we don't like their parents," so perfectly captured my sentiments that I wished that she had written her book sooner. It would have been such a compelling argument.

Stories in Use

Teacher narratives can be an important component in a variety of situations and for a variety of tasks that emphasize reflective practice. Some examples include keeping a journal, working with preservice teachers, gatherings of inservice teachers, and faculty meetings.

There is a certain satisfaction and opportunity that comes from reviewing where you have been professionally. As Peter Abbs (1974) says in *Autobiography in Education,* asking "Who am I?" and "How did I get there?" opens the door for asking "Who will I be?" and "How will I get there?" For these reasons, educators who do not keep a journal should consider starting one. A reflective journal chronicles the story of your professional life and it is probably one of the best professional development projects that you can undertake. It is also one of the best retirement gifts that you can give yourself, particularly if it is accompanied by photos, samples of children's work, and the like. A major deterrent to keeping a journal is the mistaken notion that you must write in it religiously every day, even if you have nothing noteworthy to say. It is better to be flexible yet persistent about it, to write more when you are concerned about an issue or have time to reflect, and just jot down a few phrases or nothing at all when the mood or time is not right. You may find that reviewing the strategies outlined above helps to stimulate your thinking and journal writing.

Another important piece of a teacher narrative project is to read the published versions of other teachers' journals (see Appendix A and Appendix B). Don't forget too that there are many excellent films about teachers and schools that can entertain, enlighten, and inspire: *Serafina, Stand and Deliver, The Breakfast Club,* or *Children of a Lesser God.* Equally useful and instructive are the stories of teachers from different historical eras, both written and filmed.

Narrative can also be used by teacher educators to encourage more reflective practice. Research on cognition (Rosenshine and Meister, 1992) generally recommends the following procedure:

Introduce the strategy with a concrete prompt. Begin with several examples of writing by teachers, such as student-teaching journal entries, teacher accounts of classroom experience published in professional journals, or autobiographical books by teachers.

Follow with guided practice. Introduce the notion of teachers writing their own stories by demonstrating the procedure. We have found that using some basic strategies such as literary structure (plot, theme, style, setting, characterization), journalistic style (who, what, when, where, why), or simple story elements (beginning, situation, reaction, attempt, outcome) can be used as a framework. Showing a teacher's story in several stages of revision and having a group critique it at each stage is also a good form of guided practice. We encourage readers of these different versions of the stories to answer questions like Are there any questions that remain unanswered? What would I like to hear more about? Are there any places where too much is said, where superfluous information is included? Are there ways to make the message of the story clearer? Are there literary techniques that would give the story greater impact (such as starting in the middle of the action, revealing something significant about a character as a surprise at the end, or deliberately leaving a question unanswered for some time to build interest and suspense)?

Provide different contexts for practice. Teachers who are writing their stories can benefit from different types of interaction. Making choices about the type of practice depends to some extent on how sensitive the story is. When a story is painful, yet needs to be shared, we find that teachers sometimes appreciate anonymity. If, for example, a teacher is describing a personal failure or a current conflict with a principal, she or he may not want to go public for a variety of reasons, at least not at first. One context for practice is to simply ask members of the group to make multiple copies of their typed stories, have class members select two or three randomly, and comment on them. The teacher educator or group leader is then responsible for returning the papers in private. Using this approach offers the additional benefit of freeing group members from responding out of friendship and encourages them to focus somewhat more objectively on the message. Another context for practice is the "writer's chair" concept borrowed from whole language teaching methods. In this approach, every member of the group has read the story (or, if it is short, will listen to it on the spot) and each listener or reader asks questions, gives suggestions, and lends support. Another type of context for practice is partner reading. In this approach, the writer of the story chooses someone she or he trusts to read, critique, and discuss the story.

Supplying feedback. It is essential for teachers to see how stories are crafted and how written stories differ from verbal accounts. We find that looking at a series of responses to the same work on the overhead projector (with the writer's consent, of course) is a good way to demonstrate the difference between useful and less useful feedback. In essence, this strategy is used to coach all group members in how to function as part of a community of writers. It is equally important to give the writer time to describe how he or she decided which feedback to use and how to rework the story in a way that was responsive to useful feedback. The most meaningful type of feedback occurs when teacher-authors can see their stories beginning to take on a polished and satisfying shape.

Increasing responsibility for creating new applications. The idea here is what psychologists refer to as "transfer" of learning — taking what was learned in one situation and making the adjustments necessary to apply it to another task that is similar in some but not all ways. The strategies outlined in this chapter are a good way of increasing teacher responsibility. After teacher-authors have been through the writing of a well-wrought teacher story, they should be able to choose a strategy that interests them, synthesize what they have learned about teachers' stories, and apply it to the challenge of composing another teacher narrative with a different focus and theme.

When these basic principles are applied to the preparation of preservice teachers, it is easy to see how the strategies outlined above might be useful. Researchers have found that journal writing by novice teachers promotes higher levels of thinking because authorship encourages those who are new to the field to organize, analyze, and reflect on their experiences and thoughts (Surbeck, Han, and Moyer, 1991). More specifically, an in-depth

analysis of the journal entries of preservice teachers identified
four themes: (1) understanding children, (2) awareness of appropriate practice, (3) awareness of the professional community, and (4) self-assessment/reflection (Surbeck and Han, 1993).
Interestingly, these themes reflect the major types of competence
essential for success as a teacher—knowledge of how children
develop physically, cognitively, socially, emotionally, and aes-
thetically; understanding of pedagogy, that is, effective and appropriate methods of teaching children; commitment to the
profession and socialization into the professional community;
and developing personal/professional insight, particularly with
regard to skill in self-evaluation.

Too often, when students are asked to keep a journal, they
do not really understand the purpose. They may record some
impressions or may write what they think the teacher educator
wants to read. Worse yet, they are often graded on their logs
or journals rather than using them for self-evaluation. Unless
teacher educators use the procedures for encouraging deeper
and wider "ways of knowing," then much of the value of keeping a journal is compromised.

Because teacher narratives combine thinking with feeling, they make information more relevant and memorable. This
feature of story makes it particularly useful for individuals or
groups of teachers participating in in-service activities. In a session on discipline, you might have teachers tell or write about
their most difficult conflict between two or more students, how
they responded at the time, and how they might respond today
as a result of learning more about conflict resolution. In the
hands of a skillful facilitator, sharing and discussing these situations in a collegial way is far more effective than providing a
list of helpful hints.

The small group work surrounding teachers' stories facilitates the learning process in four ways: (1) by getting participants actively involved in problem solving, (2) by requiring
group members to articulate their understandings and ideas,
(3) by supplying practice in real-life collaboration as participants
develop a rationale for their solutions, and (4) by giving participants the benefit of interacting with colleagues who are func-

tioning at different levels as they struggle with the same important issues (Rosenshine and Meister, 1992).

Administrators can use story as a way of communicating
more effectively with classroom teachers. Too often, faculty
meetings are nothing more than gathering together to hear an-
nouncements read aloud. An administrator stands before a tired,
bored group and struggles to repeat what is already on a type-
written list. Even when teachers' input is sought, only the most
vocal or adversarial usually speak up. Administrators might consider sharing the strategies contained in this chapter with teachers
and setting aside time for small groups of volunteers to share
and discuss common concerns through narrative. It may be
difficult at first because teachers are unaccustomed to anyone
showing much interest in the stories of their professional lives.
Offer to keep the stories anonymous, at least at the beginning,
to see if that will make the experience less threatening for some.
Suggest that teachers choose situations that would not be immediately recognizable as a current difficulty and instead ask
that they choose an example from another time that addresses
the same issue. These narratives could be submitted in writing, using a suggestion box format, and discussed in small groups
to build trust and collegiality.

As we collaborated on this book, our co-author Gloria
Gerbracht explained how story can be used as a focal point for
a faculty meeting.

A high school administrator who realized
the contribution of shared story experience in
educational decision making and evaluation in-
stituted "Care to Share" meetings. He based the
monthly meetings on discussions about personal
narratives supplied by the teachers. These stories then become the means for reflection—a
way for teachers to creatively participate in
their own development. The administrator
benefited as well. By supporting and leading
teachers to "work" with their stories, he inter-
acted on a regular basis with many of the finest

teachers in the district. These conversations
with teachers invited them to walk back
through their past professional experiences and
provided the administrator with a way to enter
teachers' minds and note their thoughts as they
talked about their work and practice (Millies,
1992)—for the telling of stories allows more
than reflection. It also facilitates the examination of professional development, rejuvenation,
and self-forgiveness.

Conclusion

Strategies for writing teacher narratives are an important component of this book because these narratives are an undeniable
element of reflective teaching. Among the best routes to teacher
reflection are structured journal writing, critical dialogue, examination of multiple perspectives, field experiences, and action research (Ross, 1989). It is easy to see how teachers' stories of practice address each of these ways of delving beneath
the surface to look for the deeper significance of the teaching/
learning process. This renewed emphasis on teacher narrative
is an important breakthrough in the field of education. One writing team describes the current situation this way: "Most researchers in teacher education now recognize the important role of
context, case-knowledge, deliberation of education aims/ends,
prior beliefs, wisdom-through-action, and cognitive complexity in teachers' reflective thinking" (Sparks-Langer and Colton,
1991, p. 43). Interestingly, teachers' stories are an appropriate
way of getting started with any of these reflective thinking practices as well as an avenue for attaining the highest levels of professional insight.

A

ANNOTATED BIBLIOGRAPHY OF TEACHERS' STORIES

Nancy S. Maldonado
Mariann P. Winick
Lehman College, City University of New York
(with *Joan P. Isenberg*)

Teachers play a central role in school and classroom life, yet they often feel isolated. Historically, teachers have dealt with this isolation through writing—journals, letters, and autobiographies. These stories of teachers' experiences are fascinating and at times reveal the spiritual aspects of teaching.

Teachers worldwide provide us with insights through their writings about children, school systems, and communities. The problems, as well as the successes, of teachers one hundred years ago can also be found among today's teachers. Such stories reveal the universality of the teaching experience and the common threads that bind teachers together through time and place.

The following annotated material is a selected sample of diaries, journals, and stories written by teachers. These teachers, who are our peers, mentors, heroines, and heroes, are inspirational, troubling, comforting, mystifying, and critical. We hope their stories will support, encourage, and inspire others to enrich the literature on teaching.

Ashton-Warner, S. *Teacher*. New York: Simon & Schuster, 1963. An unusual account of a teacher's work with young Maori children.

Ashton-Warner, S. *Myself.* New York: Simon & Schuster, 1967.
A memoir of the early teaching days of a New Zealand educator, revealing the conflicts between family and school life.

Ashton-Warner, S. *Spearpoint.* New York: Knopf, 1971.
A caustic portrait of an experimental school in the American
Rockies during the 1960s.

Baldwin, L. *A Yankee School Teacher in Virginia.* San Francisco:
Ayer, 1979.
Reprint of an 1884 edition of a Northern-born teacher's journal.

Brown, D. L. *Macie Katherine Southale: Her Life and Contributions
to Education.* Nashville, Tenn.: McQuiddy, 1981.
A narrative about the life and teaching experiences of an Association for Childhood Education International president
(1945–1947).

Cameron, E. *Irving Layton.* Ontario, Canada: Stoddard, 1985.
A portrait of a Canadian poet and teacher.

Channon, G. *Homework.* New York: Dutton, 1971.
A witty teacher's log of an experimental open education fifth-
grade class.

Chapman, C. *Who Am I Among So Many?* Chattanooga, Tenn.:
Chapman, 1991.
A self-published autobiography of a teacher in Tennessee,
1912–1988.

Chapman, T. *Aunt Zona's Web.* Banner Elk, N.C.: Puddingstone,
1979.
A description of the life of Arizona Hughes, a pioneering teacher.

Collins, M., and Tamarkin, C. *Marva Collins' Way.* Los Angeles: Jeremy Tarcher, 1988.
The story of Collins's work at the Westside Prep School, which
offers a classic education to black children.

Collins, M., and Tamarkin, C. *"Ordinary" Children, Extraordinary Teachers.* Norfolk, Va.: Hampton Roads, 1992.
Vignettes of students and teachers through the eyes of educational innovator Marva Collins.

Connell, R. W. *Teacher's Work.* London: Allen & Unwin, 1985.
Six Australian teaching case studies developed into composite biographies.

Cordier, M. H. *School Women of the Prairies and Plains.* Albuquerque: University of New Mexico Press, 1992.
Diaries, journals, letters, and oral histories of women schoolteachers from Iowa, Kansas, and Nebraska, 1860–61.

Covello, L. *The Heart Is the Teacher.* New York: McGraw-Hill, 1950.
An immigrant's story of his own life as a teacher and founder of the first bilingual high school.

Culbertson, M. *May I Speak?* New York: Viking Penguin, 1971.
A diary of a white teacher sent to an all-black school under court order for integration.

Cullum, A. *Push Back the Desks.* New York: Scholastic, 1967.
One year in the life of a Rye, New York, first-grade class and its intrepid teacher.

Day, B. *The Little Professor of Piney Woods.* New York: Simon & Schuster, 1955.
A story of fifty years of pioneering in black education at the Piney Woods Country Life School in Mississippi.

Deuel, L. (ed.). *The Teacher's Treasure Chest.* Englewood Cliffs, N.J.: Prentice-Hall, 1956.
Fifty stories providing views of teachers and students.

Dunn, J. *Retreat from Learning.* New York: McKay, 1956.
A brief case history of one teacher.

Dyer, T. (ed.). *To Raise Myself a Little.* Athens: University of Georgia, 1982.
The diaries and letters, 1851–1886, of Amelia Lines, a Georgia teacher.

Ernst, M. (ed.). *The Teacher.* Englewood Cliffs, N.J.: Prentice-Hall, 1967.
Recollection of catalyst teachers and the students they inspired.

Forten, C. L., and Billington, R. A. (ed.). *Journal of Charlotte Forten: A Free Negro in the Slave Era.* New York: W. W. Norton, 1981.
Journal entries, 1837–1914, of an abolitionist and teacher.

Foster, S. J. *Sarah Jane Foster: Teacher of Freed Men.* Charlottesville: University of Virginia, 1990.
A collection of journal entries and letters of a teacher of freed men.

Fuchs, E. *Teachers Talk.* New York: Anchor, 1967.
A journal technique used by beginning teachers provides a perspective on city schools.

Goldman, J. *My Life as a Travelling Home Schooler.* New York: Salomen, 1991.
Teaching experiences of the author and her uncle as home schoolers to ranchers, native Americans, Canadians, and Europeans.

Gustafsson, L. *The Death of a Beekeeper.* New York: New Directions, 1978.
A poignant account of a retired Swedish teacher as he lives and dies with cancer.

Habler, R. *I Touch the Future — The Story of Christa McAuliffe.* New York: Random House, 1987.
Life and teaching experiences of the first teacher to become an astronaut.

Hannon, J. *Never Tease a Dinosaur*. Troy, Mo.: Holt, Rinehart & Winston, 1962.
How a male elementary school teacher uses his wits to cope in a female environment.

Harris, B. K. *Karen's Nursery School Project*. Englewood Cliffs, N.J.: Julian Messner, 1955.
A nursery school assistant's fictionalized tales of daily life and professional needs.

Herndon, J. *The Way It Spozed to Be*. New York: Simon & Schuster, 1965.
One chaotic year during the 1960s at a metropolitan ghetto school.

Herndon, J. *Notes from a Schoolteacher*. New York: Simon & Schuster, 1985.
Reflections on twenty years of teaching and thinking about education.

Hoffman, N. *Woman's True Profession*. New York: McGraw-Hill, 1981.
A collection of diary and journal entries, essays, oral histories, autobiographies, and short stories of women who became teachers between 1830 and 1920.

Horton, M., Kohl, J., and Kohl, L. *The Long Haul: An Autobiography*. New York: Doubleday, 1990.
The story of Myles Horton, holistic educator and founder of the Highlander Folk School in the Appalachian mountains.

Iliff, F. G. *People of the Blue Water: A Record of Life Among the Walopi and Hansupai Indians*. Tucson: University of Arizona, 1985.
An anecdotal account of Flora Gregg Iliff, teacher of the Walopi and Hansupai Indians, 1882–1959.

Jones, T. *Where the Rainbow Waits*. Chicago, Ill.: Playboy, 1978.
An account of the daily life of a big city teacher at a one-room schoolhouse in Terlingua, Texas.

Kane, H., and Henry, I. *Miracle in the Mountains.* New York: Doubleday, 1956.
Life at the Berry schools in rural Georgia, described by dedicated founder Martha Berry.

Katai, T. *Country Teacher.* Honolulu: University of Hawaii Press, 1984.
A story based on the pre–World War I diary of a young Japanese schoolteacher.

Kaufman, P. W. *Up the Down Staircase.* Englewood Cliffs, N.J.: Prentice-Hall, 1964.
Journal and letters of a first-year teacher in an urban high school.

Kaufman, P. W. *Women Teachers on the Frontier.* New Haven, Conn.: Yale University Press, 1985.
Diaries, remembrances, and letters of nine New England women who went West in 1846 as part of the earliest U.S. Teacher Corps.

Keller, H. *Teacher.* New York: Doubleday, 1955.
A tribute to Anne Sullivan Macy "by the foster-child of her mind," Helen Keller.

Kendall, R. *White Teacher in a Black School.* Greenwich, Conn.: Devin, 1980.
A record of a teacher's experience in an all-black school.

Kennedy, M. F. *Schoolmaster of Yesterday.* New York: McGraw-Hill, 1940.
A record of three generations of teachers from one family in the 1880s.

Kohl, H. *Thirty-six Children.* New York: New American Library, 1967.
An account of a Harvard graduate's first year of teaching sixth-grade in a ghetto school.

Lopate, P. *Being with Children.* New York: Doubleday, 1975.

A report of a teacher's integration of videotaping into the school's elementary curriculum.

Manning, C. *Hill Country Teachers.* Boston: Twayne, 1990.
Oral histories of eight teachers from Texas Hill country, 1920–1960.

McDiamond, G. W. *The Inventive Mind.* Fairbanks: University of Alaska, 1986.
A collection of teachers' stories from rural Alaska.

McPherson, G. *Small-town Teachers.* Cambridge, Mass.: Harvard, 1971.
A study of nine teachers in a small New England town.

Marshall, S. *An Experiment in Education.* New York: Cambridge University Press, 1963.
An eighteen-year record of an art teacher's inspired and inspiring experiences at the Kingston County Primary Schools, England.

Miller, J. *Creating Spaces and Finding Voices.* Amherst, N.Y.: SUNY, 1991.
Dialogue journals of five public school teachers who collaborate with a university mentor as part of teacher empowerment.

Moore, R. *Welcome to X57.* New York: Putnam, 1974.
A law student's chronicle of four disturbing years of teaching and learning at a Bedford-Stuyvesant junior high school.

Morgan, L. *A Gift from the Hills.* New York: Bobbs-Merrill, 1958.
A unique story of the Penland School.

Murray, L., and Harlow, A. *Schoolhouse in the Foothills.* New York: Simon & Schuster, 1935.
The true story of Miss Ella, a teacher in a rural Tennessee mountain town.

Nash, R. M. *The Little Emigrant.* Privately published, 1970.

A record of a woman teacher's journey from childhood to adult-hood through the Dakota Territory and back East to New York State between the 1880s and the mid 1900s.

Nathan, B. *Tales of a Teacher*. Chicago: Henry Regney, 1956.
An autobiography of a pioneering California teacher, 1915–1945.

Neill, A. S. *Neill! Neill! Orange Peel*. New York: Hart, 1972.
An awe-inspiring autobiography by the pioneering educator.

Parker, J. *How to Sink a Sub*. Alpharetta, Ga.: John Max Books, 1990.
Vignettes, advice, and simple truths related to substitute teaching.

Patri, A. *Schoolmaster of the Great City*. New York: Macmillan, 1917.
The story of an Italian immigrant's rise from student to teacher to principal of a public school for the gifted in New York City.

Peters, W. *A Class Divided*. New York: Doubleday, 1971.
A record of a now-classic classroom experiment on discrimination by Jane Elliot, a third-grade teacher in Iowa.

Philips, M. *A Teacher Speaks*. New York: David McKay, 1960.
A forty-year review of classroom life and a program of solutions.

Polk, S. G. *For All Those Children Whose Lives Touched Mine*. Kingsville: Texas A & M, 1989.
Autobiographical material on both students and teachers.

Pratt, C. *I Learn from Children*. New York: Simon & Schuster, 1948.
A thirty-year intimate portrait of Pratt's work with progressive education at the City and Country School.

Raphael, R. *The Teacher's Voice*. Portsmouth, N.H.: Heinemann Educational Books, 1985.
Firsthand accounts of the daily lives of ten teachers.

Ryan, K., and Canfield, J. (eds.). *Don't Smile till Xmas; Accounts of the First Year of Teaching.* Chicago: University of Chicago Press, 1970.
Seven first-year teachers' accounts as part of a University of Chicago Master of Arts in Teaching program.

Sargent, S. *Pat Hawley, Preschool Teacher.* New York: McGraw-Hill, 1958.
A child-care program director describes the life of a nursery school teacher.

Schoolboys of Barbiana. *Letter to a Teacher.* New York: Random House, 1970.
Eight students' journals of the fascinating work of Don Lorenzo Milani, founder of a school for boys during the 1950s and 1960s, near Florence, Italy.

Seabury, D. *The Diary of Caroline Seabury, 1854–1863.* Madison: University of Wisconsin, 1991.
A collection of journal entries by a teacher and diarist, 1837–1893.

Specht, R. *Tisha.* New York: St. Martin's Press, 1976.
The story of Anne Hobbs's years of teaching Eskimos and Indians in the Alaskan wilderness beginning in 1927.

Stephans, D. M. *One-Room School.* Norman: University of Oklahoma Press, 1990.
The life and teaching experiences of Helen Hussman Morris in a one-room Oklahoma school during the 1930s.

Sterling, P. *The Real Teacher.* New York: Random House, 1972.
Edited transcripts of interviews with thirty elementary and secondary teachers in an urban ghetto school.

Sterne, E. *Mary McCleod Bethune.* New York: Knopf, 1957.
A biography of the child of slaves, focusing on her early life, her own teaching days, and the founding of a college.

Strane, S. *A Whole-Souled Woman*. New York: W. W. Norton, 1980.
The pioneering work of abolitionist Prudence Crandall, who was an educator of young black women in Canterbury, Connecticut, during the 1830s.

Stuart, J. *To Teach, To Love*. Chicago: World, 1970.
Autobiography of a teacher, school administrator, and author.

Vigdarova, F. *Diary of a Schoolteacher*. New York: Foreign Language Publications, 1954.
A true story of a first-year teacher of seven-year-olds in a USSR school.

Walcott, G. B. *The Long Way Back: An Alcoholic's Own Story*. New York: Vintage, 1987.
The life story of Gary Walcott, teacher, alcoholic, and chess player.

Warbelow, W., and Warbelow, M. *Empire on Ice*. Anchorage, Alaska: Great North West, 1990.
A chronicle of eleven years of teaching for the Department of the Interior (1945–1956) near the Arctic Circle.

Weber, J. *My Country School Diary*. New York: HarperCollins, 1946.
A journal of four years teaching in a one-room rural school before World War II.

Weiss, M. J. (ed.). *Tales Out of School*. New York: Dell, 1967.
More than a dozen vignettes of classroom life by well-known writers and teachers.

B

SUGGESTIONS FOR
PUBLISHING TEACHERS' STORIES

As you begin writing vignettes about teaching or stories about your role as a teacher/researcher, you will find three types of information helpful: guidebooks, exemplars, and outlets. Guidebooks on writing are like mentors on paper — they encourage, coach, and recommend ways of thinking about yourself. Exemplars are articles and books written in various styles that can be used as examples. Outlets refer to those publications that are amenable to publishing well-written teachers' stories.

Guidebooks: Suggestions on Writing Stories

Bateson, M. C. *Composing a Life.* New York: Atlantic Monthly Press, 1989.
Davis, D. *Telling Your Own Stories.* Little Rock, Ark.: August House, 1993.
Didion, J. *Slouching Toward Bethlehem.* New York: Dell, 1966.
Efron, S., and Joseph, P. B. "Reflections in a Mirror: Teacher-generated Metaphors from Self and Others." In P. B. Joseph, and G. E. Burnaford (eds.), *Images of Schoolteachers in Twentieth-Century America: Paragons, Polarities, Complexities* (pp. 64–77). New York: St. Martin's Press, 1994.

Elbow, P. *Writing Without Teachers*. New York: Oxford University Press, 1982.

Elbow, P. *Writing with Power*. New York: Oxford University Press, 1981.

Fischer, J. C., and Kiefer, A. "Constructing and Discovering Images of Your Teaching." In P. B. Joseph and G. E. Burnaford (eds.), *Images of Schoolteachers in Twentieth-Century America: Paragons, Polarities, Complexities* (pp. 29–53). New York: St. Martin's Press, 1994.

Fuhler, C. J. In M. D'Allesandro and others. "Writing for Publication: Voices from the Classroom." *The Reading Teacher*, 1992, *45*(6), 508–414.

Goldberg, N. *Writing Down the Bones*. Boston, Mass.: Shambhala Press, 1986.

Gomez, M. L., and Tabachnick, B. R. "Telling Teaching Stories." *Teacher Education*, 1992, *4*(2), 129–148.

Heilbrun, C. *Writing a Woman's Life*. New York: Ballantine, 1988.

Hewitt, L., and others. *Teachers' Stories: Expanding the Boundaries with the Participatory Approach*. Boston: World Education, 1992. (ED 353 856)

Hubbard, R., and Power, B. M. *The Art of Classroom Inquiry: A Handbook for Teacher Researchers*. Portsmouth, N.H.: Heinemann, 1993.

Keen, S. *Telling Your Story: A Guide to Who You Are and Who You Could Be*. New York: New American Library, 1974.

Ledoux, D. *Turning Memories into Memoirs: A Handbook for Writing Lifestories*. Lisbon Falls, Maine: Soleil, 1993.

Macrorie, K. *Telling Writing*. (7th ed.) Upper Montclair, N.J.: Boynton/Cook, 1985.

Rico, G. L. *Writing the Natural Way: Using Right-Brain Techniques to Release Your Expressive Powers*. Los Angeles, Calif.: J. P. Tarcher, 1983.

Tarshis, B. *How to Write Like a Pro*. New York: New American Library, 1982.

Thomas, F. *How to Write the Story of Your Life*. Cincinnati, Ohio: Writer's Digest Books, 1984.

Wagner, J. "The Well-Told Teaching Story: A Resource for Teachers of English." *English Education*, 1989, *21*(2), 110–125.

Exemplars: Articles and Books Written by Educators

Articles

Alejandro, A. "Like Happy Dreams—Integrating Visual Arts, Writing, and Reading." *Language Arts,* 1994, *71,* 12–21.

Barry, P. "Strong Medicine: A Talk with Former Principal Henry Gradillas." *College Board Review,* 1989, Fall (153), 2–13.

Behar, R. "Dare We Say I? Bringing the Personal into Scholarship." *The Chronicle of Higher Education, 40*(43), B1–B2.

Birdseye, T. "The Boy Who Couldn't Imagine Himself a Writer." *The Reading Teacher,* 1994, *47*(6), 478–479.

Brewster, J. C. "No More Post Offices." *Childhood Education,* 1993, *69*(5), 269–270.

Burton, R. "Reaching Troubled Children: One Teacher's Stories." *Dimensions of Early Childhood,* 1993, *21*(4), 25–28, 32.

Castle, K. "Child-Centered Teaching: Through Children's Eyes." *Childhood Education,* 1989, *65*(4), 209–212.

Chatterton, S. "On Becoming Teacher Experts: A Small Flight of Fancy on a Lesson." *Language Arts,* 1987, *64*(5), 540–541.

Chenfeld, M. B. "Flamingos in the Bathroom, Love in the Classroom." *Phi Delta Kappan,* 1993, *74*(5), 413–414.

Doremus, V. P. "Forcing Works for Flowers, but Not for Children." *Educational Leadership,* 1986, *44*(3), 32–35.

Ernst, K. "Writing Pictures, Painting Words: Writing in an Artist's Workshop." *Language Arts,* 1994, *71,* 44–52.

Fawcett, G. "Beth Starts Like Brown Bear!" *Phi Delta Kappan,* 1994, *75*(9), 721–722.

Fine, E. S. "Marbles Lost, Marbles Found." *Language Arts,* 1987, *64*(5), 474.

Hipple, M. "Journal Writing in Kindergarten." *Language Arts,* 1985, *62*(3), 255–261.

Hubbard, R. "Time Will Tell." *Language Arts,* 1993, *70,* 574–582.

Hubbard, R. "Transferring Images: Not Just Glued on the Page." *Young Children,* 1987, *42,* 60–67.

Irwin, J. M. "Finding Our Writing Voices." *The Reading Teacher,* 1992, *45*(6), 406–414.

Jalongo, M. R. "Stephanie: One Teacher's Story." *Young Children,* 1991, *46*(6), 62–64.

Lass, B. "Portrait of My Son as an Early Reader." *The Reading Teacher,* 1982, *36,* 20–28.

Merriam, S. B. "On Being a Woman Professor of Adult Education." *Lifelong Learning,* 1985, *8*(8), 6, 28.

Moriarty, K. "Learning by Doing: Lessons of a Summer Arts Program." *Music Educators Journal,* 1988, *75,* 18–22.

Siemens, L. "Does Jesus Have Aunties?" and "Who Planned it All?": Learning to Listen for "Big" Questions. *Language Arts,* 1994, *71,* 358–359.

Smith, G. "On Listening to the Language of Children." *Young Children,* 1974, *29,* 133–140.

Stamp, L. N. "On the Value of Informal Learning: The Fabric Shop." *Childhood Education,* 1993, *69*–(5), 262–264.

Tarwater, P. "Glass, Plastic, or Steel?" *Childhood Education,* 1993, *69*(5), 272–273.

Treiber, P. "I Used to Know Everything!" *Childhood Education,* 1993, *69*(5), 271.

Vance, E. "A Tree for Eric." *The Educational Forum,* 1990, *54*(3), 293–315.

Voss, M. "The Light at the End of the Journal: A Teacher Learns About Learning." *Language Arts,* 1988, *65*(7), 669–674.

Books

Ashton-Warner, S. *Teacher.* New York: Touchstone, 1963.

Ashton-Warner, S. *I Passed This Way.* New York: Touchstone, 1979.

Bateson, M. C. *With a Daughter's Eye.* New York: Morrow, 1984.

Butler, D. *Cushla and Her Books.* Boston: The Horn Book, 1975.

Calkins, L. M. *Lessons from a Child: On the Learning and Teaching of Writing.* Portsmouth, N.H.: Heinemann Educational Books, 1983.

Carter, J. M. *Confessions of a Space Cadet: The Transformation of a Teacher.* Lanham, Md.: University Press of America, 1987.

Cartwright, M., and D'Orso, M. *For the Children: Lessons from a Visionary Principal.* New York: Doubleday, 1993.

Cutuly, J. *Home of the Wildcats: Perils of an English Teacher.* Urbana, Ill: National Council of Teachers of English, 1993.

Dollas, R. H. *Voices of Beginning Teachers: Visions and Realities.* New York: Teachers College Press, 1992.

Five, C. L. *Special Voices.* Portsmouth, N.H.: Heinemann, 1991.

Fox, M. *Radical Reflections: Passionate Opinions on Teaching, Learning, and Living.* San Diego, Calif.: Harcourt Brace Jovanovich, 1993.

Freedman, S. G. *Small Victories: The Real World of a Teacher, Her High School and Their High School.* New York: HarperCollins, 1991.

French, T. *Soul of Heaven.* New York: Doubleday, 1993.

Hayden, T. L. *One Child.* Boston: Little, Brown, 1980.

Hillman, C. B. *Teaching Four-Year-Olds: A Personal Journey.* Bloomington, Ind.: Phi Delta Kappa, 1988.

Jalongo, M. R. *Creating Communities: The Role of the Teacher in the 21st Century.* Bloomington, Ind.: National Educational Service, 1991.

Kane, P. R. (ed.). *The First Year of Teaching: Real World Stories from American Teachers.* New York: Walker, 1992.

Keizer, G. *No Place But Here: A Teacher's Vocation in a Rural Community.* New York: Viking Penguin, 1988.

Marshall, S. *An Experiment in Education.* Cambridge, Mass.: Cambridge University Press, 1970.

Natkins, L. G. *Our Last Term: A Teacher's Diary.* Lanham, Md.: University Press of America, 1988.

Newman, J. (ed.). *Finding Our Own Way.* Portsmouth, N.H.: Heinemann Educational Books, 1990.

Paley, V. G. *Wally's Stories.* Cambridge, Mass.: Cambridge University Press, 1981.

Perrone, V. *A Letter to Teachers: Reflections on Schooling and the Art of Teaching.* San Francisco, Calif.: Jossey-Bass, 1991.

Rankin, E. *Seeing Yourself as a Teacher: Conversations with Five New Teachers in a University Writing Program.* Urbana, Ill: National Council of Teachers of English, 1994.

Rasmussen, M. *Listen! The Children Speak.* Washington, D.C.: United States National Committee of World Organization for Early Childhood Education, 1979.

Robertson, G. F., and Johnson, M. A. (eds.). *Leaders in Education: Their Views on Controversial Issues.* Lanham, Md.: University Press of America, 1988.

Rose, M. *Lives on the Boundary*. New York: Viking Penguin, 1989.

Rouse, J. *Provocations: The Story of Mrs. M*. Urbana, Ill: National Council of Teachers of English, 1993.

Schwartz, J. *Another Door to Learning: True Stories of Learning-disabled Children and Adults and the Keys to Their Success*. New York: Crossroad, 1992.

Upitis, R. *This Too Is Music*. Portsmouth, N.H.: Heinemann Educational Books, 1991.

Villanueva, V., Jr. *Bootstraps: From an American Academic of Color*. Urbana, Ill: National Council of Teachers of English, 1993.

Outlets: Where to Publish Teacher Stories

There are many possible outlets for well-written teacher narratives, including professional newsletters, magazines, journals, and books. Most periodicals whose primary readers are practitioners will publish stories of practice in some form at least occasionally, depending on the quality and content of the story. Increasingly, journal publications are including columns that focus on true stories about classroom experiences; these are noted below.

> *Childhood Education*
> *Day Care and Early Education*
> *Educational Leadership*
> *English Journal*
> *The Journal of Emotional and Behavioral Problems* (see especially "Voices of Youth" and "Children on the Edge")
> *The Journal of Reading*
> *Phi Delta Kappan*
> *Primary Voices, K-6*
> *Principal*
> *The Reading Teacher* (regularly features "Literacy Stories" and "Our Own Stories")
> *Young Children*

In addition to magazines and journals, you may want to consider collaborating with an experienced author or compiling and editing books of stories authored by various teachers. Some publishers that are receptive to works that rely heavily on the narrative mode are Doubleday, Heinemann Educational Books, Jossey-Bass, Viking Penguin, Teachers College Press, and University Press of America. •

REFERENCES

Abbs, P. *Autobiography in Education*. London: Heinemann Educational Books, 1974.

Adler, S. "The Reflective Practitioner and the Curriculum of Teacher Education." *Journal of Education for Teaching*, 1991, *17*(2), 139–150.

Ambrose, R. "Personal Narratives and Professional Development." *Childhood Education*, 1993, *69*(5), 274–276.

Anderson, J. A. "Cognitive Styles and Multicultural Populations." *Journal of Teacher Education*, 1988, *39*(1), 2–9.

Anderson, M. "Creating a Climate of Affirmation: Education Beyond Fear." In J. Newman (ed.), *Finding Our Own Way*. Portsmouth, N.H.: Heinemann Educational Books, 1990.

Anning, A. "Teachers' Theories About Children's Learning." In J. Calderhead (ed.), *Teachers' Professional Learning* (pp. 128–153). New York: The Falmer Press, 1988.

Applegate, J. H., Flora, V. R., and Lasely, T. J. "New Teachers Seek Support: Some People Are Supportive and Others Aren't." *Educational Leadership*, 1980, *38*, 74–76.

Argyris, C., and Schon, D. A. "Teachers' Theories About Children's Learning." In J. Calderhead (ed.), *Teachers' Professional Learning* (pp. 128–146). New York: The Falmer Press, 1975.

Ashton-Jones, E., and Thomas, D. K. "Composition, Collaboration, and Women's Ways of Knowing: A Conversation with Mary Belenky." *Journal of Advanced Composition*, 1990, *10*(2), 275–292.

Ashton-Warner, S. *Teacher*. New York: Touchstone, 1963.

Atwell, N. *In the Middle: Writing, Reading, and Learning with Adolescents*. Portsmouth, N.H.: Boynton/Cook, 1987.

Ayers, W. "Prologue." In W. Schubert and W. Ayers (eds.), *Teacher Lore: Learning from Our Own Experience* (p. v). White Plains, N.Y.: Longman, 1992.

Ayers, W. Panel discussion presented at the National Association of Early Childhood Teacher Educators Conference. New Orleans, La., November 1993.

Baldwin, J. "A Talk to Teachers." In Simonson, R., and Walker, S. (eds.), *The Graywolf Annual Five: Multicultural Literacy* (p. 4). St. Paul, Minn.: Graywolf, 1988.

Barton, B., and Booth, D. *Stories in the Classroom*. Markham, Ontario: Pembroke, 1990.

Belenky, M. F., Clinchy, B. M., Goldberger, N. R., and Tarule, J. M. *Women's Ways of Knowing: The Development of Self, Voice, and Mind*. New York: Basic Books, 1986.

Berliner, D. "Laboratory Writings and the Study of Teacher Education." *Journal of Teacher Education*, 1985, *36*(6), 2–8.

Berns, R. M. *Child, Family, and Community: Socialization and Support*. San Diego, Calif.: Harcourt Brace Jovanovich, 1993.

Bogdan, R. C. "The Soft Side of Hard Data." *Phi Delta Kappan*, 1980, *61*, 411–412.

Bonstingl, J. *Schools of Quality: An Introduction to Total Quality Management in Education*. Alexandria, Va.: Association for Supervision and Curriculum Development, 1992.

Bowra, C. M. *The Romantic Imagination*. New York: Oxford University Press, 1961.

Britton, J. *Language and Learning*. Coral Gables, Fla.: University of Miami Press, 1970.

Brown, A. L., and Campione, J. C. "Psychological Theory and the Study of Learning Disabilities." *American Psychologist*, 1986, *41*, 1059–1068.

Bruer, J. T. "The Mind's Journey from Novice to Expert." *American Educator*, 1993, *17*(2), 6–15, 38–46.

Bruner, J. S. *Actual Minds, Possible Worlds.* Cambridge, Mass.: Harvard University, 1986.

Bruner, J. "Research Currents: Life as Narrative." *Language Arts,* 1988, *65,* 574.

Bullough, R. V., Jr. "Exploring Personal Metaphors in Preservice Education." *Journal of Teacher Education,* 1991, *42*(1), 43–51.

Bussis, A., Chittenden, A., and Amarel, M. *City College Notes,* 2–7. Spring, 1974.

Butt, R., Raymond, D., and Yamagishi, L. "Autobiographic Praxis: Studying the Formation of Teachers' Knowledge." *Journal of Curriculum Theorizing,* 1988, *7*(4).

Buzzell, J. B., and Piazza, R. *Case Studies for Teaching Special Needs and At-Risk Students.* Albany, N.Y.: Delmar, 1994.

Byrnes, D. A. "Addressing Race, Ethnicity, and Culture in the Classroom." In D. Byrnes and G. Kiger (eds.), *Common Bonds: Anti-Bias Teaching in a Diverse Society* (pp. 11–22). Wheaton, Md.: Association for Childhood Education International, 1992.

Byrnes, D. A., and Kiger, G. (eds.). *Common Bonds: Anti-Bias Teaching in a Diverse Society.* Wheaton, Md.: Association for Childhood Education International, 1992.

Carter, K., and Doyle, W. Classroom Research as a Resource for the Graduate Preparation of Teachers. In A. E. Woolfolk (ed.), *Research Perspectives on the Graduate Preparation of Teachers* (pp. 51–68). Englewood Cliffs, N.J.: Prentice-Hall, 1989.

Children's Defense Fund. *Children 1990: A Report Card.* Washington, D.C.: Children's Defense Fund, 1990.

Chism, N. "Reflective Teaching." Lecture delivered at Indiana University of Pennsylvania, Indiana, Pa., March 1989.

Clandinin, D. J. *Classroom Practice: Teacher Images in Action.* London: The Falmer Press, 1986.

Clandinin, D. J., and others. *Learning to Teach, Teaching to Learn: Stories of Collaboration in Teacher Education.* New York: Teachers College Press, 1993.

Clark, C. M., and Peterson, P. L. (eds.). "Teachers' Thought Processes." In M. Wittrock (ed.), *Handbook of Research on Teaching* (3rd ed.). New York: Macmillan, 1986.

Clark, J. "To Teach Is to Learn." *The Apple,* 1993, *11*(4), 8–9.

Cochran-Smith, M., and Lytle, S. L. "Research on Teachers

and Teacher Research: The Issues That Divide." *Educational Researcher,* 1990, *19*(2), 2–11.

Cohen, R. M. *A Lifetime of Teaching: Portraits of Five Veteran High School Teachers.* New York: Teachers College Press, 1992.

Coles, R. *The Call of Stories.* Boston: Houghton Mifflin, 1989.

Connelly, M. Unpublished manuscript, Southcentral Pennsylvania Writing Project Writers' Workshop, 1993.

Connelly, M. F., and Clandinin, J. D. *Teachers as Curriculum Planners: Narratives of Experience.* New York: Teachers College Press, 1988.

Connelly, M. F., and Clandinin, D. J. "Stories of Experience and Narrative Inquiry." *Educational Researcher,* 1988, *19*(5), 2–14.

Cooper, J. E. "Telling Our Own Stories: The Reading and Writing of Journals or Diaries." In C. Witherell and N. Noddings (eds.), *Stories Lives Tell: Narrative and Dialogue in Education* (pp. 96–112). New York: Teachers College Press, 1991.

Court, D. "Studying Teachers' Values." *The Clearing House,* 1991, *64*(6), 389–392.

Cronbach, L. J. "Beyond the Two Disciplines of Scientific Psychology." *American Psychologist,* 1975, *30*, 119.

Cruickshank, D. *Reflective Teaching: The Preparation of Students of Teaching.* Reston, Va.: Association of Teacher Educators, 1987.

Csikszentmihalyi, M. *Flow: The Psychology of Optimal Experience.* New York: HarperCollins, 1990.

Daloz, L. *Effective Teaching and Mentoring.* San Francisco: Jossey-Bass, 1986.

Darling-Hammond, L. "Teacher Professionalism: Why and How?" In A. Lieberman (ed.), *Schools as Collaborative Cultures: Creating the Future Now.* Bristol, Pa.: The Falmer Press, 1990.

Darling-Hammond, L. "Reframing the School Reform Agenda: Developing Capacity for School Transformation." *Phi Delta Kappan,* 1993, *74*(10), 753–761.

Davidson, E., and Schniedewind, N. "Class Differences: Economic Inequality in the Classroom." In D. Byrnes and G. Kiger (eds.), *Common Bonds: Anti-Bias Teaching in a Diverse Society* (pp. 53–70). Wheaton, Md.: Association for Childhood Education International, 1992.

Derman-Sparks, L. "Revisiting Multicultural Education: What

Children Need to Live in a Diverse Society. *Dimensions of Early Childhood,* 1993, *21*(2), 6–9.

Dewey, J. "My Pedagogic Creed." In R. Ulich (ed.), *Three Thousand Years of Educational Wisdom* (pp. 629–638). Cambridge, Mass.: Harvard University Press, 1897.

Dewey, J. *Democracy and Education.* New York: Macmillan, 1916.

Dewey, J. *The Sources of a Science Education.* New York: Horace Liveright, 1929.

Dewey, J. *How We Think: A Restatement of the Relation of Thinking to the Educative Process.* Boston: D. C. Heath, 1933.

Dillard, A. *The Writing Life.* New York: HarperCollins, 1989.

Dimidjian, V. J. *Early Childhood at Risk: Action and Advocacy for Young Children.* Washington, D.C.: National Education Association. (ED 312 062)

Dollas, R. H. *Voices of Beginning Teachers: Visions and Realities.* New York: Teachers College Press, 1992.

Duckworth, E. "Teaching as Research." *Harvard Educational Review,* 1986, *56,* 481–488.

Dyson, A. H. "Research Currents: Diversity, Social Responsibility and the Story of Literacy." *Language Arts,* 1990, *67*(2), 193–205.

Edelman, M. W. *The Measure of Our Success: A Letter to My Children and Yours.* Boston: Beacon Press, 1992.

Eisner, E. "The Ecology of School Improvement." *Educational Leadership,* 1988, *45,* 24–29.

Elbaz, F. "The Teacher's 'Practical Knowledge': A Report of a Case Study." *Curriculum Inquiry,* 1981, *11*(1), 43–71.

Elbaz, F. *Teacher Thinking: A Study of Practical Knowledge.* New York: Nichols, 1983.

Elbaz, F. "Research on Teachers' Knowledge: The Evolution of a Discourse." *Journal of Curriculum Studies,* 1991, *23*(1), 1–19.

Erikson, E. *Childhood and Society.* (2nd ed.) New York: W. W. Norton, 1963.

Farwell, M. "The Female Hero." *Old Oregon,* 1988, *67*(4), 29–31.

Fennimore, B. S. *Child Advocacy for Early Childhood Educators.* New York: Teachers College Press, 1989.

Fox, M. *Radical Reflections: Passionate Opinions on Teaching, Learning, and Living.* San Diego, Calif.: Harcourt Brace Jovanovich College Division, 1993.

Frederick, P. "The Power of Story." *AAHE Bulletin,* December 1990, *43*(4), 3.

Fuhler, C. J. "Writing for Publication: Voices from the Classroom." In M. D'Alessandro and others, *The Reading Teacher,* 1992, *45*(6), 408–414.

Geertz, C. *Works as Lives: The Anthropologist as Author.* Stanford, Calif.: Stanford University Press, 1988.

George Mason University Case Writing Team. "Excerpts from Case Study of Jimmy Monroe." Unpublished manuscript, 1991.

George Mason University Case Study Writing Team. "When You've Taught a Little Longer." Unpublished manuscript, 1992.

Glasser, W. H. "The Quality School." *Phi Delta Kappan,* 1990, *71,* 425–435.

Gluck, S. B., and Patai, D. (eds.). *Women's Words: The Feminist Practice of Oral History.* New York: Routledge & Kegan Paul, 1991.

Gomez, M. L., and Tabachnik, B. R. "Telling Teaching Stories." *Teaching Education,* 1992, *4*(2), 129–138.

Goodman, J. "Reflection and Teacher Education: A Case Study and Theoretical Analysis." *Interchange,* 1984, *12*(2), 109–125.

Goodman, K. "Whole Language Research: Foundations and Development." In S. J. Samuels and A. E. Farstrup (eds.), *What Research Has to Say About Reading Instruction* (pp. 46–69). Newark, Del.: International Reading Association, 1992.

Grant, C., and Zeichner, K. "On Becoming a Reflective Teacher." In C. Grant (ed.), *Preparing for Reflective Teaching.* Needham Heights, Mass.: Allyn & Bacon, 1984.

Greene, M. *The Teacher as Stranger: Educational Philosophy for the Modern Age.* Belmont, Calif.: Wadsworth, 1973.

Greene, M. *The Dialectics of Freedom.* New York: Teachers College Press, 1988.

Greene, M. "The Educational Philosopher's Quest." In D. Burleson (ed.), *Reflections: Personal Essays by 33 Distinguished Educators* (pp. 200–212). Bloomington, Ind.: Phi Delta Kappa, 1992.

Grumet, M. *Bitter Milk: Women and Teaching.* Amherst, Mass.: University of Massachusetts, 1988.

Haley, G. *A Story, A Story*. New York: Atheneum, 1970.

Hardy, B. "Towards a Poetics of Fiction." In M. Meek and others, *The Cool Web*. London: The Bodley Head, 1977.

Hawthorne, R. K. *Curriculum in the Making: Teacher Choice and the Classroom Experience*. New York: Teachers College Press, 1992.

Hidalgo, N. M. "Multicultural Teacher Preparation." In T. Perry and J. Fraser (eds.), *Freedom's Plow: Teaching in the Multicultural Classroom* (pp. 99–108). New York: Routledge & Kegan Paul, 1993.

Hillman, C. B. *Teaching Four-Year-Olds: A Personal Journey*. Bloomington, Ind.: Phi Delta Kappa, 1988.

Hodgkinson, H. "Reform Versus Reality." *Phi Delta Kappan*, 1991, *73*(1), 9–16.

Hooks, B. "Transformative Pedagogy and Multiculturalism." In T. Perry and J. Fraser (eds.), *Freedom's Plow: Teaching in the Multicultural Classroom* (pp. 91–97). New York: Routledge & Kegan Paul, 1993.

Howe, H. "Reflections on Education and Schooling." In D. Burleson (ed.), *Reflections: Personal Essays by 33 Distinguished Educators* (pp. 219–231). Bloomington, Ind.: Phi Delta Kappa, 1992.

Huberman, M. *The Lives of Teachers*. New York: Teachers College Press, 1992.

Hughes, T. "Myth and Education." In K. Egan and D. Nadaner (eds.), *Imagination and Education* (pp. 30–44). New York: Teachers College Press, 1988.

Isenberg, J. P. "A Case Study of One Early Childhood Teacher's Beliefs Informing Her Practice." Paper presented at the Research Forum, Annual Study Conference of the Association for Childhood Education International, Chicago, April 1992.

Isenberg, J. P., and Jalongo, M. R. *Creative Expression and Play in the Early Childhood Curriculum*. New York: Macmillan, 1993.

Jackson, P. "Reflections on Teaching Ourselves." In D. Burleson (ed.), *Reflections: Personal Essays by 33 Distinguished Educators* (pp. 232–244). Bloomington, Ind.: Phi Delta Kappa, 1992.

Jalongo, M. R. *The Role of the Teacher in the 21st Century: An Insider's View*. Bloomington, Ind.: National Educational Service, 1991.

Jalongo, M. R. "Teachers' Stories: Our Ways of Knowing." *Educational Leadership,* 1992, *49*(7), 68–73.

Jalongo, M. R., and Isenberg, J. P. "Teachers' Stories: Reflections on Teaching, Caring, and Learning." *Childhood Education,* 1993, *69*(5), 260–261.

Jonquiere, H. P. "My Beliefs About Teaching." *Childhood Education,* 1990, *66*(5), 291–292.

Joseph, P. B., and Burnaford, G. E. *Images of School Teachers in Twentieth-Century America: Paragons, Polarities, Complexities.* New York: St. Martin's Press, 1994.

Kane, P. R. (ed.). *The First Year of Teaching: Real World Stories from American Teachers.* New York: Walker, 1992.

Kazemek, F. E. "Stories of Our Lives: Interviews and Oral Histories for Language Development. *Journal of Reading,* 1985, *29,* 211–218.

Keen, S. "The Stories We Live By." *Psychology Today,* 1988, *22,* 46–47.

Keizer, G. *No Place But Here: A Teacher's Vocation in a Rural Community.* New York: Viking Penguin, 1988.

Kilpatrick, W. "The Moral Power of Stories." *American Educator,* 1993, *17*(2), 24–35.

Koerner, M. E. "Teachers' Images: Reflections on Themselves." In W. Schubert and W. Ayers (eds.), *Teacher Lore: Learning from Our Own Experience* (pp. 44–60). White Plains, N.Y.: Longman, 1992.

Kohl, H. *36 Children.* New York: New American Library, 1967.

Kowalski, T. J., Weaver, R. A., and Henson, K. T. *Case Studies on Teaching.* White Plains, N.Y.: Longman, 1990.

Krall, F. R. From the Inside Out — Personal History as Educational Research. *Educational Theory,* 1988, *38*(4), 467–479.

Lampert, M. "How Do Teachers Manage to Teach? Perspectives on Problems in Practice." *Harvard Educational Review,* 1985, *55*(2), 178–194.

Leinhardt, G. "What Research on Learning Tells Us About Teaching." *Educational Leadership,* 1992, *49*(7), 21–24.

Livo, N. J., and Rietz, S. A. *Storytelling: Process and Practice.* Littleton, Colo.: Libraries Unlimited, 1986.

Low, A. M. *Dust Bowl Diary.* Lincoln: University of Nebraska Press, 1984.

McDonald, M. A. "Reconstructing Narratives of Teachers." *ADE Bulletin,* 102, Fall 1992.

MacDonald, R. E. *A Handbook of Basic Skills and Strategies for Beginning Teachers: Facing the Challenge of Teaching in Today's Schools.* White Plains, N.Y.: Longman, 1991.

MacIntyre, A. *After Virtue: A Study in Moral Theory.* South Bend, Ind.: University of Notre Dame Press, 1981.

McLaren, P. "The Liminal Servant and the Ritual Roots of Pedagogy." *Language Arts,* 1988, *65,* 164–179.

McLean, V. S. "Learning from Teachers' Stories." *Childhood Education,* 1993, *69*(5), 265–268.

Mandler, J. M., and Johnson, N. S. "Remembrance of Things Passed: Story Structure and Recall." *Cognitive Psychology,* 1977, *9,* 111–151.

Matthews, J. *Escalante: The Best Teacher in America.* New York: Henry Holt, 1988.

Mattingly, C. "Narrative Reflections on Practical Actions: Two Learning Experiments in Reflective Storytelling." In D. A. Schon (ed.), *The Reflective Turn* (pp. 235–257). New York: Teachers College Press, 1991.

Melnick, C. R. "The Out-of-School Curriculum." In W. H. Schubert and W. C. Ayers (eds.), *Teacher Lore: Learning from Our Own Experience.* White Plains, N.Y.: Longman, 1992.

Millies, P. S. "The Relationship Between a Teacher's Life and Teaching." In W. Schubert and W. Ayers (eds.), *Teacher Lore: Learning from Our Own Experience* (pp. 25–43). White Plains, N.Y.: Longman, 1992.

Morrison, R. *Song of Solomon.* New York: Knopf, 1977.

Murray, D. M. *Shoptalk: Learning to Write with Writers.* Portsmouth, N.H.: Heinemann Educational Books, 1990.

Newman, J. (ed.). *Finding Our Own Way.* Portsmouth, N.H.: Heinemann Educational Books, 1990.

Noddings, N. *Caring: A Feminine Approach to Ethics and Moral Education.* Berkeley: University of California Press, 1984.

Noddings, N. "Stories in Dialogue." In C. Witherell and N. Noddings (eds.), *Stories Lives Tell: Narrative and Dialogue in Education* (pp. 157–170). New York: Teachers College Press, 1991.

Ohanian, S. Quoted in E. Schuster, "In Pursuit of Cultural Literacy." *Phi Delta Kappan,* 1989, *70,* 539–542.

Ornstein, A. C. "The Trend Toward Increased Professionalism for Teachers." *Phi Delta Kappan,* 1981, *63*(6), 196–198.

Paley, V. G. *Wally's Stories.* Cambridge, Mass.: Cambridge University Press, 1981.

Papalia, D. E., and Olds, S. W. *A Child's World: Infancy Through Adolescence.* New York: McGraw-Hill, 1990.

Pasch, M., and others. *Teaching as Decision Making.* White Plains, N.Y.: Longman, 1991.

Perrone, V. *A Letter to Teachers: Reflections on Schooling and the Art of Teaching.* San Francisco: Jossey-Bass, 1991.

Perry, T., and Fraser, J. W. "Reconstructing Schools as Multiracial/Multicultural Democracies: Toward a Theoretical Perspective." In T. Perry and J. W. Fraser (eds.), *Freedom's Plow: Teaching in the Multicultural Classroom* (pp. 3–26). New York: Routledge & Kegan Paul, 1993.

Peterson, P. L., and Comeaux, M. A. "Assessing the Teacher as a Reflective Professional: New Perspectives on Teacher Evaluation." In A. Woolfolk (ed.), *Research Perspectives on the Graduate Preparation of Teachers* (pp. 132–152). Englewood Cliffs, N.J.: Prentice-Hall, 1989.

Picasso, P. "Conversation." In H. B. Chipp (ed.), *Theories of Modern Art: A Sourcebook by Artists and Critics.* Berkeley: University of California, 1971.

Pinar, W. *Contemporary Curriculum Discourse.* Scottsdale, Ariz.: Gorsuch Scarisbrick, 1988.

Polanyi, M. *Personal Knowledge.* London: Routledge & Kegan Paul, 1958.

Polkinghorne, D. E. *Narrative Knowing and the Human Sciences.* Albany: State University of New York Press, 1988.

Price, H. H. *Beliefs.* London: Allen & Lewin, 1969.

Resnick, L. "Cognition and Instruction: Recent Theories of Human Competence." In B. L. Hammonds (ed.), *Master Lecture Series: Vol. 4 Psychology and Learning* (pp. 123–186). Washington, D.C.: American Psychological Association, 1985.

Reunzel, D. "Woman on a Mission." *Teacher,* August 1993, 26–31.

Rogers, C. "Towards a Theory of Creativity." *ETC: A Review of General Semantics,* 1954, *11,* 249–260.

Rogers, C. *Freedom to Learn.* Columbus, Ohio: Merrill, 1986.

Rose, M. *Lives on the Boundary.* New York: Viking Penguin, 1989.

Rosen, B. *And None of It Was Nonsense.* Portsmouth, N.H.: Heinemann Educational Books, 1988.

Rosen, H. *Stories and Meanings.* Sheffield, England: National Association for the Teaching of English, 1987.

Rosenblatt, L. *Literature as Exploration.* Portsmouth, N.H.: Heinemann Educational Books, 1983.

Rosenshine, B., and Meister, C. "The Use of Scaffolds for Teaching Higher-Level Cognitive Strategies." *Educational Leadership,* 1992, *49*(7), 26–33.

Ross, D. D. "First Steps in Developing a Reflective Approach." *Journal of Teacher Education,* 1989, *40*(2), 22–30.

Ross, D. D. "Action Research for Preservice Teachers: A Description of Why and How." *Peabody Journal of Education,* 1989, *64*(3), 131–149.

Rouse, J. *The Completed Gesture: Myth, Character and Education.* Morris Plains, N.J.: Skyline Books, 1978.

Rubin, L. *Artistry in Teaching.* New York: Random House, 1985.

Ryan, K. *The Induction of New Teachers.* Bloomington, Ind.: Phi Delta Kappa, 1986.

Sadker, M., and Sadker, D. "Sexism in the Classroom: From Grade School to Graduate School." *Phi Delta Kappan,* 1985, *67*(7), 512–515.

Sapon-Shevin, M. "Ability Differences in the Classroom: Teaching and Learning in Inclusive Classrooms." In D. Byrnes and G. Kiger (eds.), *Common Bonds: Anti-Bias Teaching in a Diverse Society* (pp. 39–52). Wheaton, Md.: Association for Childhood Education International, 1992.

Schelechty, P. *Schools for the Twenty-First Century.* San Francisco: Jossey-Bass, 1990.

Schön, D. A. *The Reflective Practitioner: How Professionals Think in Action.* New York: Basic Books, 1983.

Schön, D. A. *Educating the Reflective Practitioner: Toward a New Design for Teaching and Learning in the Professions.* San Francisco: Jossey-Bass, 1987.

Schön, D. A. (ed.). *The Reflective Turn: Case Studies on Educational Practice*. New York: Teachers College Press, 1991.

Schubert, W. H. "Our Journeys into Teaching: Remembering the Past." In W. H. Schubert and W. C. Ayers (eds.), *Teacher Lore: Learning from Our Own Experience* (pp. 3–10). White Plains, N.Y.: Longman, 1992.

Schubert, W. H., and Ayers, W. C. *Teacher Lore: Learning from Our Own Experience*. White Plains, N.Y.: Longman, 1992.

Shafer, R. "Narration in the psychoanalytic dialogue." In W.T.J. Mitchell (ed.), *On Narrative*. Chicago: University of Chicago, 1981.

Shulevitz, U. *Writing with Pictures*. New York: Watson-Guptill, 1985.

Shulman, L. "On Research on Teaching: A Conversation with Lee Shulman." In R. S. Brandt, *Educational Leadership*, 1992, *49*(7), 14–19.

Silko, L. M. *Ceremony*. New York: Penguin, 1986.

Smith, C. A. *From Wonder to Wisdom: Using Stories to Help Children Grow*. New York: Viking Penguin, 1989.

Smith, F. "Learning to Read: The Never-Ending Debate." *Phi Delta Kappan*, 1992, *73*(6), 432–441.

Smith, J. "Setting the Cat Among the Pigeons: A Not So Sentimental Journey to the Heart of Teaching." *English Education*, 1991, *23*(2), 68–126.

Sparks-Langer, G. M., and Colton, A. B. "Synthesis of Research on Teachers' Reflective Thinking." *Educational Leadership*, 1991, *48*(6), 37–44.

Spodek, B. "Implicit Theories of Early Childhood Teachers: Foundations for Professional Behavior." In B. Spodek, O. N. Saracho, and D. L. Peters (eds.), *Professionalism and the Early Childhood Educator* (pp. 161–171). New York: Teachers College Press, 1988.

Surbeck, E., & Han, E. "Becoming a Child-Sensitive Teacher: Can Journal Writing Help?" *Journal of Early Childhood Teacher Education*, 1993, *14*(2), 4–10.

Surbeck, E., Han, E., & Moyer, J. "Assessing Reflective Responses in Journals." *Educational Leadership*, 1991, *48*(6), 25–27.

Swick, K. J., and Hanes, M. L. *The Developing Teacher.* Champaign, Ill.: Stipes, 1987.

Takaki, R. *A Different Mirror: A History of Multicultural America.* New York: Little, Brown, 1993.

Tappan, M. B. "Narrative, Authorship, and the Development of Moral Authority." In M. B. Tappan and M. J. Packer (eds.), *Narrative and Storytelling: Implications for Understanding Moral Development* (pp. 5–25). San Francisco: Jossey-Bass, 1991.

Tappan, M. B., & Brown, L. M. "Stories Told and Lessons Learned." In C. Witherell and N. Noddings (eds.), *Stories Lives Tell. Narrative and Dialogue in Education* (pp. 171–192). New York: Teachers College Press, 1991.

Tappan, M. B., & Packer, M. J. (eds.). *Narrative and Storytelling: Implications for Understanding Moral Development.* San Francisco: Jossey-Bass, 1991.

Taylor, P. *Normative Discourse.* Englewood Cliffs, N.J.: Prentice-Hall, 1961.

Tennyson, W. W., & Strom, S. M. "Beyond Professional Standards: Developing Responsibilities." *Journal of Counseling and Development,* 1988, *64*(5), 298–302.

Twitching, J., and Demuth, C. (compilers). *Multicultural Education: Views from the Classroom.* London: British Broadcasting Corporation, 1985.

Vance, E. "A Tree for Eric." *The Educational Forum,* 1990, *54*(3), 293–315.

VanMaanen, J. *Tales of the Field: On Writing Ethnography.* Chicago: University of Chicago, 1988.

Wanner, S. Y. *On With the Story: Adolescents Learning Through Literature.* Portsmouth, N.H.: Heinemann Educational Books, 1994.

Wassermann, S. *Serious Players in the Primary Classroom.* New York: Teachers College Press, 1990.

Wassermann, S. *Getting Down to Cases: Learning to Teach with Case Studies.* New York: Teachers College Press, 1993.

Webster's New World Dictionary of the American Language. New York: Simon & Schuster, 1984.

Wells, G. *The Meaning Makers: Children Learning Language and Using Language to Learn.* Portsmouth, N.H.: Heinemann Educational Books, 1986.

White, H. "The Value of Narrativity in the Representation of Reality." In W. Mitchell (ed.), *On Narrative* (pp. 1–15). Chicago: University of Chicago Press, 1981.

Witherell, C., and Noddings, N. *Stories Lives Tell: Narrative and Dialogue in Education.* New York: Teachers College Press, 1991.

Yonemura, M. "Teacher Conversations: A Potential Source of Their Own Professional Growth." *Curriculum Inquiry,* 1982, *12*(3), 239–256.

Yonemura, M. *A Teacher at Work.* New York: Teachers College Press, 1986.

INDEX

ADDRESS SERVICE REQUESTED

TO: Tonya Rutkowski
925 Texas Hill Rd.
Huntington, VT
05462

MAY BE OPENED FOR POSTAL INSPECTION IF NECESSARY

____ PARCEL POST
____ PREINSURED ____ EXPRESS COLLECT
$ ____ VALUE ____ EXPRESS PREPAID

LIBRARY MAIL

DEMCO